THE TIES THAT BIND

Questioning Family Dynamics and Family Discourse in Hispanic Literature

---

Edited, with an Introduction and Notes by
Sara E. Cooper

University Press of America,® Inc.
Lanham · Boulder · New York · Toronto · Oxford

Copyright © 2004 by
University Press of America,® Inc.
4501 Forbes Boulevard
Suite 200
Lanham, Maryland 20706
UPA Acquisitions Department (301) 459-3366

PO Box 317
Oxford
OX2 9RU, UK

Library of Congress Control Number: 2003109232
ISBN 0-7618-2649-1 (paperback : alk. ppr.)

For my family...

The family I was born into, thanks to my great fortune and my parents' persistence, without whom I would never have known the joys of being a granddaughter, daughter, and sister.

The family I have chosen, especially my life partner CJ and the friends who have sustained me through the many phases of this project.

Contents

Preface

The Ties That Bind: Questioning Family Dynamics and Family Discourse in Hispanic Literature is a project many years in the making. As a Master's student at the University of Texas at Austin, I came upon a short story by the Brazilian author Edla van Steen that would change my life. Books had always been my first love, and I had frequently found in them balm for my troubled soul, much needed inspiration, and proof that the human race had some redeeming qualities. However, at that point in my life, being in the midst of a radical process of personal inventory and amends for past wrongs, I was ready to integrate the different areas of my existence at a much deeper level. Reading the poignant and disturbing portrayal of family in "Cio" brought me to contemplate seriously my own upbringing, the social institution of family, and the way that scholars approach the family in literature. With the blessing of my faculty advisor, Naomi Lindstrom, I went in search of a theoretical apparatus that would allow me to discuss what I thought I was seeing in the short story. After exhaustive hours with the MLA International Bibliography, I was extraordinarily fortunate to find a resource in the English Department of UT; Jerome Bump would be my introduction to Family Systems Theory (FST) and a fresh new way to study and teach literature in the classroom. Soon I had met (via e-mail) the main proponents of a literary methodology based on FST, especially John V. Knapp, who proceeded to initiate me in this latest wave of literary criticism. At that time there were no critics in my own field of Hispanic literature who were utilizing this approach.

Ironically, after having sparked my interest, the Edla van Steen tale did not make its way into this collection. By the time I completed my doctoral work some years later, I had found an absolute wealth of literature and film that dealt with family function and dysfunction, communication, evolution, definition, and social purpose. I also began to see more literary criticism remarking on the family, although truth be told it was difficult to find any structuring imaginary that would serve to contextualize and situate the emerging studies. Being enthralled with the flexibility and subtlety of FST, I became determined to search out other scholars in the area of Spanish and Latin American literature who were using (or looking for) such a methodology.

My call for papers elicited, if not a deluge, at least a respectable number of abstracts that showed great promise. Through a long process of creation, sharing sources, and propitious meetings, the very best of the abstracts have been developed into the essays in this collection. On the way I have found colleagues for whom I hold the greatest admiration and affection, and together we have made the next step toward what could be a burgeoning trend in literary criticism. As befits my own eclectic tastes and due to my hesitance to place undo restrictions on scholarly creativity, this collection of essays shows the influence of many critical approaches other than Family Systems Theory. I believe that the integration of critical theories according to the dictates of the literary text makes for a vibrant and living body of scholarly work; thus, our work here attempts to utilize those elements that contribute the most to the textual readings.

My original purpose with this book was simple: collect the works of interesting critical voices beneath the umbrella of a Family Systems approach. I also have hoped to be able to spark interest in the FST methodology for the next generation of scholars. The resulting collection has exceeded my expectations, in that I have also found a community of intellectuals that continue to inspire my own work. Through the work of editing these essays, I have been able to further elucidate my own ideas and come to a greater understanding of the concepts that underlie a systemic approach to literature (and life). I will always be grateful for the experience.

Acknowledgements

I wish to acknowledge the help and motivation given to me by the many friends and colleagues who consistently come to my rescue.

Thanks to Naomi Lindstrom for her many insightful comments and suggestions during the very beginning phases of my work with Family Systems. Your observations as a top-notch scholar (who had never worked with FST) helped me to spell out definitions and concepts without (I hope) boring the general reader.

Jerome Bump has been an incredible resource and inspiration to me for several years. Thank you, Jerry, for bringing your heart and beautiful spirit into the dangerous arena of academia, which you have made a better and safer place for people like me.

To John V. Knapp, thanks for all the reading lists and for treating me like a colleague. Also, I gratefully acknowledge your work in fashioning an intellectual community based on concepts of family and communication. You have taught me so much.

Enormous appreciation is due to my family, especially Jenny, June, and Will (may he rest in peace), who have tolerated my tedious analysis of our own interactions and communication over the last years. The same goes for my incredibly supportive friends and recovery community. You have made it possible for me to be a human being as well as an academic, which is no mean feat.

Thanks to Sarah Hammill, my brainy and rebellious student, for the great conversations as well as research assistance. Mil gracias a Obdulia Corona, who helped proofread the chapters in Spanish, and to Gale Carrillo for her patience. Special thanks to CJ Trebra for proofreading all my work and gently pointing out opportunities for improvement. That is the very least that you give me.

While these generous souls have not stinted in their generous aid, any remaining errors are of course due to my own failings.

Excerpts from *The Two Mujeres* are used with permission of Aunt Lute.
Excerpts from *Memorias de Leticia Valle* and *Julia* are used with permission of Lumen Press.
Excerpts from *Un aire de familia* are used with permission of Silvia Italiano.
Excerpts from *El cuarto mundo* are used with permission of Editorial Planeta Chilena.
Excerpts from *El ingenioso hidalgo don Quijote de la Mancha* are used with permission of Editorial Planeta Chilena.

1

Introduction:
Questioning Family Dynamics
and Family Discourse
in Hispanic Literature and Film

Sara E. Cooper

Tie Me Up, Tie Me Down: Or, the Ubiquity and Perversity of Family in Hispanic Literature and Film

The obvious (and intentional) referentiality of this subtitle to the controversial Pedro Almodóvar film *Átame* (1989)—released in the United States as *Tie Me Up, Tie Me Down*—is meant to stir up a complex response in the reader. In the film, a yet to be internationally famous Antonio Banderas plays a psychiatric patient and orphan who, released from the institution, tries to find family "normality" through the use of force. He kidnaps a model, Marina (played by Victoria Abril), so that she may get to know him and realize that he would be a good husband for her and a good father for her children. The sexual tension that emanates from the two characters is made even more polemical by the film's blatant sado-masochistic elements: in addition to various scenes incorporating physical violence, Marina spends much of the movie tied to the bed by her own request, because she admits that she can't be trusted. In the true Almodóvaresque tradition, what emerges is a social and psychological portrait of Spanish culture that emphasizes the ephemeral or illusive quality of family normality and suggests links between interpersonal relationships, violence, alienation, dysfunction, questions of dominance/submission, and unrealistic social expectations created by mass media. Banderas, in his role as Ricki, embodies a concentrated and easily culpable example of the family or social "problem," which is complicated by the fact that his "victim" (and much of the audience) ends up sympathizing with his plight, his innocent wish to create a family, and even his ingenuous belief that he can solve a life of disconnection with one extreme action. Nonetheless, the possibility of a happy ending, with Marina welcoming Ricki into her extended family, is extremely unsettling. The audience knows that nothing is that simple, that the apparently simple normality achieved by the protagonists is inevitably temporary if it exists at all. In this way, *Átame* reflects a reality of the modern world—family relationships and interpersonal dynamics are not homogeneous or uncomplicated; rather, they are often as perverse as they are ubiquitous.

The centrality of family in social and political spheres is a reality beyond question, a reality that influences the cultural production in all parts of the globe. As such, family has been a recurring theme in Hispanic film and literature since its inception and throughout every literary movement in Spain and Latin America, including the upsurge of writing by U.S. born or immigrant Latino/as. Despite hundreds of thousands of examples to the contrary, many readers accept as fact the idea that literature reflects a traditional and fairly universal image of the Hispanic family: an enormous network of kinship supporting and passing on a clearly established conventional and conservative value system. In this imaginary family system, gender roles would be distinctly defined, sexuality would be unproblematic (and never include incest or homosexuality), and the family would be an institution that maintained the social and political hierarchy. However, delving into the rich literary production of writers of Spanish or Latino origins, one is immediately struck by the images of a subversive or perverse domestic sphere and the prevalence of and myriad variations on family dysfunction and rebellion. Even many of those works that depict a traditionally defined and socially controlled family either subtly undermine or explicitly denounce the inherent injustice and dysfunctionality of such a construction.

Examples abound on both sides of the Atlantic; space limitations dictate that only a few can be mentioned here. The parody of traditional family composition and dynamics, as well as changing social and family expectations, is manifestly present in much of Miguel de Cervantes' work, most dramatically (and lengthily) in both volumes of *Don Quixote* (1604 and 1615).   By the same token, the entire picaresque genre sets forth the family as the original site of learning for its troublemaking protagonists, and picaresque novels from Spain and Latin America constantly reflect the hypocrisy of aristocratic and religious ideals pertaining to the family.

To cite just one case, the main character in Francisco de Quevedo's *Lazarillo de Tormes* (1554) ends up in a marriage of convenience with a woman whose reputation is less than sparkling in order to protect himself from legal prosecution for his life of crime and dissipation.   He acknowledges the poetic justice of this and insinuates that his situation is much more the norm than the perfect family fiction upheld by Spanish culture.

Turning to literature from the 19ᵗʰ and 20ᵗʰ centuries, the proliferation of works by women writers gives a new slant to the literary representation of family—here I will mention only a handful. The Cuban novelist and proto-feminist Gertrudis Gómez de Avellaneda y Arteaga situates her tragic *Sab* (1841), an indictment of slavery and the parallel oppression of women, within the family home of the protagonist Miss Carlota; in so doing, she portrays the family as a conscious agent of the establishment that must be challenged.   In another novel that subtly exposes and criticizes the limited role of woman as wife and mother, Teresa de la Parra's *Ifigenia* (1924) traces the protagonist's road of rebellion and ultimate submission to societal and family strictures.   In one of many poems recalling the family, the Mexican writer Rosario Castellanos offers implicit criticism in "Economía doméstica," where in some corner of her spotless home the poetic narrator has lost her capacity for tears and need through "la regla de oro que me dio mi madre" (the golden rule my mother gave me; 292 my translation).   The importance and complexity of familial influence on the formation of personal and social identity is further explored in Castellanos's prose, such as in the novel *Balún Canán* (1957) and the short story collection *Album de familia* (1971).   Puerto Rican Rosario Ferré is famous for her scathing depiction of society and family, as in the novel *Maldito amor* (1986) and her collection of short fiction and poetry *Papeles de Pandora* (1976).   Then, the magical realist novel *La casa de los espíritus* (1982) is Isabel Allende's saga of a complex family dynasty that suffers and serves as witness during Chile's brutal political transition of the 1970s.   Works by the Mexican/Chicana authors Sara Levi Calderón (*Dos mujeres* 1990) and Cherríe Moraga (*Giving up the Ghost*; *The Hungry Woman: A Mexican Medea*) as well as Uruguayan Cristina Peri Rossi's short story "El testigo" (1991) introduce a lesbian family dynamic that is not able to escape the

violence and oppression of the larger sociopolitical context. By the
same token, modern Spanish women writers such as Carmen Laforet,
Carmen Martín Gaite, Rosa Chacel, Ana María Moix, and Esther
Tusquets interweave commentary on how the family is affected by
Franco-era and pre-or post-Civil War society with intricate and
penetrating exploration of changing roles of gender and sexuality in
Spain.[1] The rise in popularity and critical acclaim of films by Hispanic
women means that in this genre too do we see a woman's perspective
of the family system, as in the case of *Camila* and *De eso no se habla*
by the noted director María Luisa Bemberg.

Obviously, the modern (or postmodern) author's preoccupation
with family does not at all place her/him into a strictly feminine
discourse. On the contrary, issues of kinship and family structure are
relevant to both sexes, and are also abundantly present in the works of
male authors of the past two centuries. Referring to even the most
well-known and canonical literature one recalls, for instance, Benito
Pérez Galdos' genius in representing family dynamics in novels such as
Doña Perfecta (1876), *La familia de León Roch* (1879), his masterpiece
Fortunata y Jacinta (1886-87) and *Misercordia* (1897), in which an
aging servant devotes her life to the ungrateful family she serves.
Federico García Lorca looks intensely at the painful yet fundamental
role of women and family in Andaluz culture in the dramas *Bodas de
sangre* (1935) and *La casa de Bernarda Alba* (1936). Often viewed
from a psychological point of view, José Camilo Cela's *La familia de
Pascual Duarte* (1942) offers a unique delineation of social and family
brutality and dysfunction. More contemporary works reflecting the
fascination with communication and dysfunction in family include
novels by Luis Goytisolo and Rafael Sánchez Ferlosio and plays by
Alfonso Sastre and José Luis Alonso de Santos. In Latin American
literature by men, one could point to the portrait of aristocratic family
life in the Chilean Alberto Blest Gana's novel *Martín Rivas* (1862), the
multigenerational and incestuous lineage in the Colombian Gabriel
García Márquez's epic novel *Cien años de soledad* (1967), the
confusing yet character-forming family relationships in the Peruvian
José María Arguedas's novel *Los ríos profundos* (1958), and the
representation of blatant family dysfunction by authors like the
Uruguayan Mario Benedetti and the Peruvian Mario Vargas Llosa. For
writers such as García Márquez and Arguedas, the family is not only a
thematic concern; rather, the family make-up and dynamic are integral
to the formation of the narrative structure. Such is the case, too, with
much of the cinematographic production of Spain and Latin America,

as can be seen in almost all of Almodóvar's works, Carlos Saura's film versions of Lorca's masterpieces, and other contemporary classics like *La historia oficial* (Argentina) and *Lucía* (Cuba). Then too, writers such as the Argentine Manuel Puig and Chilean José Donoso transgress virtually every taboo about family and social systems. As a case in point Donoso's novel, *Lugar sin límites* (1966), juxtaposes gay male homosexuality, prostitution, class conflicts, and relationships of power between the sexes in order to question and subvert ideals of family construction and interaction. Short stories and novels by Chicano and Latino authors such as Rolando Hinojosa Smith and Tomás Rivera depict the struggles of immigrant families in the United States, a theme also pivotal in films such as *El Norte*, *My Family/Mi familia* and *...Y no se lo tragó la tierra (...And the Earth Did Not Devour Him)*.

Given the enormous corpus of works that treat the central theme of family, it is not surprising that representations of family dynamics and relationships in literature are increasingly a topic in contemporary scholarship. Some more prominent examples include the work of noted critics Harriet Turner (*Family Ties and Tyrannies: A Reassessment of Jacinta*), Marianne Hirsch (*The Mother/Daughter Plot*), and Roberto Reis ("Representations of Family and Sexuality in Brazilian Cultural Discourse"). However, relatively few critics explicitly name the *family* as the focus of their discussion, preferring to speak simply of motherhood, marriage, or societal restrictions (to name a few related themes); nonetheless, it is clear that each of these topics is intimately tied to the institution of family. For instance, feminist critics of Latin American literature like Lindstrom, Waldman, and Mathieu underline the ideas of lack, alienation, anguish, and power struggles in the family, but without discussing family as a system or institution. One avenue that remains open is the study of women *within* the family group, their patterns of *interactions* and their *cooperation* in the maintenance of the family system. This opportunity exists as well in the discussion of the genre of the *bildungsroman*, where critics tend to focus upon the protagonist as an individual rather than as the member of a family system that profoundly impacts her psychosocial development. Indeed, the critical silence about family *per se* is quite provocative in itself, suggesting that there exists some unspoken taboo about delving too deeply into the subject. Whereas it is clearly acceptable to go into great detail in protesting the inequities of marital life or the suffering intrinsic to the mother-daughter relationship, there is seldom more than a general mention of the nuclear or extended kinship system. To this point it appears that Hispanic literary criticism has been much more interested in the study of the man/woman's role or voice in opposition to or in isolation from his/her surroundings. The critical gamut should be stretched to include more direct treatment of the family system as an issue crucial to both gender and sexuality.

In summation, there is without a doubt much more to be explored in terms of how literature delimits, describes, or distorts the family. Within the corpus of fiction by Iberian, Latin American, and U.S. Latino writers, the family has been discussed, defined, lauded, and maligned. Hearth and home have been symbolized as the safe haven and refuge of the working man, a caring space where children are nurtured and taught how to grow into adults, and the shelter in which women not only are guarded from the dangers of the public arena, but also have been designated as having a certain amount of power and voice. In contrast, literature also has shown family to be a socially constructed prison cell, a set of limitations that chafes and destroys, and a place where unimaginable violence and cruelty are perpetrated. The critic Denis Jones has said that *every* story inescapably narrates the family (111). Indeed the family is the basic system of society, in which we learn how to communicate or miscommunicate, how to interact with others, and how to define our own roles in both the private and the public spheres. In view of the family's fundamental social importance, it becomes possible both to concede an elemental validity to Jones's exuberant statement and to explain why the family is a theme that never loses its relevance in literature. If the family can be seen as both the space where socialization (normalization) occurs and the seat of social or political rebellion, where roles of sex and gender are both established and subverted, and where communication skills are honed or destroyed, then the literature that represents the family must be explored with some exceedingly flexible yet powerful critical tools.

Hispanic film and literature provide an abundance of examples of family as story, family shape mirrored in narrative structure, and family dynamic seemingly competing with narrative, dramatic, and cinematographic style to achieve the highest level of complexity--as well as vying for the attention of the reader. Often these literary representations of family, both positive and negative, are accompanied by more or less clearly enunciated approval or disapproval, often perceived in the tone, irony, juxtaposition of words and images, or even direct commentary by narrator or literary characters. A focus on how the family should or does function and what it should or does mean, both for society and for the individual, will be a fruitful area for critical discussion. Whatever surfaces, it will be of paramount importance to constitute clear theoretical parameters within which the structure and dynamic of families in literature may be studied. One of the objectives of this introduction will be to outline some possible parameters for this undertaking.

The Slipknot: Shifting Definition(s) of Family

Before outlining a theoretical framework for the study of family in literature and film, the definition of the term *family* deserves a closer examination. The idea that a family is something more than people who share common blood is an integral concept in the current exploration. Think of the ever-present maxim *family values*, used as a rallying cry by the radical right. This phrase is uttered as if there were a certain meaning universally ascribed to it, a genuine semantic value that could guide or referee the ongoing debate over whether *family values* have become corroded, corrupt, or even missing from our contemporary society. Yet the psychiatrist Ross Speck suggests that even such seemingly specific terms as *nuclear* or *extended* family "are not as clear cut or descriptive as every day usage would suggest" (68). The interpretation of *values* can be even more elusive, requiring the internalization of and adherence to some religious, philosophical, legal, or personal code of ethics. What is purported to be clear, unquestionable, universal, and timeless is in truth a very slippery question indeed. The relevance of the family values issue to this study of Latin American literature and the history of family is the following: even though the expression *family values* is used by some to defend a patriarchal, biological, and static view of family, it actually suggests something totally different. In fact, family, kinship, and household can't be reduced to biological ties or a universally accepted system of interactions. The objective of this section is to establish an elemental understanding of the concept of the family itself, and how this concept or definition has changed over time. The historical transformations of the family remind us that the definition of a traditional family reflects the changing sociocultural reality over time and that alternative family systems have always existed as part of the evolutionary process.

A foundational text on the composition and function of the family is Friedrich Engels's *The Origin of the Family, Private Property and the State* (1942; 1st ed. 1884).[2] In his discussion of the history of the family, Engels specifically contrasts the modern family structure (somewhat to its detriment) with other previously predominant patterns. In short, the family structure evolved slowly from a group or communal marriage where all persons enjoyed the responsibilities and privileges of marriage with all others to the "monogamous family," characteristic of civilization --or recorded history--, with a stronger marriage tie breakable only by the man, who also retained the "right of conjugal infidelity." According to Engels, this type of family "is based on the supremacy of the man, the express purpose being to produce children of undisputed paternity; such paternity is demanded because these children are later to come into their father's property as his natural heirs" (55). The author points out that this latter, patriarchal family was originally more a construct based on economics, grouping together those related by blood, marriage, or ownership.

Using Karl Marx's *Capital* as well as Morgan, Engels ties together and summarizes the undermining of the gentile constitution at the transition from barbarism to civilization. As soon as commodities, then surplus, then money appear, a *class* division emerges based on who has more rather than simply who will do what. Inheritance becomes more complicated, men gain more power, communities grow and merge, and a state politic is created that diminishes kinship and domestic labor and privileges acquisition of goods. At the same time slavery and serfdom are created to increase the labor force while allowing the concentration of wealth and power in individual hands. Individual men are then given supremacy over all beings in their home, without being subjected to an equally binding responsibility as to the well-being of these persons, thereby completely perverting the previously predominant structures of the family (145-50).

Offering a distinct slant on family evolution, Martine Segalen posits that the family is not a passive social institution, forced to change by outside elements; rather, it is "a site of resistance capable of adapting to different situations" (378). As such, both the needs and the capabilities of families have an impact on society. Segalen, like many others, stresses the plurality of *families* in place of a false unified *family* structure, acknowledging differences across class levels and units and means of production. The nineteenth century saw the emergence of the bourgeois family ideal, which as Michel Foucault noted was soon embraced even by the poverty class and working class culture. Including a gender-based division of labor and intensified focus on the children, the new family ideology also had a strong moral component. According to Segalen, the family:

> was defined as the place of order, the conveyor of a powerful normative model, every discrepancy from which was considered a dangerous form of social deviance. In this crucible were refined the values necessary for individual achievement, the fruit of moral virtues

which had been inculcated in the course of a long process of socialization. (393)

In other words, in addition to serving as a conduit for goods, services, and information, the kinship structure now represented the limits of the virtuous private sphere in opposition to the social disorder of the public sphere. In particular, after the First World War, the beautification of the interior became a productive cultural and commercial enterprise (Segalen 400). If the female role was sanctified as that of caretaker of this sacred space, it began to be devalued as soon as paid servants took over the housekeeping and child care in more affluent homes. That, combined with new access to higher education and economic shifts that made working outside of the home more profitable than homemaking, opened the door for a growing number of women to enter the work force (Segalen 407). Women's increased economic strength, the heightened access to contraceptives, and the appearance of new legislation have made divorce more attainable and frequent, which is one factor that causes many to lament the demise of the family. Notwithstanding these many changes, Segalen counters that "if the couple is in crisis the family, as an institution which unites the generations, is sturdy. Cohabitation, divorce and extramarital births have ceased to be deviant forms, and have been integrated into the whole process of family relationships" (411).

In keeping with the work of Engels and Bernand and Gruzinski, the anthropologist Sir Edmund Leach, Lawrence Stone, and Edward Shorter have professed the belief that the so-called *nuclear* family -- comprised of two parents and their children-- is historically unusual and certainly neither the only possible configuration nor intrinsically the most desirable.[3] In radical opposition is Ferdinand Mount, whose *The Subversive Family* (1982) is centered almost entirely upon refuting this idea along with certain others that he terms "myths" of the family.[4] He states energetically that "the nuclear family is universal. Wherever more complicated forms exist, the nuclear family is always present as well" (53). Interestingly, Mount posits this ubiquitous nuclear family as the primary revolutionary force in history. Rather than being the seat of tradition and socialization into a dominant hierarchy, the family "is the ultimate and only consistently subversive organization. Only the family has continued throughout history and still continues to undermine the State [and the Church]" (1). Mount describes a cycle in which new political, religious, or intellectual entities first attempt to lessen the family's importance, then as the family does not cede ground for long, its adversary slowly accepts, ceases to fight, and eventually even tries to recuperate the family as symbolic of itself (e.g. the family as Christian, Republican, or Communist) (3-4). Yet why, indeed, should the family ever be such a target of antagonism for the rising political, ideological, or religious institutions? Simply because in its ideal manifestation, family responsibility holds a higher priority than political action or religious community service. Mount insists that *this* is the subversive power of the family; that is, to consistently uphold a set of values in direct opposition to the power hierarchies and oppression intrinsic to external social and political groups.[5]

As the definition, constitution, and function of family have evolved in the European and Euro-American context, outside influences have informed how this occurred in different geographic and sociocultural spheres. Assuming that any definition of family, no matter how flexible or heterogeneous, will be equally accurate in the study of distinct literary texts, is short-sighted; thus, the specificity of a cultural and historical context will be addressed in each of the essays in this collection. Nonetheless, some general points pertaining to Latin American family systems should be made now.

When speaking of the evolution of the Latin American family, for instance, one must also address specifically the influence of early indigenous beliefs and practices. Bernand and Gruzinski suggest that the nomenclature used by precolonized Mexico questions the essentialist nature of the word *family*. There were various phrases to indicate groups or subgroups of kinship and economic and social ties: "*nahua* (a production and consumer group possessing a common residence) [. . .], *cencalli* (whole house), *cencaltin* (people of the same house), *cemithualtin* (people of the same house, of the same courtyard), *cenyeliztli* (people who are together, and *techan tlaca* (household)" (163). By the same token, constitution of the domestic group, practices of endogamy and exogamy, and matrimonial practices varied widely by region and by class throughout Meso-America (163-64). Despite their immense contributions to historiography, chroniclers such as Fray Bernardino de Sahagún (1499-1590) tended to distort and misunderstand the indigenous customs, and colonizers began to manipulate and control the indigenous groups, leaving us with a rather confused idea of what family and kinship meant in precolombian America (Bernand and Gruzinski 164).[6] The strict limitations that characterized the Western family were soon implanted in the "New World." Despite resistance along many lines, ties between spouses, like those between parent and child, were intensified, while connection to the community (including the previously existent female community of the household) was lessened; both *mancebas*, or concubines, and bastards became part of the new marginalized classes in colonial Meso-America (182-83). In this way the family system both apparently solidified European control and secretly maintained subversive indigenous customs.

The contemporary Argentine psychologist Salvador Minuchin asserts that the function of the family in society is the "support, regulation, nurturance, and socialization of it's members" (14). This function is relatively new, as the Colombian sociologist Guillermo Paez Morales stresses in his study of the family in Colombia. In the past, the traditional family was expected to control sexuality and preservation of the species, transmit family and cultural traditions, assign status, model formal relationships, provide care and education to children and food to the entire family, and furnish a space for leisure and religious practice. As Paez Morales wishes to imply that the family is disintegrating in contemporary times, his description of the modern family limits the functions of family to controlling sexuality and preservation of the species. He marks community and cultural contact as weak and posits that there is little control, continuity, communication, or connection built into current family systems. As much as his criticisms mirror the lament of the decline of family values, his opinion is inconsistent with contemporary social norms as well as ideals held up by family therapists and theorists.

Viewing Family Function: The Psychological Framework

Viewing the family as an emotional as well as an economic and social unit is one of the basic premises of Family Systems Theory (FST), which is instrumental in this collection of essays. From an FST perspective, successful families are those that fulfill all necessary functions to a satisfactory degree.

A case in point, family psychologist Murray Bowen defines families mostly on the basis on their systemic emotional and psychological interactions. The defining lines of family are thus predicated on emotional oneness rather than bloodlines, so that servants or family friends could possibly be more enmeshed than actual relatives (107). Bowen thus broadens the term family to include those persons who emotionally interact with each other in a systemic manner, who are most affected by the emotions and behaviors of their "family members". The psychologist R. D. Laing concurs that whether part of the bloodline or chosen as a spouse, each member belongs insofar as he or she plays a part in the family drama, however unknowingly. In other words, according to Laing, the important element of family is an instinctual continuance of the historical family patterns. For the anthropologist Kath Weston, the material, social, and emotional support may be even more significant than cohabitation or biological ties. Weston, equating love with kinship, looks at families "organized through ideologies of love, choice, and creation" (27). She explains that "grounding kinship in love de-emphasized distinctions between erotic and non-erotic relations while bringing friends, lovers, and children together under a single concept" (107). In this scenario, the mutual sense of responsibility and the wide range of support found in the family would be based on love and affection rather than on a duty to those joined by blood.

On the contrary, blood ties do not guarantee a loving or supportive environment at all. When patterns of behavior within the family group reveal a hierarchy, a system based on fear and oppression, on the subjugation and/or manipulation of its constituent members, or when some family members neglect, abuse, or ostracize others, we may well ask whether this group of people should be termed a family at all. At the very least, we may ask whether the system sufficiently fulfills the various purposes of family, for instance the "mutual obligations of help, protection, and assistance" or other mutual responsibilities of "services, affection, respect and attention."

When the reader encounters a family portrayed in literature, she instinctually interprets and analyzes that family in accordance with her own experience and cultural context. A reader who is informed in sociological or psychological discussions of family may also measure or understand the family according to those precepts. I suggest *reading* the fictional family, in other words interpreting or understanding it, however it is depicted in the text—rather than judging it according to an arbitrary and limited definition of family. As stated above, the Hispanic family is most emphatically not a homogeneous or static construction, although many prefer to think so and thus ignore or discount any group that may not reside within traditional boundaries of kinship. I refer in particular to so-called *alternative* fictional families, for instance the queer families portrayed in works by Esther Tusquets, Cristina Peri Rossi, José Donoso, Sara Levi Calderón, and others; in many cases, a critical inquiry of family patterns can establish fresh inroads to important texts or facilitate an analytical appreciation of formerly marginalized works. The reader is able to enter a discussion of the dynamics, dysfunction, and discourse of the family portrayed in a literary piece; in addition, she may probe the narrative, drama, or verse for the answer to relevant questions. What do the families mean to the literary characters who comprise them? What do they mean to the narrator, to the poetic voice, to the narrative, or even to the author of the literary work? And how do these possible meanings concur or clash with the reader's image of family? How are they informed by or how do they try to subvert the dominant discourse of social and interpersonal relationships, of gender roles, and of the structures of family in a particular culture? In addressing these issues of family in literature, we will open further the door to the exploration of the literary text.

Family Systems Psychology

Neither Freudian nor Lacanian-inspired literary criticism addresses these issues, because psychoanalysis as a science focuses on the individual. When one deals with family issues, in many instances it is necessary to analyze not just an individual and his/her problem or experience, but rather one must view each family member that participates (actively, passively, or by maintaining silence or distance) in the family dynamic and find out what this dynamic reflects or hides. Through bringing together as many family members as possible and visually attending what happens between them, what is said and how it is expressed (and accompanied by what gestures), what is never uttered, and how each person responds to the others, family therapists and researchers have begun to theorize a psychology of the family as a system. Since many narrative texts offer a multiplicity of voices and descriptive modes that all contribute to the portrayal of a/the literary family, I believe that the FST paradigm may serve both as an impetus and a critical device for the reader to garner and order these disparate elements that configure the textually represented family. This critical introduction will not attempt to answer outright the questions outlined above, but rather will discuss a possible method of literary criticism, based on Family Systems Theory (FST), that will allow the questions to be addressed both in general and in regards to specific texts. This collection of essays then provides some initial examples of critical inquiry based on an application of Family Systems ideas.[7]

The advent of Family Systems has been key in the evolution of psychology and therapy, and FST has a great deal of influence in the psychological community, yet most literary critics are not familiar with the breadth and depth of its analytic potential. In order to apply Family

Systems Theories to the literary text, or to value a systemic approach, it will be helpful to be familiar with certain basic concepts of its principal practitioners.[8] Especially germane is the FST vocabulary, which will be used without much additional explanation in the critical analyses to follow. While a study of this length does not permit a complete discussion of the history, theoretical basis, terminology, and usage of a field as vast as FST, this introduction will provide an overview of the most salient or representative ideas that are particularly relevant for the literary critic.

Family systems is related to a general systems perspective, here summarized succinctly by the sociologist Margaret Hall:

> Systems thinking is a holistic or comprehensive context for the study of all kinds of phenomena. This approach tries to account for the complex interplay of many influences, variables becoming focused in different formulations and propositions. [. . .] In systems thinking there is an express attempt to avoid arbitrarily singling out one variable as a cause and another variable or other variables as effects. In lieu of what is considered to be a piecemeal cause-effect approach to describing reality, systems thinking documents patterns of action or interaction and sequences of events in as broad a context as possible. (23)[9]

In the 1950s and early 1960s, systems thinking began to influence a broad range of scientific endeavors, including the social sciences of psychology and psychiatry, spurring the concurrent development of Family Systems Theory by a number of separate theorists/clinicians and/or research groups, especially Gregory Bateson at the Mental Research Institute Group (Bavelas 100; Schwartzman 1) and Murray Bowen (Hall 21; Kerr and Bowen viii). This is one of the reasons that FST is in truth a group of theories, sometimes complementary and other times somewhat contradictory, rather than one specific school or theoretical construct. As a side note, it is difficult to say whether FST came about when clinicians began to generalize and theorize about insights they had gleaned from their practice, or whether counseling psychologists started testing out certain theoretical notions in clinical settings. From the history of the various groups, it seems as though both processes were operating to some extent. Whichever the case, the theorizing and clinical application of a family-centered approach to psychology was a major divergence from the predominant ideas and practices of the time.

In contrast with previously predominant social science models, which try to isolate and define the material structure of psychopathology, *systems thinking* --as may be inferred by its origin-- sees more value in contextualizing the *problem* and examining the conjunction of elements that may justify or explain its occurrence. To be explicit, FST not only advocates studying the patient *within her family system*, but also requires a cognizance of the more inclusive sociocultural and/or political systems that circumscribe the family (Schwartzman 5, 10-13). While further development of FST has acknowledged inference to be a necessary interpretive tool, what remains key for the FST practitioner is the focus on *observable behavior* and *communication* as a way to understand the larger issues that implicate not only the individual patient but also each part of the family system to which she belongs. As the understanding of the family system begins to include more constituent elements, the observer simply has more material to use in her interpretation and analysis.

One general systems concept that is reflected abundantly in family systems writings is that any change in one part of a system necessarily occasions changes or reactions in the rest of the system, reactions that are not usually haphazard or indecipherable when seen within their context. Through the psychologist Murray Bowen's research it became clear that families, "while they had widely different values, attitudes, personalities, etc., still played out the same fundamental patterns in relationship" (Kerr & Bowen 10). Bowen wished to develop a theory that would both describe and account for the systemicity of the family, a theory that possessed the rigor and precision of a science (Kerr & Bowen 11). In general he confirmed that family functioning was more a continuum than an easily divisible dichotomy of "sick" and "healthy" or "functional" and "dysfunctional." Bowen elucidates that in general, relationships are governed by the (im)balance of two equally crucial life forces, individuality --the wish and ability to follow one's own directives --and togetherness-- the wish and ability to follow the directives of others (Kerr & Bowen 64-65). Relative to this is the degree to which we can consciously mediate our responses to those forces; *self-differentiation* is the acquired competence in maintaining objectivity about one's own and others emotional, feeling, and intellectual reactions, and acting out of a *choice* to be guided by either self-interest or the interest of the group. A higher level of self-differentiation allows more flexibility and less symptom development in times of crisis within relationship, whereas lower levels of self-differentiation in a family are manifested in quicker emotional perception of threat, more intense accompanying anxiety, and more extreme emotional measures to counteract the threat and anxiety (Kerr

& Bowen 71, 79).[10] Basically, the more well-differentiated a person is, the more she will be able to be an individual and at the same time comfortably be part of a group shared with other individuals.[11]

Less differentiated families may manifest general anxiety as dysfunction of a spouse, marital conflict, or impairment of a child (Bowen 168). The one(s) who "carry" the family dysfunction as symptoms do so because they are the main foci of the family's anxious attention (and projections) as well as because they are the most apt to "give up self" in helping to achieve family equilibrium. Symptom development is an extreme measure that reflects a limited family (and personal) adaptability to internal and external pressures (169).[12]   A nuclear family's low levels of differentiation and adaptability and accompanying high levels of chronic anxiety do not occur overnight, nor do they occur in a vacuum. Rather, they are mainly the product of the multigenerational emotional process, by which one generation transmits through relationships its own levels of anxiety, self-differentiation, and ability to deal with change or difference.

For instance, Bateson has theorized that schizophrenia results from dysfunctional patterns of communication and interpersonal relations, most specifically from the double bind (Sander 186; Marantz Cohen *Daughter's* 14-16). Bateson, et.al., describe the double bind as the perception of consistently conveyed contradictory messages, from persons believed to be crucial to the listener's survival, accompanied by the injunction not to question or escape the messages' contradictions. The result of chronic double-binding is that the "victim" will at some point cease to distinguish between the logical levels of the messages, will lose the ability to correctly interpret even clear messages from outside sources, and will in fact resort to radical "solutions" to the confusion and stress such as hallucinations and catatonia (251-64).

Despite discomfort and dysfunction, families usually try to keep things as they are. Don D. Jackson first coined the phrase *family homeostasis* to describe a process found regularly in any family system. In general terms, a family naturally attempts to sustain a balance in relationships; the first reaction to change will be an instinct to try vigorously to preserve the status quo. Failing that, the family will reach toward a new perceived (and relatively) comfortable balance. The maintenance of homeostasis occasions both overt and covert action on the part of family members, which can be manifested in attempts to close off the family system from outside influence or closely control any such interaction. In the further scrutiny of the concept of homeostasis, some theorists have found particularly paradoxical the sociological family functions that must at the same time maintain family connection/coherence and yet teach or foster individuation in each member (Marantz Cohen *Daughter's* 18).

Impelled by clinical experience, Virginia Satir began to incorporate the idea of the family as a system that should be treated together. Her joint goal was that the therapist would be able to learn the "rules governing [the] family group" (x), and through therapy the family members would be able to understand (and perhaps change) their behaviors that contributed to the problem (the identified patient's symptoms). Since Satir believes that the entire family system is invested in maintaining even a clearly dysfunctional homeostasis (2), because of each member's own particular needs, insecurities, neuroses, etc., she shifts the psychological perspective by 180 degrees (27-44). She sees the identified patient as manifesting an outward sign of the intrapsychic and interpersonal problems present within the family system, and tries to interpret how the "symptoms" or "sickness" are preserving --while paradoxically revealing-- the family's secrets, agendas, and processes. Thus what may appear sick or crazy to an outside observer may be performing a needed function within its dysfunctional system. In some cases, for example, Satir suggests that:

> The behavior of a problem child may be eminently functional within the family, because it allows the marital partners to keep the focus on the child as troublemaker and divert suspicion from the real troublemaker, which is their own conflicted relationship. (37)

As follows logically, the parents and other family members have a role in fostering the very behavior that in its extreme form they must admit to be odd, crazy, or even dangerous. Without being remotely aware of it, they send out verbal and nonverbal messages that induce or reinforce the established role played by each family member. Then at the first hint of a change in the status quo, including the temporary relief of symptoms in the identified patient, they will instinctively react in some way to stabilize the pattern that has worked for them in the past (35-40).

Arguably Satir's greatest theoretical contribution to FST is the work she has done with Communication Theory, which defines communication as all verbal and non-verbal interactions or transactions within a social context. Satir argues that communication techniques are eminently illustrative of interpersonal functioning, and their study "can help close the gap between inference and observation as well as help document the relationship between patterns of communication and symptomatic behavior" (63). Clear communication, necessary in order to give and receive information about our surroundings and our place within them, is made difficult not only because words have multiple denotations and connotations, but also because they are merely abstractions that do not correspond directly to their referents (64-65). Therefore, a functional communicator must be able to avoid overgeneralizations or sweeping assumptions, ask for and provide clarification or qualification when appropriate, send relatively complete and coherent messages, and be aware of whether or not communication actually occurs (65-74). In terms of the non-verbal aspects of communication, Satir posits that:

> A person simultaneously communicates by his gestures, facial expression, body posture and movement, tone of voice, and even by the way he is dressed. And all this communication occurs within a context. When does it take place? Where? With whom? Under what circumstances? What is the contract between the persons carrying on the interchange? [. . .] The receiver must assess all the different ways in which the sender is sending messages, as well as being aware of his own receiving system, that is, his own interpretation system. (75)

Also, communication has at least two levels and two purposes, the latter being to convey information and to request something of the receiver, otherwise referred to as the command aspect of a message (78). The two levels include the denotative, or literal content, and the metacommunicative, which includes additional information about the message's literal content as well as commentary on the social context and the interpersonal relationship of those involved in the communication process. Satir asserts that humans not only must communicate (by words, silence, or gestures), they also can not refrain from metacommunicating (by words, silence, or gestures) (76); at the highest level of abstraction, "all messages. . .can be characterized as 'validate me' messages. These are frequently interpreted as 'Agree with me,' 'Be on my side,' 'Validate me by sympathizing with me,' or, 'Validate me by showing me you value me and my ideas'" (81).

Sometimes communication is simply *contradictory*, being inconsistent on one level, such as when a person says overtly, "I love you and I hate you." Satir separates as more serious *incongruent* communication, when the disparity occurs on different levels of communication. For instance, there may be inconsistency between the denotative message, the verbal metacommunication, and the non-verbal metacommunication: "The sender may say 'Come closer, darling,' then stiffen, and then say, 'I want to make love" (83).   As stated above, for some people it feels too dangerous or foreign to communicate directly or overtly, but rather they have been taught or indirectly influenced to communicate via contradictory and incongruent, or even incoherent messages. When a dysfunctional communicator does not know how to elicit clarification, or is under an injunction not to question unclear or mixed messages (e.g. in a double bind situation), and has a faulty perception of what may be expected of her in a social context, the information she receives will be incomplete at best, occasioning confused and inappropriate reactions. According to Satir, "difficulty in communication is closely linked to an individual's self-concept, that is, his self-image and self-esteem" (94); if he views any hint of different-ness in others as threatening his identity and existence, then communication will be treated as a war zone where he must constantly be on the attack or on the defense.   In families with an identified patient, the patterns of (mis)communication usually embody just such an embattled tone.

The founder of Structural Family Therapy, another approach based in systems thinking, is the Argentine Salvador Minuchin.[13] Minuchin emphasizes the impact humankind's social context has on his behavior, especially since the onset of the technological age in the twentieth century has challenged old views of the human being as a hero with unlimited resources to recover and dominate.

The rapid and extensive social changes occurring in today's urban industrial society have minimized some of the previously crucial functions of the family, but have intensified the major remaining function--that of supporting family members psychosocially and preparing them to live and adapt within their existing socio-economic culture "in transition" (46-47).   This being the case, a family's functioning is in a sense reflective of and accountable to both its members and its community, the latter comprising the larger system to which the family belongs. Family interactions directly influence the attitudes and beliefs of family members, it is obvious, but the psychological impact of the family dynamic is greater than such a statement might suggest. Since the structure of the family is extremely resistant to change, in some way this prohibits it from carrying out its necessary social and psychological functions.   However, a well-functioning family, while perhaps conflictual, will still help its members to learn to behave acceptably in a variety of social situations and positions of power, and to deal adequately with the normal stressors and transition periods of life.

Theorists like Minuchin, Bowen, Bateson and Satir built the foundation for understanding the family as a system that is more than just the sum of its parts.   Family Systems Theory explores functionality, communication, interpersonal boundaries, the impact of external or internal changes, and the connection of physical, emotional, and psychological development.   The underlying premise is that a family is and thus will act as a system.   In sum, Family Systems Theory provides a multifaceted and well-developed set of parameters within which one may assess and interpret the complexities of family dynamics and their connection to the sociocultural context.

Connecting the Cords: The Advent of FST Literary Criticism

Despite the abundance of Hispanic films and literary texts that are centered on either traditional or alternative families, there exists no systematized method of studying the family as it appears in these works.   As suggested above, critical analyses have not ignored the idea of family, although commentary has tended to be either more limited in scope or simply without a broad organizing methodology.   For instance, some Freudians have studied examples of the family romance in literary works; other critics have focused on mother-daughter relationships in particular texts.   Such studies are quite valuable, but at the same time they do not come close to uncovering the fullness of the family-literature connection in Spain, Latin America, and the Latino U.S.   Each literary work that is centered around family offers an immense range of subject matter that can prompt critical study.   For example, one may ask more sociological questions such as whether a testimonial text like *Me llamo Rigoberta Menchú y así me nació la conciencia* (1983; *Rigoberta Menchú*) is attempting to portray the Guatemalan indigenous community as the predominant family system. Along other lines, one may wish to probe the relation between narrative construction and family dynamics in a novel like the Puerto Rican Magali García Ramis's *Felices días, Tío Sergio* (1986; Happy days, Uncle Sergio).   Taking yet another tack, one could delve into the psychological transition of the family system during the process of immigration in a film like *El Norte* (1983).   The possibilities are practically endless. Hispanic literature abounds with representations of incestuous families, abusive families, enmeshed families, and idealized families.   There are clear interpersonal alliances that challenge social norms and there are family patterns that resist changes reflected in the broader cultural context.   Some texts compare and contrast distinct family systems, thus critiquing or questioning either the traditional or the alternative family structures, or both. Clearly, even one very complex text might give rise to any number of new studies in its own right. Yet the issues manifested by this proliferation of family representations in literature transcend the specificity introduced by individual texts. An expansive and flexible theory of literary criticism of the family is needed to put some order to the critical discussion without unduly restricting the field of study. Family Systems Theory offers an engaging, intellectually interesting and critically productive framework within which to explore the complexity of family in literature.

How, then, can the psychological terminology and therapeutic framework of FST be adapted to a methodology of literary criticism? To what extent is a FST-based criticism being employed now, and what are the objectives and tenets of a Family Systems textual reading? To begin to answer these questions, I will first provide a selected overview of the corpus of critical works proceeding under a FST framework.[14]

Apparently the first to examine fictional families using a systems framework was psychoanalyst and family therapist Fred M. Sander, who began writing on family systems in the early 1970s. In the tradition of many psychoanalysts (including of course Freud), Sander utilizes dramatic plays to illustrate the theoretical paradigms and clinical practices he employs in family therapy, thus underlining the value of interdisciplinary studies combining psychology and literature. Sander's *Individual and Family Therapy: Toward an Integration* (1979) traces the emergence of family therapy and discusses interactive, intrapsychic, and interpersonal relations within families. Since "often it is the artist who intuits and reflects these creative revolutionary conceptions of ourselves" (xvi), Sander communicates many of his psychological observations through literary examples, both in the classroom and in his writings. Just as the plays he has chosen illustrate the theoretical material he wishes to introduce, his family systems reading of these texts provides fresh insight for the literary critic. First Sander looks at Shakespeare's *Hamlet*, beginning with the query: "What's the matter with 'What's the matter with Hamlet?'?" (6).[15] While he allows that *Hamlet* was "portraying and exploring the emergence of a more modern man in whom the external interpersonal battlefields become internalized to a marked degree" (7), and therefore has been excellent material for psychoanalytic interpretation, he notes that there are certain questions outside of that paradigm that must be raised, such as, "Why could Claudius not control his urge to kill his brother? What led Gertrude into an adulterous and hasty incestuous

marriage to her brother-in-law? What was the nature of the family
system that allowed the enactment of the oedipal crime?" (6) Perhaps
the most fascinating thought proffered in this chapter is the linking of
Hamlet's supposed madness and the reactions and reflections this
causes in others to the phenomenon of the *identified patient*, who is
often scapegoated for all family trouble and at the least deflects
attention from other family members' dysfunctional behaviors.

> Through displacements or projections of their own
> preoccupations and points of view, the characters in the play put forth
> loss, anger, ambition, motives of revenge, and the irreducible taint of
> madness itself, as partially correct causes of Hamlet's disorder. These
> theories in turn defend each of them against further awareness of their
> own conflicts. Polonius does not want to examine his anxiety and
> jealousy over the possible loss of the only woman in his life, Gertrude
> need not look further into the implications of her hasty remarriage.
> Claudius can psychopathically attempt to eliminate the anticipated
> retaliation for the murder of his brother, and finally Hamlet himself can
> deny his murderous impulses, all by focusing upon *his madness*. (14)

Despite Hamlet's statement that he would counterfeit madness to
achieve his own ends, the rest of the family accepts and somehow
delights in his lack of reason, each claiming a part in its causation or
planning to use it in some form or fashion. The fact that the literary
critic, in focusing the brunt of her attention and explication on the
designated family problem, could be in unknowing collusion with the
rest of Hamlet's family is an irony too delectable to ignore.

One of the first literary scholars who incorporated FST into critical
readings of narrative is Paula Marantz Cohen in "Stabilizing the Family
at Mansfield Park" (1987). In this article on Jane Austen's 1814 novel
Mansfield Park, Marantz Cohen's argument rests on the premise that in
the Mansfield Park family, "individual behavior only has meaning
when studied in relation to the behavior of all other family members"
(671). Marantz Cohen recognizes the particular relevance to the novel
of such concepts as the Oedipal complex and Lévi-Strauss's theories on
incest, which would reflect a Lacanian reading, but she asserts that "the
personal dynamic and the family dynamic interlock to reinforce each
other," thereby making it necessary to study the latter in more detail
(672). To do this she utilizes Family Systems Theory. An emerging
truth in Cohen's essay is that Austen's novel portrays the nineteenth-
century shift from a looser-knit kinship structure (of the protagonist's--
Fanny--family of origin) to a more self-contained, insular, and even

enmeshed family, like that into which Fanny is incorporated (674). In contrast to a traditional, linear family hierarchy, Fanny's new family places value on its members by virtue of their relational or affective ties to others within the system (675). Marantz Cohen sees Mansfield Park as a thematization of the closed family system as a social (and literary) ideal of the historical period; the family laments "unwanted contractions of our family circle" as vigorously as it guards against foreign intrusions, continuously shifting and reacting until finally an equilibrium is reached through the marriage of Fanny to her cousin Edmund, signified as so strong an affective bond that the family feels stable (676-77). This steadfast connection is brought about by a family dynamic which places Fanny in the role of scapegoat and links her every pleasure to the instances in which Edmund briefly takes her part, owing to his own feelings of guilt (680). Marantz Cohen suggests that a particularly effective reading of the novel is possible when one eschews a study of Fanny's deep-rooted need for this masochistic pleasure in favor of an exploration of how her personal drives interact with the family's need for a member exactly like her (681). Marantz Cohen sees Fanny's submission and compliance as a springboard to power, just as conversely the family patriarch Thomas becomes balanced without having to relinquish his dominant role; in this way Fanny is symbolic of the woman who gains in personal and social power through a shift in family dynamics on a macrosystemic level (689-90).

Marantz Cohen deals with FST more extensively in her book *The Daughter's Dilemma: Family Process and the Nineteenth Century Novel*. Her introduction very briefly introduces major concepts of some theorists, such as Bateson's double bind, Jackson's family homeostasis, and Bowen's enmeshment vs. cutoff, triangulation, and multigenerational model for mental illness, all notions that she will apply to the Victorian novels under study.[16] Still, for the most part the FST approach is limited to discussing the dramatic content of the novels and the relationship this has with the novelists' own life experience. There are many other aspects of the novels that could be explored using FST, particularly the more formal elements of the narrative. For instance, one could mine the subtleties of language used in the novels, commenting upon the fascinating dialogue and even the narration as communicational acts, for which Virginia Satir's communication theory would seem appropriate. The strengths of Maranz Cohen's critical work include the insightful manner in which the author employs Family Systems ideas to explicate the motivations of key characters in the novels, and even more importantly the fact that in a couple of instances she offers a reading that differs radically from the extant criticism of the work in question. As an example, her innovative treatment of Emily Brontë's novel *Wuthering Heights* (1848) reconsiders the importance of the "peripheral" character Nellie Dean and repositions the novel into a believable and congruent sociohistorical context, effectively arguing for a reevaluation of its place within the literary canon (107-109; 98-99). Without a doubt Marantz Cohen makes an interesting sociological case as to the changing and crucial role of the daughter in both literature and culture in the Victorian age.[17]

One of the most valuable attributes of John V. Knapp's monograph *Striking at the Joints* is the convincing and concrete commentary on how contemporary psychology sheds light on literary texts. Knapp dedicates one chapter to an FST analysis of two novels, D.H. Lawrence's *Sons and Lovers* (1913) and Henry Roth's *Call it Sleep* (1934), which he claims provides a "more interesting reading" of the principal characters and their family dynamics (60). Knapp's reading of *Sons and Lovers* draws heavily from all three schools of FST, the historical, structure/process, and experiential (65), with perhaps some preference for the work of Minuchin and Bowen. Knapp shows that the "early emotional and sexual ruination" of the protagonist, Paul, cannot be explained solely by a too intense an attachment to his mother, but rather that his distress is a symptom of a completely dysfunctional household where each member, his father and brother included, have a part in perpetuating Paul's inability to form a healthy relationship with a significant other (64). Indeed, the young man mirrors attitudes and behaviors that he has seen in each family member, and in fact that both of his parents have brought with them from their families of origin. A critical focus on Paul's relationship with his father brings to light the way narrative strategies are employed to represent the older man's affective involvement with his family, while at the same time reflect Paul's perception of his father as absent or at least emotionally invisible in his life. Here the critic is encouraged to explore the constructions of language and expressions that either make evident or attempt to conceal family interactions downplayed in other psychological paradigms. Knapp's reading is an example of how utilizing a FST approach to some literary works will allow for a more thorough study of their complex narrative strategies. Equally important, by viewing the novel in this manner the reader may become privy to a much richer understanding of each character's motivations and contributions in the family battles being waged, and in the end have a much more balanced picture of the protagonist's psychological experiences.

A scholar of Anglophone literature, Jerome Bump has begun to employ Family Systems in quite a different manner, in both criticism and teaching. Bump shows a familiarity with a wide range of family theorists while maintaining a preference for the less theoretical version connected to John Bradshaw, a popular speaker whose ideas have reached a wide public via the mass media. In general, Bump tends to favor a reader-centered approach to literature, with FST being used as a tool that allows the reader to access not only the text, but also his or her own personal and/or experiential relationship with the text.[18] By way of illustration, in "*Jane Eyre* and Family Systems Therapy" (1993) he discusses teaching Charlotte Brontë's novel with a methodology reminiscent of bibliotherapy, in which the therapist guides her client in the reading of chosen narrative or poetic texts in order to promote identification, self-awareness, or even catharsis.[19] Bump describes "how a new reader-centered psychological approach to literature, combined with awareness of sexism, classism, and racism, has made reading *Jane Eyre* a powerful, deeply relevant personal experience for me and many of my students" (130-31). Bump points out the relevance of FST in a discussion of the dysfunctional family, of which there have been countless examples in world literature, and encourages students to use textual passages as the impetus to discover and explore their own experiences of the transgenerational repetition compulsion, triangulation, threats of abandonment, rigid role assignment, physical or emotional abuse, and other such family dynamics. In the case of *Jane Eyre*, the protagonist is observed in various phases of personal and family development. The FST approach facilitates a deeper understanding of the interconnectedness of Jane's experience of abuse and her low self-esteem, her acceptance of the roles of scapegoat and lost child, and ultimately her social and emotional dependence upon a dominant male--Rochester. Each family member is studied in terms of his/her stated feelings, reactions, mode of speech, and contribution to the maintenance of the family homeostasis. While no one character can be blamed for the tone of cruelty in the family interactions, nor for the family's need to persist in a status quo that thrives on systemic suppression and oppression, neither can any character be seen as an innocent bystander or victim with no personal responsibility. A true innovator in the classroom, beyond initiating frank exchanges about these sensitive topics, Bump goes so far as to structure and model functional interactions between members of the class "family," thereby providing a counterbalance to the negative examples found in *Jane*

Eyre, Wuthering Heights, and many of the individual histories related by himself and his students (131-32).[20]

Finally, the 1997 volume of *Style,* a thematic issue entitled *Family Systems Psychotherapy and Literature/Literary Criticism* (31.2, March 1998), edited by John V. Knapp and Kenneth Womack, is a heterogeneous collection of essays that greatly strengthens the current field of FST literary analysis and suggests the growing appeal of critical studies of the family in literature. The volume includes an introduction to Family Systems literary criticism by Knapp, a survey article by Bump, and four other essays that demonstrate the wide-ranging applicability of a FST-based criticism. James M. Decker examines triangular enmeshment and frustrated attempts at self-differentiation in "'Choking on my Own Saliva': Henry Miller's Bourgeois Family Christmas in *Nexus.*" In response to extant criticism on Miller that emphasizes his anti-capitalist leanings, Decker submits that the author (and the author's literary persona--the protagonist Henry Miller) may find much of his resistance and anger coming from "a deeper conflict within his own family" (270).

Judith Ann Spector's contribution, "Anne Tyler's *Dinner at the Homesick Restaurant*: A Critical Feast," credibly argues in favor of FST as a critical tool in writing and in the classroom. Before entering the analysis of Tyler's novel, Spector explains the basic attraction of this methodology:

> My own students understand 'family systems theory'--at least on an informal basis--because they have lived it on a conscious level; they understand dysfunctional families. [. . .] What is more important, they expect literature to teach them about their own lives as well as about universal truths regarding human behavior. What is remarkable about contemporary family systems theory as a means of interpreting literature is that it can meet both of those expectations. (310)

Spector's exclusive concentration on the textual analysis allows her to weave a multilevel analysis of *Dinner at the Homesick Restaurant* as an example of the "intergenerational transmission of symptoms."

In the same vein, Gary Storhoff argues that FST provides new insight and balance to a critical study of Toni Morrison's most enterprising novel. In "Anaconda Love: Parental Enmeshment in Toni Morrison's *Song of Solomon*" Storhoff first delineates the multigenerational progression of family patterns that bears upon the behavior of the main characters. Building on this foundation, he then examines how the author portrays the procreative family systems of this younger generation, coming to the conclusion that Morrison "does not privilege Pilate's unconventional, matriarchal, marginalized family unit over Macon and Ruth's conventional, patriarchal, bourgeois nuclear family, as critics often claim" (291). Storhoff's probing of the characters' psychological complexities, especially Macon and Ruth's son Milkman, both on an individual level and in relation to their immediate and extended family, reframes Milkman's "marvelous epiphany" as a surprising and encouraging deviation from the over-involvement that was his patrimony.

Womack contributes the volume's most complex essay, "'Only Connecting' With Family: Class, Culture, and Narrative Therapy in E. M. Forster's *Howard's End.*". Whereas many psychological literary critics have been satisfied to mirror the therapeutic role and provide an interpretation of the mental and emotional processes of the characters, which is certainly of value, this study proceeds to situate the literary work within a larger social context--an endeavor that is also supported by the systems approach. Womack thus posits a thesis that combines a commentary on family dynamics with that of larger social systems that function similarly to family, and furthermore substantiates an intertextuality between *Howard's End* and the "*Principia Ethica* (1902), G. E. Moore's Bloomsbury-era manifesto on the social and ethical rewards of friendship and aesthetic experience" (256). Mining the innovative writings of Michael White as well as other traditional proponents of FST, Womack examines the connection between psychology, family, social structure, and narrative.[21]

The first article to apply Family Systems to Hispanic literature, Cooper's "Cristina Peri Rossi's 'The Witness': A Study in Utopia and Infiltration" looks at subversion in the lesbian family. The lesbian family system portrayed in "The Witness," originally painted as utopic by the young male narrator, is infiltrated by violence and power struggle attributed to the patriarchy. Cooper shows that the communication, generational roles, and power dynamic within this lesbian family contribute just as much to the violence as any external influence. This reading interrogates the assumption that a lesbian family would be inherently different than a heterosexual one and complicates the reader's urge to place blame on the young man, even though he is the one to manifest violence and sexual aggression at the story's climax. The article posits that the story, a socially relevant and complex narration, opens up the field of contemporary Latin American literature to include a new sub-genre: the lesbian and gay family narrative.[22]

How to Tie the Knot, or a Practical Guide to an FST Approach

The usefulness of a FST methodology seems to be clearly indicated by its growing visibility in publications in the field of literary and cultural criticism and by the increasing complexity of FST-based literary analyses. While there is as of yet no official manifesto that outlines a set of specific requirements or tenets of "good FST criticism," the main objectives and strategies of the methodology are possible to cull from a study of extant critical literature (including the essays in this collection). A key concept in FST criticism is the systemicity of the family group; one might say that even in literature (or perhaps, especially in literature) a family is more than the sum of its parts. The foremost requisite of the proposed methodology, then, is that any FST study should not ignore the family and social system by focusing too closely on the individual. Whereas much psychological literary criticism successfully zeroes in on the protagonist of a novel, for example, in order to investigate minutely his or her pathological characteristics, childhood development, or thought processes (to mention but a few possibilities), that will not be the sole issue here. On the contrary, the methodology of this study will consistently encourage a study of the entire family --however that may be defined or represented in the individual text(s)-- both as a system in its own right and as a subsystem of larger social groups. This focus does not in any way preclude or denigrate the psychological study of individual characters in the texts discussed; on the contrary, such a complementary study will often seem particularly necessary. Nonetheless, the consideration of the family as a special kind of group, and a curiosity as to the communication and other interworkings therein will take precedence here. Similarly, for the purposes of this study in particular, the methodological approach must be open to and useful in the analyses of a wide range of families. The films and texts to be discussed portray ideal families, gay families, dysfunctional families, and "broken" families, yet they do not necessarily presuppose a *real* norm from which these examples stray. Rather, the narratives engender a complex questioning of family and society that would escape a methodology too ensconced in a limited definition of family.

While harvesting all the insights offered by an interdisciplinary approach, the methodology should be primarily a vehicle for literary criticism. This means a focus on the literary elements of a text, including but not limited to its structure, tone, narrative voice, use of metaphor and other figurative language, use of imagery, lexicon, plot, and temporal or spatial innovation. The structure of many texts mirrors the structure of the family portrayed within, for example being overly rigid and closed, or conversely having extremely diffuse boundaries, or perhaps, having different members of the family competing to be heard as the narrative voice. The narrator's use of language can reflect a dysfunctional system of communication, encoding messages with metaphor or a disjointed stream of consciousness. This may be underlined by the inclusion of dialogue or narrated interactions between family members that substantiate the reader's suspicions of the family's (lack of) functionality. A decided emphasis on the family can be achieved by locating the action in the private arena of the domestic space, where flashbacks and projections can parallel a family's inability to live in the present. While these are but examples of the narrative strategies to be foregrounded in a family systems analysis, they should suffice to suggest the inherently literary nature of the study of family in literature.

As the FST critic "reads" the textual family (whether in narrative, drama, film, or other cultural production), a primary focus should be the discourse, or in other words the system of communication represented in the text. FST provides a point of entrance to the dysfunctional communication so abundantly manifested in literature, for instance when the protagonists' utterances conflict directly with their revealed thoughts or described actions, or when they seem to act or speak (or remain silent) in a manner that does not befit the social context put forth in the work. While these confusing textual interactions may reflect many authorial intentions, such as a social criticism of gender or class oppression, a satire of an individual's or a group's rhetoric, or a parody of another existing text, they also may point (intentionally or not) to the character's psychological development and current role within the family system. Delving into this issue can give the reader further insight into both the character and the sociocultural milieu that supports and encourages the repression or distortion of communication.

In the analysis of some contemporary texts, an FST-based criticism will often dovetail with other currents in literary theory in its focus on the structure of the literary work. As may have become apparent in the review of family systems informed criticism, FST appears to offer a high degree of compatibility with the particular concerns of contemporary literary studies. In particular, much post-modern literary criticism pays attention to the apparent textual incoherence and the schism between an easily discernible literary reality and a lapse into the realm of literary fantasy. This reflects the sociocultural environment (and the complex state of the family) at the transition into the twenty first century, in which a constant barrage of images and information bears witness to the rapidity of technological change and the impossibility of finding a single "reality" that is stable or reliable. In this way, literature is merely mirroring the fractured perception of life and the accompanying emotional distress and psychological confusion that may be the reader's own experience. A systemic psychological approach offers plentiful insight into the postmodern text or postmodern family.

One related issue that is often raised in contemporary criticism is the unreliability of the narrator and the implications for interpreting the literary text as truthful, falsified, or somewhere in between. Sander observes that "where Freud gathers the pieces of the total situation from his patient, the family therapist seeks such data by direct observation. The departure from the rules of the confidential doctor-patient relationship is here as radical as when Freud departed from the model of professional conduct of his time" (26). In general, this results in a study of the multiple voices in the text. However, I see an interesting complication for the literary critic when dealing with a text narrated in the first person. Although FST would encourage the attempt to garner information by direct textual observation of dialogue and behavior, this attempt is obviously thwarted to some degree when the narration is explicitly or implicitly related by one person. Indeed, even when the narrator is purported to be omniscient, or is an amalgamation of disparate voices, one has to take into account the fallibility or incompleteness of any narration. Interestingly enough, in a certain way this approximates the job of the therapist in session, to sort through the perspectives that are put forth, to see the truth of interaction through the lies, omissions, and hidden or explicit agendas of the family members, and then to remain conscious of her own expectations, experiences, biases, etc.--finally trying to emerge with the most inclusive interpretation of the family system. This challenge of finding the interpersonal relations --in other words, the multiplicity-- in the first-person narrator, and dealing with the ever-present subjective filter of any narrator, may offer another interesting twist to family systems criticism.

These, then, are the basic criteria for a family systems critical methodology for literary analysis: interdisciplinarity with the fields of contemporary family psychology and family sociology; an awareness of the cultural context of the text (and the families portrayed within); attention to the whole system of family rather than to only one of its members; emphasis on the systemicity of family in terms of interpersonal dynamics, communication, and interaction with the social system at large; and a close textual reading that comments upon its literary strategies. In general, such a study will be prompted by the critical and/or social questions suggested by the specific text rather than standing alone as a psychological investigation of the characters or even the work as a whole. This will be the prevailing framework of the readings proposed in this study, an outline of which follows.

Unraveling Family Discourse and Dynamics: The Essays

In "Shifting Families and Incest in Chacel and Moix," Ellen Mayock examines the techniques used in two novels to foreground the intricate play of family shifting and incest in Spanish post-War narrative. Using a systems-based analysis, the author traces the rejection of traditional perspectives of family, society, and politics in Rosa Chacel's *Memorias de Leticia Valle* (1945) and Ana María Moix's *Julia* (1970). Mayock posits that the female protagonists of Chacel and Moix exile themselves from the traditional family system by creating new social groups, or "social kinship family" as introduced by social scientist David Popence. Each protagonist must then come to terms with her orphandom or self-exile from the family, must reconcile her biologically female body with an intellectually and emotionally androgynous mentality, and must evaluate her own stance against that of society as she becomes party to strains of incest within the family system. Mayock demonstrates how narrative elements combine to create a "non-heterosexual rhetoric" in which the daughters/ protagonists shift their identity, their family position, and their gaze to encompass a new reading of gender roles in Spanish family and society. In this study of emotional triangulation and psychological movement, the narrative cords of the novels are shown to be tortuously and insidiously imbricated within the web of the family system.

Family Systems Theories provide new insight into perhaps the most traditional and well-read of all Spanish literary texts in Don Miller's "Dysfunction, Discord, and Wedded Bliss: Baroque Families in *Don Quixote*." His insightful essay juxtaposes the family and conjugal ideals set forth in various prescriptive texts of the Spanish Medieval and Golden Age periods with the representations of family and marriage in Cervantes' masterpiece. Taking care not to impose an anachronistic ideology onto the *Quixote*, Miller distinguishes between dysfunction as it is understood in contemporary psychology and what might be called "social dysfunction," or the transgression and subversion of family norms as set forth by the dominant discourse of the time. Miller asserts that the Spanish bard's "focus on the realities of inharmonious and conflictive family life clearly satirizes the marital bliss and familial symmetry proposed by his ecclesiastical and philosophical predecessors." The article turns to some of the most humorous scenes of the *Quixote* to exemplify the text's success in inverting the gender roles and family dynamics of the Spanish Golden Age and in the creation of a topsy-turvy, Baroque system of family and marriage that unties the perfectionist Renaissance ideology.

Miyam Criado explores the portrayal of a mother/daughter relationship in the context of the struggle for discourse in "Matrofobia y matrilinealidad en *Un aire de familia* de Silvia Italiano." Pointing out the pervasive theme of matrophobia in literature by Spanish American and Iberian women writers, Criado explains that only dead mothers are characterized as a possible positive influence on their daughters' development. (The rest are depicted as pitiful caricatures of a social class and/or constructed as devouring monsters whose only desire is to control every aspect of their daughters' lives.) The author's essay rests on the assumption that Italiano departs from this paradigm and the daughter-centric literary tradition, deconstructing the patriarchal structures on which a daughter's discourse is constructed in order to create an alternative space for the mother's voice and authority. One can envision a revitalized narrative genre in which the mother is no longer a victim silenced by age and gender, a passive (if aggressive) member of the family system, but rather a positive force to be reckoned with. Criado demonstrates how the novel reveals and denounces the patriarchal economy and its destruction of matrilineal bonds as a way to perpetuate the status quo. Her essay is hopeful in that it unearths a social call to arms implicit in Silvia Italiano's *Un aire de familia*, ironically a plea for the reinstitution of the bonds that unite women in family.

A darker and more disturbing vision of family and society emerges in "Dysfunctional Family, Dysfunctional Nation: *El cuarto mundo* by Diamela Eltit," by Lea Ramsdell. Her reading shows how "the artifice of Agusto Pinochet's nationalistic discourse, in which he unabashedly held his wife and himself up as the mother and father figure in Chile, is laid bare by the writer Diamela Eltit." Ramsdell utilizes Judith Butler's definition of gender as performance to interpret the novel's main characters, twin siblings of supposedly different genders and their parents. They are shown to be completely unable to reproduce the binary oppositions of *machismo/marianismo* set forth by Chile's leader and first lady, thereby failing to fulfill the functions assigned to them in the national (and family) project. As pointed out by Ramsdell, "The culmination of this resistance to overarching public dogma is the pregnancy that results from the incestual relationship between the twins." Obviously the resultant family is abnormal, transgressive, and offensive rather than productive, loyal, and predictable. However, Ramsdell suggests that the novel ends with the conception of an alternative family system, one that despite its incomprehensibility may have both the strength and the extreme potentiality of subversion needed to contravene the imposed nationalistic/familial doctrine of dictatorial Chile.

The essay "Familia y comunidad como bases del proceso de adaptación social en tres largometrajes chicanos" reflects the feminist and politically aware criticism of its author, María Claudia André. Here she explores the process of acculturation and life experiences of three Hispanic families in their quest to settle in the United States in the films *...Y no se lo tragó la tierra (...And the Earth Did Not Devour Him)*, *El Norte* (The North), and *My Family, Mi Familia*. The films suggest the significance of a solid family unit/bond required for the Chicano and Guatemalan refugees in order to survive the trauma of migration, transculturation, and exile. André posits that while each of the migrant and immigrant families eventually manages to settle and establish in the United States, not all are equally successful in this venture. Due to the lack of emotional and psychological support, the siblings in *El Norte* fail to accomplish the same goal, miserably failing in spite of their enthusiasm and courage. First delving into the communication dynamics and emotional conflicts among family members, as well as the men's and women's roles within the family system, the essay then turns to a critical reading of the cinematic depiction of Hispanics/ Latinos/ Chicanos and the representation of the Other. The complexities of cross-cultural relations between cultural identity and space present a challenge to the immigrants' quest for identity and recognition within American society, which is further complicated by the influence of Chicano narrative discourse on the family system.

Dinora Cardoso's "*Celestino antes del alba*: The Family as Agent of the Community" is a reading of Cuban family and society in the 1968 novel by Reinaldo Arenas. The traditional Cuban family rests on certain principles associated with the head of the family. A double standard of morality allows men to carry on discreet, adulterous relationships as long as they do not cause a scandal, while the wife is barred from such relations. Even children do not escape the arbitrary nature of society, "illegitimate" or "natural" children being summarily discarded and stripped of their birthrights. Cuban society of the mid twentieth century had established a type of social and family hierarchy based on gender and sexual preference that is exposed in Reinaldo Arenas's *Celestina antes del alba*. In the novel the unconventional behavior of women and children is castigated not just by society at large but rather by a dictatorial male (or father) figure; in essence, the family acts as an agent of the community in repressing these alternate sexualities. By the same token, it is by codifying, writing, and leaving a historical account of the alternate experiences, in the language of the oppressor, that some modification of the system has been made. Using a feminist Foucauldian lens, Cardoso's essay explores the family dynamics and discourse in *Celestina antes del alba* as a double-edged sword that both protects and destroys sexual proscription.

The theme of alternative sexualities continues to be central in the last essay of the collection, "Queering the Family Narrative in Contemporary Latin American and Latino Literature." Cooper's wide-ranging study reviews the wealth of literary texts (and films as literature) that represent a queered, abnormal, and/or sexually transverse idea of family or kinship. While the field of Hispanic literature has been enriched by the relatively recent emergence of gay and lesbian-focused critical works, such as those by David William Foster, Sylvia Molloy, Robert Irwin, Amy Kaminsky, Emilie Bergmann, Paul Julian Smith, Daniel Balderston, Roberto Reis, and Elena M. Martínez, among others, no critical work as of yet has focused pivotally on the problematic of a queer family discourse. The works discussed in Cooper's essay can be read as queer family narrative both for their portrayal of gay, lesbian, or alternatively gendered/sexed family dynamics and for their intertwining of the ideas of queer family and narrative (both existing due to the creative efforts of their "authors"). If, as Adrienne Rich posits, "cultural imperialism . . . [is] the decision made by one group of people that another shall be cut off from their past, shall be kept from the power of memory, context, continuity," (xii) then narratives like Manuel Puig's *The Kiss of the Spider Woman*, Sara Levi Calderon's *The Two Mujeres*, and Magali García Ramis' *Happy Days, Uncle Sergio* are anti-imperialistic and subversive acts that explode the silencing of the queer family. Here the juxtaposition of Family Systems Theories and Queer Theory suggests a direction for future research and the fruitful possibility of more detailed studies of the works mentioned.

In essence, this collection of essays is meant to be just that—the initial inroads into the study of the family system in Latin American, Spanish, and Latina/o literature. If the exploration found within is necessarily incomplete, considering the enormous body of works that could possibly fit within the scope of its project, then hopefully the ideas set forth here will provide an interesting challenge to be met by current and future scholars. If this book can contribute to the critical dialogue on Hispanic literature, and if it can bring into the discussion the systemic quality of the family (within) narrative and dramatic production, then it will have been a resounding success.

NOTES

[1] One excellent collection of short stories that features stories about family by Spanish women writers is *Madres e hijas*, ed. Laura Freixas, Barcelona: Anagrama, 1996.

[2]Ferdinand Mount recalls that scholars such as Germaine Greer and Shulamith Firestone rely on Engels's evidence of the impermanence of the nuclear family in their attempts to create women-friendly alternatives to the patriarchal order (9-10, 242, 244-5).

[3]Leach's famous pronouncement that the nuclear family "is a most unusual kind of organisation and I would predict that it is only a transient phase in our society" is cited in Mount (38-39), who as well includes mention of Stone's *The Family, Sex and Marriage in England 1500-1800* (1979) and Shorter's *The Making of the Modern Family* (1977).

[4]In Mount's chapters on "Matchmaking and Lovemaking" and "The Troubadour Myth" he attempts to substantiate his vehement disagreement with C. S. Lewis's *The Allegory of Love* (1936). Also in answer to Engels, Mount argues that what this latter terms "modern sex love" is not at all a recent phenomenon, but is documented in writing and oral history across the ages. Although his proofs are less than compelling, the point he makes that the un-moneyed classes have been much freer in courting and marrying for "love" rather than from social or economic constraints is certainly valid. Nonetheless, this point had already been made, if not developed, by Engels.

[5]As an aside, Eli Zaretsky argues that the opposition of family and state is a relatively modern construct stemming from the Western world's adherence to the capitalist ideology. Like other feminists, she questions the dichotomy of the public and the private, maintaining that the relationship between family and state has always been an intimate one, albeit never static or one-sided in terms of influence. (188-224) When entering the discussion of families in literary texts, it will be interesting to ponder the contradictory assumptions presented by Mount, Engels, and feminists like Zaretsky.

[6]Sahagún was a Franciscan missionary, historiographer and philologist who preserved pre-historic literature and testimonials. He established himself in opposition to Fray Bartolomé de las Casas over the representation and treatment of the indigenous population in the New World. His major contribution to Latin American literature and history is the treatise *Historia general de las cosas de Nueva España*, published posthumously in 1829.

[7] The approach proposed here takes into account that while the family in literature is a construct of language, i.e. of words on the page, *the family* as a more general term is also a construct that has been influenced by sociological, psychological, historical, and linguistic elements (and perhaps many others). It is inevitable that these constructs of family, both the literary and the sociocultural, are connected, and a study of the first will be greatly enhanced by a firm understanding of the latter. Therefore, one crucial element of this methodological framework will be its interdisciplinarity, or its attention to details of a sociological, historical, psychological, and linguistic nature. It may seem pedantic to insist that an understanding of *the family* is as instrumental as a comprehension of literary analysis in the interpretation of certain elements in contemporary literature. However, while most scholars certainly would be able to enjoy and understand much of this study without a further grounding in some sociological and psychological concepts, they may not fully appreciate the value and complexity of this interdisciplinary methodology. For this reason, I believe that the amount of space given here to issues that are not merely literary in focus will be justified by virtue of its providing the critic --already well-versed in literary history, theory, and criticism-- with the requisite background information to completely contextualize and understand the analyses presented in these pages.

[8] For a history of Family System Theory, see Hall, Knapp, Bowen, and L. von Bertalanffy.

[9]For further study of general systems theories, see L. von Bertalanffy, who is named by Hall, as well as by most other scholars who discuss the history of systems thinking.

[10]Bowen marks the contrast between basic and functional differentiation. The former is more individual, passed on through generations, and subject to little variation, whereas the latter depends on the person's relationship system and may be influenced to rise or fall quickly by any number of factors, be they social, physical, situational, etc. The reciprocal element of relationships may induce one family member to temporarily "give up" some of their functioning ability, which seems to be "borrowed" by other members, making it even more difficult to gage any person's basic or functional differentiation in a limited time frame. The higher the basic level of differentiation, the less volatile or subject to wide fluctuations is the functional differation. (97-99)

[11]For a feminist critique of Bowen's idea of differentiation, see Carol Gilligan. Her works dealing with psychological theory and women's and girls' development contain insightful and poignant discussion of the possible

difference in the psychological needs of men and women. While Gilligan raises some significant questions, part of her quarrel with the concept of differentiation seems based on an erroneous equation of differentiation and separation, or lack of connection, which does not take into account the distinction that Bowen makes between these terms.

[12]According to Kerr and Bowen, the idea that one person can manifest symptoms of anothers' anxiety is based on two assumptions: "there is a mind-body link, such as that shown to exist between the central nervous system and the automatic nervous system, the immune system, or the endocrine system; and there is a person-person link, substantiated by clinical observations consistent with people's emotional functioning being interrelated" (181-2).

[13]Minuchin's structural family therapy is essentially a systemic therapeutic approach that strives to change family functioning by changing a family's perspective, or perception of their reality. Since the focus of this paper is not therapeutic change, this section introduces some of the terminology and ideology behind Minuchin's work without dwelling on the role of the therapist as catalyst, which nonetheless is a major topic of his writing.

[14] Additional FST-based criticism not discussed here includes Frank Morral's article "D.H. Lawrence's Alcoholic Family" (1992); Amy Mashberg's Ph.D. dissertaton on the dysfunctional communication in novels by Honoré de Balzac, and a subsequent article focuses on co-dependency and obsession in the celebrated novel *Madame Bovary* (1856) by Gustave Flaubert; and psychologist Scott Johnson's readings of *The Laocoon* and Franz Kafka's long story *The Metamorphosis*.

[15] In the course of his book Sander also delves into a number of other plays, including T.S. Eliot's *The Cocktail Party* (1949) and *The Family Reunion* (1939), Edward Albee's *Who's Afraid of Virginia Woolf?* (1969), and Oscar Wilde's *Salome* (1891).

[16]Marantz Cohen treats Samuel Richardson's *Clarissa*, Jane Austen's *Mansfield Park*, Emily Brontë's *Wuthering Heights*, George Eliot's *The Mill on the Floss*, and Henry James's *The Awkward Age*.

[17]Marantz Cohen extensively quotes from Freud, Foucault, Lévi-Strauss, Philippe Aries, and Margaret Mead; this gives the work in its entirety a more eclectic and sociological rather than a FST or even merely psychological bent.

[18]While this article concentrates on the personal gratification of a FST-influenced textual reading, the author reiterates a point echoed strongly in Knapp, that there is a possibility for literary criticism and family systems psychology to have a mutually beneficial interaction, reminding the reader that family psychologists such as Jackson and Foley have analyzed literature to provide illustration and exemplification of their theories just as literary critics have utilized FST to look at literary texts (131).

[19] In the field of Family Systems criticism, Bump has also authored "D.H. Lawrence and Family Systems Theory" (1991) and a panoramic article in the special FST issue of *Style*: In "The Family Dynamics of the Reception of Art", Bump suggests systems readings of novels by Tyler, Oates, Morrison,

Kingston, Heller, Updike, Ferro, Leavitt, Plante, Chute, Smith, Conroy, Humphrey, Furman, McMillan, Larsen, Islas, Hinojosa, Garcia, Banks, Winthrop, Smiley, and Allison. Bump points out that these novels may embody the family as system due to their appearance during the same time period in which FST gained such preeminence in the therapeutic practice.

[20]In another article, "Reader-Centered Criticism and Bibliotherapy: Hopkins and Selving," Bump discusses the profitability of using literature to instigate memory retrieval, destroy patterns of denial, and open channels for communication within the formal/therapeutic sphere of Family Systems Therapy. While his essay is not specifically related to the present study, it is worthwhile to note that his argument successfully links literary representations of the family with contemporary psychology in yet another manner.

[21]Knapp and Womack have edited a new collection of FST criticism, entitled *Reading the Family Dance: Family Systems Therapy and the Literary Study,* that is forthcoming from the University of Delaware Press in 2003.

[22]A Family Systems Theory perspective in the study of family in literature is beginning to be more evident in academic conferences as well. As one example, a panel on Family Systems and Literature appeared at the 1999 Narrative Conference of the Society for the Study of Narrative Literature (SSNL), co-sponsored by Dartmouth College and The University of Vermont (April 29-May 1, 1999). The essays presented at this panel included "Toni Morrison's *The Bluest Eye* and Family Systems Theory" by Bump, Knapp's, "Family Systems Theory and Shakespeare's *Hamlet*: A New Synthesis," Denis Jonnes's study "Flannery O'Connor and the American Postwar Family System," and Sara Cooper's "Recovering Roots: Alternative Family Systems in Marilene Felinto's *The Women of Tijucopapo*."

Works Cited

Allen, Katherine R., and David H. Demo. "The Families of Lesbians and Gay Men: A New Frontier in Family Research." *Journal of Marriage and the Family* 57 (Feb 1995): 111-127.

Allende, Isabel. *La casa de los espíritus*. Barcelona: Plaza & Jones, 1985.

Átame. Dir. Pedro Almodóvar. Spain: El Deseo S.A., 1989.

Arguedas, José María. *Los ríos profundos*. Madrid: Cátedra, 1998.

Bateson, G., et al. "Toward a Theory of Schizophrenia." *Behavioral Science* 1 (1956): 251-64.

Bavelas, Janet Beavin and Lynn Segal. "Family Systems Theory: Background and Implications. *Marriage and the Family* 32:3 (Summer 1982): 99-107.

Bernand, Carmen, and Serge Gruzinski. "Children of the Apocalypse: The Family in Meso-America and the Andes." Burguière 161-215.

Bertalanffy, L. von. *General Systems Theory: Foundations, Development, Applications.* New York: Braziller, 1968.

Blest Gana, Alberto. *Martín Rivas.* Oxford: Oxford UP, 2000.

Bowen, Murray. *Family Therapy in Clinical Practice.* New York: Jason Aronson, 1978.

Bump, Jerome. "D.H. Lawrence and Family Systems Theory." *Renascence* 44.1 (Fall 1991): 61-80.

---. "The Family Dynamics of the Reception of Art." *Style* 31.2 (1997): 328-50.

---. "*Jane Eyre* and Family Systems Therapy." *Teaching Jane Eyre.* Eds. Diane Hoveler, and Beth Lau. New York: MLA, 1993. 130-38.

---. "Reader-Centered Criticism and Bibliotherapy: Hopkins and Selving." *Renascence* 42.1 (Fall 1989): 65-86.

Burguière, André, et al. *A History of the Family: The Impact of Modernity.* Trans. Sarah Hanbury Tenison. Oxford: Polity P, 1996.

Burgos, Elizabeth. *Me llamo Rigoberta Menchú y así me nació la conciencia.* Barcelona: Seix Barral, 1983.

Camila. Dir. María Luisa Bemberg. Meridian, 1995.

Castellanos, Rosario. *Album de familia.* Mexico City: Fondo de Cultura Económica, 1971.

---. *Balún Canán.* Mexico City: Fondo de Cultura Económica, 1957.

---. "Economía doméstica." *Poesía no eres tú.* Mexico City: Fondo de Cultura Económica, 1972.

Cela, José Camilo. *La familia de Pascual Duarte.* Barcelona: Ediciones Destino, 1955.

Cervantes, Miguel de. *El ingenioso hidalgo don Quijote de la Mancha.* Barcelona: Planeta, 1992.

Cooper, Sara E. "The Lesbian family in Christina Peri Rossi's 'El testigo': A Study in Utopia and Infiltration." *Tortilleras: Hispanic and Latina Lesbian Expression.* Eds. Lourdes Torres and Inmaculada Pertusa. Forthcoming from Temple Press Fall 2002.

James M. Decker. "'Choking on my Own Saliva': Henry Miller's Bourgeois Family Christmas in *Nexus*." *Style* 31.2 (1997): 270-89.

De eso no se habla. (*I Don't Want to Talk About It*) Dir. María Luisa Bemberg. Columbia Tristar, 1995.

Donoso, José. *El lugar sin límites.* Mexico City: Joaquín Mortiz, 1966.

El Norte Dir. Gregory Nava. Independent Productions, 1984.

Engels, Friedrich. *The Origin of the Family, Private Property and the State: In the Light of the Researches of Lewis H. Morgan.* 4th ed. New York: International Publishers, 1942.

Ferré, Rosario. *Maldito amor.* New York: Vintage Español, 1998.

---. *Papeles de Pandora.* New York: Vintage Español, 2000.

Foster, David William and Roberto Reis, eds. *Bodies & Biases: Sexualities In Hispanic Cultures and Literatures.* Minneapolis: U of Minnesota P, 1996.

Foucault, Michel. "The Order of Discourse." *Untying the Text: A Post-Structuralist Reader*. Ed. Robert Young. Boston: Routledge and Kegan Paul, 1981. 48-51.

García Lorca, Federico. *Bodas de sangre*. Madrid: Cátedra, 2001.

---. *La casa de Bernarda Alba*. Madrid: Cátedra, 2001.

García Márquez, Gabriel. *Cien años de soledad*. Madrid: Cátedra, 2001.

García Ramis, Magali. *Felices días, Tío Sergio*. San Juan, Puerto Rico: Editorial Antillana, 1986.

Gilligan, Carol. *In a Different Voice: Psychological Theory and Women's Development*. Cambridge: Harvard UP, 1982.

Gómez de Avellaneda y Arteaga, Gertrudis. *Sab*. Madrid: Cátedra, 1999.

Hall, C. Margaret. "Family Systems: A Developing Trend in Family Theory." *The Sociology of the Family (Sociological Review* Monograph 28) Ed. Chris Harris. Staffordshire: U of Keele, 1979.

Hirsch, Marianne. *The Mother/Daughter Plot: Narrative, Psychoanalysis, Feminism*. Bloomington: Indiana UP, 1989.

La historia oficial. Dir. Luis Puenzo. Pacific Arts Video, 1986.

Jackson, Don D. "The Question of Family Homeostasis." *Psychiatric Quarterly Supplement* 31 (1957): 79-90.

Johnson, Scott. "Structural Elements in Franz Kafka's *The Metamorphosis*." *Journal of Marital and Family Therapy* 19.2 (1993): 149-57.

---. "*The Laocoon*: Systemic Concepts in a Work of Art." *Journal of Marital and Family Therapy* 18.2 (1992): 113-24.

Jones, Denis. *The Matrix of Narrative: Family Systems and the Semiotics of Story*. New York: Mouton de Gruyter, 1990.

Kerr, Michael E., and Murray Bowen. *Family Evaluation: An Approach Based on Bowen Theory*. New York: W.W. Norton, 1988.

Knapp, John V. *Striking at the Joints: Contemporary Psychology and Literary Criticism*. New York: UP of America, 1996.

Knapp, John V. and Kenneth Womack, eds. *Family Systems Psychotherapy and Literature/Literary Criticism* Spec. issue of Style 31.2 (1997).

Laing, R. D. *The Politics of the Family*. New York: Vintage, 1972.

Levi Calderón, Sara. *Dos mujeres*. México: Diana, 1990.

---. *The Two Mujeres*. Trans. Gina Kaufer. San Francisco: Aunt Lute Books, 1991.

Lindstrom, Naomi. *Women's Voice in Latin American Literature*. Washington, D.C.: Three Continents P, 1989.

Lucía. Dir. Humberto Solás. ICAIC, 1968.

Marantz Cohen, Paula. *The Daughter's Dilemma: Family Process and the Nineteenth Century Novel*. Ann Arbor: U of Michigan P, 1991.

---. "Stabilizing the Family at Mansfield Park." *ELH* 54.3 (Fall 1987): 669-93.

Mashberg, Amy. "Co-Dependency and Obsession in *Madame Bovary*." *Dionysos* 2.1 (Spring 1990): 28-40.

---. "Dysfunctional Communication in Balzac's Family Systems." Diss. U of Texas at Austin, 1991.

Mathieu, Corina S. "Argentine Women in the Novels of Silvina Bullrich." *Latin American Women Writers: Yesterday and Today*. Eds. Miller, Yvette E. and Charles M. Tatum. Pittsburgh: Latin American Literary Review, 1977. 68-74.

Minuchin, Salvador. *Families and Family Therapy*. Cambridge: Harvard UP, 1974.

Moraga, Cherríe. *Giving up the Ghost*. Albuquerque, NM: West End, 1986.

---. *The Hungry Woman: A Mexican Medea*. Albuquerque, NM: West End, 2001.

Morral, Frank. "D.H. Lawrence's Alcoholic Family." *Dionysos* 4.1 (1992): 27-35.

Mount, Ferdinand. *The Subversive Family: An Alternative History of Love and Marriage*. London: Jonathan Cape, 1982.

My Family/Mi familia. Dirs. Gregory Nava and Anna Thomas. New Line Studios, 1995.

Paez Morales, Guillermo. *Sociología de la familia: Elementos de análisis en Colombia y América Latina*. Bogotá: U Santo Tomás Centro de Enseñanza Desescolarizada, 1984.

Parra, Teresa de la. *Ifigenia*. Mexico City: Editora Nacional, 1977.

Pérez Galdos, Benito. *Doña Perfecta*. Madrid: Cátedra, 2001.

---. *La familia de León Roch*. Buenos Aires: Losada, 1948.

---. *Fortunata y Jacinta*. Madrid: Cátedra, 2000.

---. *Misericordia*. Madrid: Cátedra, 2000.

Peri Rossi, Cristina. "El testigo." Fernández Olmos and Paravisini-Gebert 93-99.

de Quevedo, Francisco. *Lazarillo de Tormes*. Madrid: Cátedra, 2000.

Reis, Roberto. "Representations of Family and Sexuality in Brazilian Cultural Discourse." Foster and Reis 79-114.

Rich, Adrienne. Foreword. *The Coming Out Stories*. Eds. Julia Penelope Stanley and Susan J. Wolfe. Watertown, Mass: Persephone P, 1980. xi-xiii.

Sander, Fred M. *Individual and Family Therapy: Toward an Integration*. New York: Jason Aronson, 1979.

Satir, Virginia. *Conjoint Family Therapy*. Palo Alto: Science and Behavior Books, 1964.

Schwartzman, John, ed. *Families and Other Systems: The Macrosystemic Context of Family Therapy*. New York: Guilford P, 1985.

Segalen, Martine. "The Industrial Revolution: From Proletariat to Bourgeoisie." Burguière 377-415.

Speck, Ross. "Social Networks and Family Therapy." Schwartzman 63-83.

Spector, Judith Ann. "Anne Tyler's *Dinner at the Homesick Restaurant*: A Critical Feast." *Style* 31.2 (1997): 310-27.

Storhoff, Gary. "Anaconda Love: Parental Enmeshment in Toni Morrison's *Song of Solomon*." *Style* 31.2 (1997): 290-309.

Turner, Harriet. "Family Ties and Tyrannies: A Reassessment of Jacinta." *Hispanic Review* 51.1 (1983): 1-22.

Waldman, Gloria Feiman. "Three Female Playwrights Explore Contemporary Latin American Reality: Myrna Casas, Griselda Gambaro, Luisa Josefina Hernández." *Latin American Women Writers: Yesterday and Today*. Eds. Miller, Yvette E. and Charles M. Tatum. Pittsburgh: Latin American Literary Review, 1977. 75-84.

Weston, Kath. *Families We Choose: Lesbians, Gays, Kinship*. New York: Columbia UP, 1991.

Womack, Kenneth. "'Only Connecting' With Family: Class, Culture, and Narrative Therapy in E. M. Forster's *Howard's End.*" *Style* 31.2 (1997): 255-69.

Zaretsky, Eli. "The Place of the Family in the Origins of the Welfare State." *Rethinking the Family: Some Feminist Questions*. Eds. Barrie Thorne and Marilyn Yalom. New York: Longman, 1982. 199-224.

2

Shifting Families and Incest
in Chacel and Moix

Ellen Mayock

*We have neither the time nor the space needed to create a soul for ourselves,
and the mere hint of such activity seems frivolous and ill-advised.
Held back by his aloofness, modern man is a narcissist--
a narcissist who may suffer, but who feels no remorse.*

Julia Kristeva cited in Kelly Oliver,
Family Values *(227)*

*The mother herself is and remains absent even to herself.
The place she inhabits is vacant.
Although she produces and upholds the subject,
she herself remains the matrix, the other, the origin.
And the child's own narrative--
the narrative of our culture--rests on that "othering."*

Marianne Hirsch, The Mother/Daughter Plot *(168)*

Leticia Valle and Julia, two protagonists of the Spanish post-War period, capture the essence of the suffering narcissist who must create her own child's narrative as a path first away from her intimate family relationships and then back to the family. The epigraphs introduce an exploration of the female protagonist and her familial relationships, especially as they relate (respectively) to paternal portrayal in Rosa Chacel's *Memorias de Leticia Valle* (1945) and to maternal portrayal in Ana María Moix's *Julia* (1968). These two novels provide fertile ground for an examination of identity through the protagonist's relationship to her family and/or shifting families and the incestuous nuances suggested therein.

In an article about family ties in *Fortunata y Jacinta*, Harriet Turner states that narrative point of view "place[s] the family at the beginning of the story...[and] refract[s] early events through their perspective" (6). This essay investigates how narrative point of view establishes a framework for family relationships and shifting in the two novels, including observations on the original families, the "extended kinship families" (Popence cited in Thompson, 812) sought out by or imposed upon the protagonist, and the third and final shift of each of the protagonists.[1] The shifting relates directly to Bowen Family Systems Theory: "In a 1966 paper, he [Bowen] explained that the family was a system because a change in one part produces compensatory change in other parts of the family" (Papero 4). The two fictional protagonists develop according to the intimate familial connections they develop and thus act out Papero's statement that "organism and environment evolve together" (17).

Each description and event in Chacel's and Moix's novels influences subsequent events and, more specifically, the development or regression of the protagonists. Elements such as narrative voice, tone, structure, plot, and stylistics function together to create a textual organism which displays the function and dysfunction of fictional Spanish families. Chacel and Moix represent the Spanish "woman writer [who] transmits the essence of her perception in terms of alienation and confusion. In that perception the fragmented family repeatedly appears as the symbol and metaphor of a ruptured society" (Schyfter 23). The remarkable influence of real-life family systems is constantly reflected in Spanish literature.[2] Several sociologists who research family structure in Spain emphasize the fundamental role of the family in Spanish culture and history:

> La familia es, ante todo, un grupo pequeño en el que se producen interacciones muy frecuentes e íntimas, que dan origen a una estructura de relaciones muy peculiar y diferenciada de la de otros grupos, y que tiene consecuencias sociales de gran envergadura por el papel tan relevante que desempeña en la sociedad; particularmente, por la función que cumple en la socialización de sus miembros. Esa estructura de relaciones es normalmente desigual y conflictiva, por lo que se ha convertido en el blanco real de los ataques a la familia como institución. Pero, con independencia de esta problemática, de mayor calado teórico e ideológico, es indudable que el mal funcionamiento manifiesto de esas relaciones tiene repercusiones del más diverso tipo sobre sus miembros. (Campo Urbano and Navarro López 135)

David Rehrer adds:

> Risk, uncertainty, and death; dysfunctional and resilient
> families; family loyalties, brokered marriages, social and moral
> strictures; survival and stability; property, wealth, and poverty.
> The themes are always the same: the family, always the family.
> (2)

The "real-life" Spanish family and the concomintant familial themes are literarily manifested as a consistently compelling plot motivator and nexus of character types, relationship function and dysfunction, and significantly heart-wrenching conflict.

The fictional Spanish families studied here appear in two novels that span the Spanish post-War period and mirror the unique social constraints of the era. Chacel's *Memorias de Leticia Valle*, written in 1945 but not published in Spain until 1971, offers a protagonist whose separation from her original family reflects the author's self-exile from Francoist Spain. Ana María Moix published *Julia* 23 years after the initial publication of *Memorias de Leticia Valle*.[3] The eponymous protagonist, although from a much younger generation than her Chacelian counterpart and from the supposedly more liberal ambience of cosmopolitan Barcelona, also must confront issues of family, gender identity, and socially imposed norms. While Chacel's exile from Spain was resolutely physical, Moix's exile seems to be of a more emotional nature, as she lives in Spain but always in a marginalized way. This emotional exile manifests itself in *Julia* as deeply frustrating and complex. Moix grew up in the Spain of the 1960's, an era which Rehrer states was as backwards or perhaps more so than the Spain of 1920, thus emphasizing the slow pace of social modernization: "Economic backwardness and the political and social scars of a Civil War were central to the lethargic pace of Spanish modernization" (272). It is within this context that both Chacel and Moix write their somewhat inverted Bildungromane.[4]

The physical and/or emotional positioning of the protagonist at the beginning and end of each of the narrations is significant both in terms of displaying a link to one of the two parents and establishing narrative perspective. Bowen and Papero establish that the term *nuclear family* "stems from the observation that families appear to have an emotional center or nucleus to which family members (and other non-related individuals) are responsively attached. From this viewpoint the family can be defined as the total number of individuals attached to an emotional nucleus" (Papero 26). The two psychiatrists assert that the mother is most typically the emotional nucleus of the nuclear family (Papero 28). The absence of a mother in *Memorias de Leticia Valle* is the nucleus of the narration, as Leticia's father can not function in a parental capacity without Leticia's mother, and Leticia, their offspring, must learn to function as an individual far more mature than her age would suggest.   In *Julia* the mother is forcefully present as the emotional nucleus of the family: her adulterous affair creates a separation from the father; she dispenses parental love in an erratic and unsettling manner; she dotes on the ailing brother Rafael; she mercilessly teases Ernesto and Julia, the physically healthy siblings. Julia learns to depend overly much on maternal love and is unable to mature beyond the six-year old Julita whom the reader meets at the beginning of the narration.

At the very beginning of the novel, Leticia Valle aggressively regards her physically present but emotionally absent father in his big armchair. By the end of the novel, Leticia has shifted into two different families and has appropriated her father's position in the armchair. Leticia, the compelling "I," occupies the place of the father after fomenting a scandal of incest and death.   She, like modern man in the epigraph by Julia Kristeva, has difficulty forcing herself to feel the remorse that society once had dictated as obligatory.   Chacel frames the narration with these parallel images and succeeds in forging a first-person narration whose "I" is powerful and capable of directing the reader's gaze in the exact direction of her own--towards the world without and, in an equally compelling manner, towards her world within.

Moix, on the other hand, draws the reader directly into the psyche of the protagonist, Julia.   The reader immediately becomes acquainted with the protagonist's interiority, her constant feelings of suffocation, the duality of Julia/Julita, and Julia's all-consuming attraction towards and nightmares about her "Mamá."   In addition, there is an early and metaphorically related account of the rape of Julita at the age of six by a family friend, thus complicating the web of family turmoil Julia already confronts and reinforcing the need for escape into another "self."[5]   By the end of the narration, Julita conquers Julia, thus consolidating a dual protagonist into a dominant one and stagnating the remaining Julita in her incestuous obsession for Mamá.   The third-person narration emphasizes the dual and decentered, and yet suffocatingly narcissistic "I," while the reader focuses almost exclusively on gazing *at*, rather than *with* and *at* (as in *Leticia Valle*) the protagonist.

Leticia Valle begins and ends her narration with her thoughts about turning 12 years old. The plot is enclosed by these musings, and the narration offers an explanation, at times clear and at other points quite allusive, of the intervening events of Leticia's year of separation from her original family, her intellectual development, and her loss of innocence.   As she starts to think about turning 12, she cannot help but turn towards the past year and the vision of her father in his armchair:

> Cuando quiero decirme a mí misma algo de todo lo que sucedió, sólo se me ocurre la frase de mi padre: «¡Es inaudito! ¡Es inaudito!» Me parece verle en su rincón, metido en su butaca, cogiéndose la frente con la mano y repitiéndola, y yo, desde el mío, diciéndelo sin decirle: «Eso es lo que yo estaba queriendo decirte siempre. Yo no sabía decir que todo lo mío era inaudito, pero procuraba dártelo a entender, y tú de todo decías que no tenía nada de particular. Claro que si ahora lo que ha pasado te parece inaudito es porque sigues creyendo que anteriormente nada tenía nada de particular». (7)

This initial interior monologue portrays the typical barriers of communication that characterize the relationship between Leticia and her father.   Leticia is aware of her different, stronger-than-average, willful, intellectual nature and has wanted her father, or anyone, to know her in just that way.   She soon learns that only catastrophic events will awaken her alcoholic father to some kind of response or action.   He has just participated in the war in Morocco, and his diegetic disillusionment reflects the extradiegetic mass frustration of the novel's post-Civil War time of publication.   Leticia's first family--absent mother, alcoholic father, and enabling aunt--is comparable to the image of the father "metido en su butaca": monotonous, static, stagnant.[6]   This family suffers from the "closeness-distance cycle" (Bowen in Papero, 38), and the extreme fluctuation in levels of intimacy causes the low-functioning father's inability to grasp a message sent, as Leticia phrases it, "diciéndole sin decirle."   Leticia's father and aunt eventually become frustrated and confused by Leticia's outwardly rebellious character.   They feed her rebellion with passivity, saying simply, "Haz lo que quieras" (30-31) and indirectly providing for her a childhood with more freedom of physical and intellectual movement than most young girls enjoyed at the time.   Grau-Lleveria confirms:

> Leticia es producto de la desintegración de la familia como núcleo de transmisión de comportamientos.   En esta desintegración Leticia goza de unas libertades que, enmarcadas en un contexto más tradicional, serían del todo imposibles: "...pero no fue eso lo único que cambió; hubo un cambio desconcertante: yo dejé de ser el centro de la casa... No puedo decir que estuviera descuidada, pero empecé a tener una libertad que antes no había tenido (22-3)." (208)

Once Leticia recognizes the incapacitation and lack of involvement of the adult figures in her household, she is compelled to look outside the walls of the traditional family home for a new and more satisfactory family.[7]   Julia's original family is more in line with the traditional nuclear family as it was emerging in the 1950's and '60's (Campo Urbano and Navarro López 137). She has a mother, a father, and two older brothers. Nevertheless, strained family ties and estrangement between the two parents soon reveal themselves in the narration and help to launch Julia's flow of memory and evaluation of a past gone horribly astray. Julia's mother is the portrait of the new bourgeoisie. Her vital concerns are superficial and always oriented around the self. In this sense, Julia's mother destroys the traditional real-life model of self-abnegation and self-sacrifice of the Spanish mother.[8]   David Rehrer observes the role of the Spanish mother during the 1960's:

> More than any other member of the family, mothers were the chief source of cohesion within the family and their importance was recognized by all. Yet women were more directly affected by the transformations rocking Spanish society than any other members of the family. (274)

Julia's maternal grandmother, the traditional "abuela de la mantilla" (Martín Gaite, *Usos amorosos*), attempts to rule the embattled household by imposing her conservative values and concern for the *qué-dirán*. Julia's mother, however, is separated from Julia's father, thus demonstrating that she does not comply with the Falangist norms of the post-War era. She entertains several lovers, and seems focused more on the latest fashion and her own diversion than on her family's concerns:

> Mamá siempre se mostraba dispuesta en lo referente a comprar cosas nuevas para la casa y hacer cambios en las habitaciones, sobre todo si era Julia quien lo pedía. Se quejaba, en cambio, de que Julia jamás tuviera iniciativa para comprarse un vestido, o unos zapatos, arreglarse el pelo o cualquier cosa por el estilo que Mamá calificaba como pruebas de feminidad. (124-25)

Julia, who lives in "un extraño y peculiar universo llamado Mamá" (47), always offers abundantly more filial love than she receives in maternal love. The reader learns early in the narration that "desde siempre, Julia tuvo la sensación de que Mamá la quería a temporadas" (16). Julia's mother, in fact, calls Julia "mi fea" (Moix 18) and states that Julia smells her like a dog (19). "Mamá" also often promises to bring home a gift for Julia and then forgets saying, "Se ha pasado el tiempo tan aprisa" (21). Nichols argues convincingly for Julia's mother as the figure of the *femme fatale*:

> Pero este enamoramiento, típico de niños de corta edad y generalmente inocuo, también se volvió anormal, pues Mamá era la quintaesencia de la *femme fatale*, cuyo único interés (aparte ella misma) estribaba en conquistar a los hombres. Inconscientemente, Mamá aumentó la infatuación de sus hijos varones, prefiriéndolos a Julita y torciéndolos a ellos en el proceso. (120)

The figure of Julia's mother, as "matrix, the other, the origin" (see epigraph by Hirsch), appears and reappears in the narration depending on Julia's need to conjure up her real image or a representative image in the form of shifting maternal figures (schoolmates, teachers, aunts).

Julia therefore lives with a restrictive grandmother, a distant and undependable mother, and a father whose occasional presence in the home only brings more unrest and discordance due to his embattled relationship with Julia's mother and the distance created by his absences. The strain between the two parents and the resultant anxiety felt by the children reflects the Family Systems phenomenon that Bowen calls the triangle:

> The triangle is best seen in a moderate degree of stress. At that point the pattern unfolds clearly yet does not tend to spill over into other interlocking relationships, which occurs when anxiety is high. When anxiety is great, the basic triangle can no longer contain and dissolve the tension, which spreads through the web of interlocking triangles. (Papero 49)

The tension between Julia's parents and between Julia and her mother incite Julia to seek a "pact" with her father when her father returns to the family home:

> Bajo la aparente confabulación con Mamá, Julia trataba de hallar en Papá la muestra de su alianza. La encontraba. A veces, ligera: un simple movimiento de cabeza, un vago ademán con las manos, una mirada de reojo. Julia creía encontrarla y significaba para ella la última esperanza de que Papá aún le pertenecía en algún modo, de que Papá permanecía más ligado a ella por su pacto secreto que a ellos por la convivencia diaria. (31)

In addition, Julia has a preening, insecure, and often cruel older brother named Ernesto. Ernesto imitates Julia's mother in a variety of ways, and many allusions are made (interestingly enough, often through the voice of the servants) to Ernesto's struggle with homosexual desire and a need to comply with the externally imposed image of the "macho ibérico." Ernesto and Julia both are too focused on their mother, Ernesto in a mimetic manner and Julia in a futile search for love and semiotic, unspoken understanding. Julia finds unconditional love only in the figure of her ailing brother Rafael: "Julia recordaba aquel mes y medio con su hermano en casa de don Julio, como el principio de una complicidad amistosa con Rafael, el inicio de una unión que la muerte desharía al cabo del tiempo" (100).

Despite the moments of pleasure that Julia enjoys in Rafael's company, the movement of the plot dictates that Rafael must die, leaving Julia/Julita alone with her internal conflict of identity defined by an early violation of selfhood, a lack of healthy family relationships and, more specifically, by a lack of mutual bonding with her mother. The Julia/Julita duo can be separated and her drive towards self-voyeurism can diminish only when Julia's thoughts comfortingly turn to the memory of Rafael:

> El recuerdo de Rafael la ligaba a un tiempo pasado que sentía como suyo, vivido por ella. Todo lo demás quedó como una película vista entre sueños, cuya protagonista se llamaba Julia y tenía su mismo rostro, pero no era ella en realidad. El recuerdo de Rafael la llenaba de paz, una tristeza muy dulce la envolvía. (127)

Leticia and Julia are in clearly unfortunate family situations. The freedom Leticia gains in her family's lack of parental care and her resultant accelerated maturation allows her to seek actively a sphere in which she can evolve and find temporary contentment. This sphere is the home of Daniel and his wife, Luisa. While Leticia is able to remove herself physically from her original stagnant surroundings, Julia has the power only to remove herself emotionally, by means of "el motor de la memoria" and a strange, almost corporal, separation from self:

> Fue un instante de estupor, como si ella no estuviera en ninguna parte, como si a pesar de no existir pudiera contemplar, y se llamó a sí misma, se preguntó por ella. Se extrañó de su cuerpo. Supo que entonces, en aquel momento preciso, terminaba un tiempo que podía remontar poniendo en marcha aquel singular vehículo que era la memoria. (48)

Julia is relieved of this heavy, often unbearable introspection only when her parents take her away from the original family to live with her grandfather, Don Julio, for five years. Therefore, each of the protagonists is extracted from her original family situation in order to set up an extended kinship family.

Leticia and Julia seek in their extended kinship families both duplication and transformation. Leticia wants to experience life with parental figures, but not the ones she has known until her twelfth year. Julia wants access to a real mother and father, but she knows somewhere in her subconscious that her replacement families will be just that: temporary replacements for a less than ideal family that has never been able to love her enough.[9] Leticia seeks a new family with a more predatory attitude than Julia, who is either thrown to a new set of relatives or links herself to female figures in a loneliness too intolerable for any other remedy. Leticia exerts a centrifugal force: she hoists herself upon her extended kinship family and upsets their routine. The "real" nature of these relationships creates the potential as well for "real" danger (Leticia's stained honor; Daniel's suicide). Even Leticia's silences seem to have a mighty voice that wordlessly communicates her preferences, delights, and frustrations. Julia, on the contrary, is a centripetal force. Everything she experiences outwardly turns itself inward to make for a too-alive inhalation of worry and lack. Her external relationships cause harm only to herself as Julia/Julita. Her silences stem from her unhappy perception of her place in the world, her dissatisfactions, her power struggle, her interior stagnancy in the mental embodiment of Julita, and the emotional and intellectual death of Julia, who at an earlier age had had the potential to realize herself within a mature, self-confident identity. The narrator recounts Julia's struggle:

> Había intentado matar a Julita, y sólo ella permanecía. Un sopor agobiante empezó a invadirla. Antes de dormirse, pensó que quizá algún día pudiera vencerla, y ser ella, Julia, quien la condujera de nuevo a la punta rocosa, solitaria de la playa, acercarse al mar, tenderse en la arena y soñar sin miedo, por vez primera, en una hermosa fiesta que le aguardaba en alguna parte. Pero lo supo, de pronto, con una certeza absoluta, implacable: mentir, a partir de aquel momento, resultaba absurdo, innecesario. Había intentado matar a Julita y sólo ella permanecía, sólo ella permanecía ya. (187)

The plural selves of the protagonists, their silences, and their desires create a connection to the members of the extended kinship family, giving rise to duplications of and transformations from the original family. Leticia incorporates herself, in the true bodily sense of the word, easily into the lives of the young archivist Daniel and his wife Luisa.[10] Daniel and Luisa offer much: they are young, intelligent, talented, energetic--all characteristics Leticia seeks to develop in herself. This family is certainly "new and improved," for Luisa not only replaces Leticia's aunt but also represents Leticia's long-absent mother, while Daniel's forceful, attractive character is the polar opposite of the passive and sickly figure of Leticia's father in the armchair.

Leticia first develops an intricately complex relationship with Luisa, who, significantly, "no parecía castellana" (32) and who "parecía una chica pequeña" (35). Luisa's "otherness"-- not looking Castilian and being a grown woman who looks like a little girl-- foments an immediate passion and attraction in Leticia. Both Leticia's constant hunger (she mentions that "en aquellos días no pensaba más que en comer" and labels this obsession "un hambre loca" [23]) and her attraction to that which was not part of her original home are revealed when Leticia narrates:

> Pero no sólo manipulábamos en la cocina; goloseábamos continuamente. Yo en mi casa no lo había hecho jamás y ella me enseñó. Fuese lo que fuese, todo lo probábamos, hasta las cosas que no se le ocurriría a uno nunca comer entre horas. (36)

The hunger to which Leticia refers represents a real physical hunger as well as an already recognized desire to learn and to distinguish herself. It also foreshadows the manifestation of Leticia's sexual voraciousness in her seduction of Daniel.

Leticia's relationship with Luisa is complex. Luisa at first seems to be a maternal figure: she has a small son; she cooks, cleans, sews, and plays the piano. Luisa's domain is the home, and Leticia is attracted to that normalcy. As Leticia slowly insinuates herself into Luisa's domestic life, Luisa states that "Leticia es mi mejor amiga y yo estoy encantada de tenerla conmigo a todas horas" (41). Luisa and Leticia have moved from a mother-daughter relationship to one of peers, best friends. Their connection evolves further as Leticia becomes the mother figure and Luisa's diminutive features and voice retreat into the background, thereby infantilizing the character of Luisa and stripping her of any familial power she may have had. The following quote exemplifies the changing dynamic between Leticia and Luisa:

> --Podría muy bien ser tu madre. Y yo repuse: --Pues, a veces, me parece que por dentro podría yo ser la suya. Contestó en el mismo tono: --En ese caso voy a tener que respetarte. -- ¡Oh!, no diga usted esa palabra repugnante. (78)

Leticia becomes more impatient with the domestic sphere and in fact develops "un asco de ser mujer que me quitó la fe hasta para llorar" (49). At the same time, the reader is aware of the frequent characterization of Leticia as a socially gendered "masculine" character. For example, several references are made to her "ademanes varoniles", and Daniel states slyly to Leticia: "--Me parece que si tú fueras un caballerito tendrías el arte de hacer regalos a las damas, y me parece también que a ti te gustaría mucho algunas veces ser un caballerito" (73). Chacel's typical interplay of male/female identity and imagery is extended with Leticia's narration of her fantasies through "a veces una gruta, a veces una selva" (79-80). Mangini cites Roberta Johnson on this point about gender in Chacel:

> As Roberta Johnson says of both Chacel's autobiography and the novel: "The fictional as well as the autobiographical girl negotiates a precarious position between finely chiseled masculine and feminine stereotypes. Chacel forges an eroto-aesthetics that shifts the female-obsessed unidirectional male vanguard gaze to a diffused female gaze (or sphere of attention)." (131)

Leticia becomes the androgynous embodiment of a Luisa/Daniel hybrid: she replaces Daniel as husband as she surrenders herself to sexual thoughts about Luisa (imagining her with a sword [112] instead of a cooking implement in her hand and fixating on "aquel abrazo, aquel beso más largo que lo acostumbrado" [99]). Then she becomes a more powerful version of Luisa as she seduces Daniel. Leticia's existence, like Virginia Woolf's writing, "involved a dual origin and a dual destination, both paternal and maternal" (Hirsch 108). The moment of seduction is not spelled out but is quite clear when Leticia narrates: "en aquel momento no había entre él y yo ni distancia ni secreto" (129).

Chacel chooses two female names that begin in "L" to emphasize the replaceability of the two characters and the triangular, incestuous nature of this extended kinship family. The true "desdoblamiento" takes place when Leticia states:

> ...me uní, me identifiqué con Luisa en aquel momento, recorrí su alma y sus cinco sentidos, como se recorre y se revisa una casa que nos es querida. Vi todo lo que había en su pensamiento, percibí lo que sentían sus manos, sentí el sentimiento que se imprimía en su voz. (144)

As would befit each of these two "I" characters, Leticia is the active "I" linked with the verbs in these sentences, while Luisa is the possessive pronoun being acted upon. The narrator goes on to state that Luisa's look was saying exactly: "Quieres quitarme lo único que tengo" (148), thus stating and not stating, just as the "diciéndole sin decirle" at the beginning of the narration, that Leticia has successfully replaced Luisa in her seduction of Daniel. Soon after this scene, Leticia comments indirectly on Luisa's passivity, lack of voice, and transferral of power to Leticia: "Pero no cantaba nunca porque tenía muy poca voz y porque además el cantar no era para su carácter. Acaso por eso mismo deseaba tanto que yo cantase" (150).

The specific references to personality traits and family ties in the extended kinship family are precisely what create and nuance the taboo of incest. If Luisa and don Daniel were not cast in the roles of mother-sister-best friend-daughter and father-teacher-protector, respectively, the "only" scandals would be adultery and loss of innocence. Chacel's triangle reflects the movement of the Family Systems triangle:

> In the basic unit of two parents and a child, therefore, three interlocking attachments are at work at any given moment--that of the breeding pair and of each parent with the child. Each relationship can influence every other through the mechanism of shifts in functional state in each individual and the responsiveness of the others to those shifts. (Papero 33)

The careful construction of intricate family-oriented social ties establishes a framework in which Leticia conquers Daniel, commits emotionally real incest, and must return to a life defined by its unchanging landscape and uninteresting adult figures.

Immediately following the scandal, Leticia moves in with her aunt, uncle, and cousin. The aunt and uncle have as their "mission" to erase Leticia's sin and inculcate traditional family values, even if all three consider it too late for that. Leticia narrates: "Mi tía Frida sigue creyendo que soy una buena chica; tanto ella como su marido se han impuesto como misión el convencerme de ello" (167). Leticia, however, is not certain how she feels about being "saved" by this third family, who places the blame for Leticia's wandering on Leticia's father:

> Tú no tienes la culpa de lo que ha pasado: eso tenía que pasar, si no hubiera sido por esto, habría sido por otra cosa. En fin de cuentas, el único responsable es tu padre por no haberte puesto desde hace tiempo en un ambiente adecuado. (167)

The "ambiente adecuado," of course, restores the sense of the social and familial status quo (a functioning father and a present mother) and leaves Leticia with the sad sense that she will never again experience love. Julia follows a trajectory similar to that of Leticia but without the apparent control that Leticia at times exercises over her own destiny. Julia's original family has never been a model of happiness or unity. When Julia's father is at home, the parents' conversations turn immediately to barbed words: "Tu antipatía alcanza los límites de la grosería. Y tu excesiva simpatía resulta insoportable" (46). Julia as usual feels isolated and foreign, not only within the family environment but also within her own self. Julia wonders: "¿Dónde estaba Rafael? Una fotografía enmarcada en plata le recordó que Rafael había muerto. Se sintió desconocida entre desconocidos" (47). Despite the grandmother's fervent efforts to have at least the appearance of a "normal" household, none of the family members is willing to mold her- or himself to the Falangist principles the grandmother holds so dear. While Rafael is sick, the narrator recounts that "la abuela Lucía le obligaba a rezar el rosario cada mañana y cada noche: Uno, para la recuperación de Rafael y, otro, para evitar el escándalo" (110).

Julia's shift away from her original family begins long before her physical move to her paternal grandfather's home, where she is empowered in socially masculine ways reinforced by the Franco regime--hunting, talking politics, criticizing the family, learning Latin, exploring the library--by her grandfather Julio. As Julia is unable to recover from her childhood rape or find the maternal love she so desires and without which she is incapable of self-realization, she draws further within. Schumm addresses the representations of Francoist Spain in *Julia*:

> While it is Víctor who rapes Julia, Julia's family--a metaphoric microcosm of the patriarchal and fascist attitudes prevalent in Spain at that time--ignores and even continues the violation. Julia's maladjusted parents are the first descendants of Franco's rule (represented by Julia's dictatorial grandmother Lucía and Don Julio), and the effect upon Julia is even more intolerable, forcing her to employ a schizophrenic solution to her 'unliveable situation' in society (see Laing, *Experience* 79). (163)

Since the beginning of the narration the reader has been aware of the active, frenetic, frightened pace of Julia's inner world. This internal activity is cloaked in an external passivity--an aggressive drive towards sleep, monotony, and silence (obvious images of death which presage

Julia's attempted suicide).   At home Julia has become what Martín Gaite has termed the "chica rara" (*Usos amorosos* and *Desde la ventana*), while at school she has become "la que no habla" (111). Instead of loving her all the more, Julia's mother admonishes her, "No tienes amigas porque eres rara, no hay quien te soporte, no tienes simpatía" (35), thus placing herself among those who do not tolerate Julia.   Julia is unable to find a way out of her externally imposed and self-reinforced solitude:

> No sabía cómo remediar el aislamiento que ella misma había provocado.   Aunque le daba rabia, se esforzaba en aparentar que la terrible soledad en que la envolvía el colegio no le importaba en absoluto, e incluso se mostraba orgullosa de haberla conseguido.   (111)

The only temporary relief Julia finds from her "terrible loneliness" is captured in her relationship with a series of female characters.   The narrator informs the reader from the start that Julia has had a constantly conflictive relationship with her mother ("Luego la odió.   La odió durante mucho tiempo con mezcla de rencor y devoción [13]).   The protagonist comforts herself from her "Mamá" nightmares by wrapping herself in "la imagen de Eva" (24), the last of the series of women for whom Julia has an abiding attraction.   Julia needs a mother, rejects the mother, and searches for a replacement, a rhythm established from the beginning of the novel and sustained throughout.   Julia, however, never transforms the new relationships she develops.   Each connection with a female figure repeats and reinforces the failures she has had with her own mother, thus manifesting literarily the following Family Systems phenomenon:

> To the degree that responsibility for self is not attained, a need for another is established.   This need for another governs the degree to which the individual attaches to others throughout life. [. . .] This set of relationships to caretakers, established in the primary triangle, becomes a template for future relationships of equal intensity, generally with mate and offspring.   Said somewhat differently, all future relationships become variations on a theme. (Papero 34)

Julia spends five years at her grandfather's house with her *tía* Elena, whom she plays with and comforts in bed, just as she had done at times with her own mother: "Mamá gritaría Julita, Julita, y jugarían las dos en la cama" (21).   The connection cannot last, however, as Julia grows and Elena grapples with a heterosexual love in her small town. Julia is both attracted to and repelled by her classmate Lidia.   Lidia rules Julia, likes to play with her hair, and, like Julia's mother, also labels Julia a "bicho raro" (147). The two other female characters who replace Julia's mother are adult role models, a teacher and a university professor. When Rafael dies, Miss Mabel, the headmistress of Julia's grade school, comforts Julia and then realizes that the crumbs of feeling she has offered to the protagonist have been gobbled up and that Julia is voraciously searching for more. Finally, Julia completes the incestuous circle by falling in love with her professor, Eva, who also happens to be a former love of Julia's father. Eva helps Julia to enjoy work and to find hours of contentment, but these are contingent upon Eva's presence. Julia cannot stand alone. She still has found neither a maternal figure nor a peer friendship to fill the void that defines her entire existence. While Leticia Valle's sexual transgression results in Don Daniel's suicide and Leticia's restoration to "normal" family life, Julia's incestuous drives are more emotional than physical. Again, rather than the centrifugal forces of Leticia Valle, the circumstances and events in Julia's life exert a centripetal force on her, resulting in Julia's attempted suicide and restoration to the unhappy life of her original family.

Julia realizes by the end of the narration that she has succeeded in a lifelong alienation of the male figures who have surrounded her (179-80). She has a dream in which one male figure replaces another, thus reflecting her real attempts to replace her mother. When Julia awakens, she knows instinctively that the male figures were her dead brother Rafael. Schumm comments that: "Readers can extend these metonymic links further to see that Julia's family continues the violation of her sense of self" (162). The death of Rafael and the chilly distance of Julia's mother are the two familial phenomena that most entrench Julia in unhappiness and insecurity. Brooksbank Jones summarizes the effects on Julia:

> The frame freezes with Julita neither excluded nor included, guarding the threshhold, with the family inside suspended in sleep, as the soundlessly colliding stones double her conflict and her petrification. ("Sacrifice" 30)

Moix's use of stream of consciousness, temporal inconstancy, and driving repetition helps to reinforce the repeated isolation in which the protagonist is trapped. She is born, searches for her mother, finds only a lack of love, cannot separate herself from her mother until love is realized, collects and glorifies mother figures with whom she has a temporary relationship of maternal and sexual qualities, and is ultimately stagnated in the death of the older Julia and the survival of the girl Julita. Julita must punish herself for the lack of mother-love in her life: "Y, sobre todo, recordaba la imagen rebuscada en su mente para tener ganas de llorar: Mamá muerta. Este pensamiento sirvió para mortificarse una y otra vez hasta sentirse satisfecha" (57).

The desire and controlled gaze which manifested themselves as hunger and gluttony in *Memorias de Leticia Valle* become in *Julia* a faltering gaze demonstrated by the protagonist's emptiness and drive towards deprivation. Both protagonists have a powerful sense of "multiple selves" (a phrase coined by Virginia Woolf) as they each view themselves acting and being acted upon. Leticia Valle, the first-person narrator, "sees herself," while the third-person narrator Julia watches herself and Julita and the play between the two.

Rosa Chacel successfully creates the role of a "niña-mujer" whose uncanny intuition about herself and human nature (a result of her position as a highly functioning daughter of an alcoholic father and an absent mother) leads her to an inversion of the typical man-girl seduction story, an inversion which so mars the man's reputation that *he* is the one to commit suicide. The novel's time of publication during the immediate post-War lends itself to a look at the death and/or absence of male figures and a unique manner of portraying men and a female protagonist bequeathed with traditionally masculine and feminine traits. Ana María Moix's depiction of the "mujer-niña" at first seems to reinforce traditional views of female victimization but instead subverts it through a liberated view of the mother figure and other female role models. *Julia* was published in the late 1960's, not long after the publication and revelations of Friedan's *The Feminine Mystique*, thus establishing a natural context for a look at the "modern" woman still entrenched in and yet at times removed from articulation of the only-maternal. The discourse breaks ground because it is heterogeneous and allows for non-heterosexual rhetoric in which the daughter "writes" the mother and her numerous selves. Sociologist Stephanie Coontz states that "families have always been in flux and often in crisis; they have never lived up to nostalgic notions about 'the way things used to be'" (Coontz in Thompson, 811). The general "societal anxiety" (Papero 60) that influences family systems in the Spain of the post-War period translates into an anxiety about modernization, socially imposed gender roles, and a general concern for the *qué-dirán*. These themes are amply demonstrated in the intricate play of family shifting and triangles of incest in the textual systems of *Memorias de Leticia Valle* and *Julia*.

NOTES

[1]It is important to note that family structure and events in the two novels echo certain occurrences from the adolescent years of their authors.

[2]Hirsch's assertions about family functioning in Wolf's *A Model Childhood* apply also to the two novels discussed here: "At every moment in the text, the personal familial issues are intertwined with public political ones. The family becomes society's primary agent of socialization and subject-formation. Even the activity of writing is a familial gesture: a daughter writing about her parents, a mother writing for her daughter(s)." (156)

[3]In an interview with Geraldine C. Nichols, Moix expresses a true appreciation for Chacel's fiction (104). She also is impressed with Virginia Woolf (105), a link and influence easy to place in Moix's fiction.

[4]In this study of family ties and incest in Chacel and Moix, I draw terminology both from psychoanalytic theory and Family Systems Theory in order to introduce a discussion of constructs of family and gender within the repressive climate of post-War Spain. The works cited by Hirsch, Oliver, Papero, Bowen, Campo Urbano and Navarro López, and Rehrer have been of invaluable help in the orientation of this study.

[5]See Schumm's "Progressive Schizophrenia in Ana María Moix's *Julia*" for an excellent discussion of Julia's rape and its effects on her plural personalities. See also references to Bowen's studies on schizophrenia in Papero (65).

[6] Hirsch comments on the absent mother: "Women writers' attempts to imagine lives for their heroines which will be different from their mothers' make it imperative that mothers be silent or absent in their texts, that they remain in the prehistory of plot, fixed both as objects of desire and as examples not to be emulated" (34). She states later: "Ironically, if daughters knew their mothers' stories, they might *not* repeat them But for that suppressed mother-daughter connection to make its way into fiction, either the oedipal origins of plot would have to be reimagined and transformed, or oedipal paradigms abandoned altogether. Narrative itself would have to be enabled, at least in part, by maternal presence rather than absence" (67).

[7] Grau-Lleveria divides the narration into three sections: the first a letter to Leticia's father; the second, a confession; and the third, "una afirmación del ser de Leticia, de su voz y de su identidad" (203). These three divisions correspond nicely with the three family shifts I describe here.

[8]David Rehrer discusses contemporary transformations in Spanish economy and society as compared to traditional roles for women only recently challenged: "It is hardly likely that Spanish families could have remained untouched during times of such intense social, economic, and political transformations. They were, though some aspects of family life were more affected than others. The changing role of women in Spanish society was a key link between families and social, economic, and political change. The importance of the role played by women for the family cannot be underestimated: the entire family life cycle was predicated on their reproductive process, their contribution to the household budget was fundamental, and their role in the education and socialization of children made

them essential for the entire process of social reproduction" (274).
[9] Both protagonists suffer the same problems of identity and involvement as does Gwendolen in Eliot's *Daniel Deronda*: "Gwendolen's inability to sympathize and identify with the mothers causes her violent rejection of the plots in which they are enmeshed. In psychological terms, she affirms boundaries through distance and separation and struggles against identification. This attempted break with female plot, however, only succeeds in enmeshing her more firmly within it." (Hirsch 78)
[10]Elizabeth Scarlett states about *Memorias de Leticia Valle* that "el cuerpo femenino se aprovecha como arma en una batalla en que se disputan el saber y el poder" and that "el escribir duro, cosa que Rosa Chacel llevaba a cabo a la perfección, desafiaba al predominio masculino con una actitud iconoclasta inaudita" (115). The corporeal presence of the protagonists as element of power and desire for control is emphasized both in *Memorias de Leticia Valle* and in *Julia*.

Works Cited

Bellver, Catherine G. "Division, Duplication, and Doubling in the Novels of Ana María Moix." *Nuevos y novísimos*, ed. Ricardo Landeira and Luis T. González-del-Valle. Boulder, CO: Society of Spanish and Spanish-American Studies, 1987.

Brooksbank Jones, Anny. "Ana Maria Moix and the Sacrifice of Order." *Letras Femeninas* 23.1-2 (1997): 27-40.

---. "The Incubus and I: Unbalancing Acts in Moix's *Julia*." *Bulletin of Hispanic Studies* 52.1 (January 1995): 73-85.

Campo Urbano, Salustiano del and Manuel Navarro López. *Análisis sociológico de la familia española*. Barcelona: Ariel, 1985.

Chacel, Rosa. *Memorias de Leticia Valle*. Barcelona: Lumen, 1993.

---. *Memoirs of Leticia Valle*, translated by Carol Meier. Lincoln: U of Nebraska P, 1994.

Feminism and Families, ed. Hilde Lindemann Nelson. New York: Routledge, 1997.

Fernández Utrera, María Soledad. "Construcción de la 'nueva mujer' en el discurso femenino de la vanguardia histórica española: *Estación. Ida y vuelta*, de Rosa Chacel." *Revista Canadiense de Estudios Hispánicos* 21.3 (Spring 1997): 501-21.

Grau-Lleveria, Elena. "La silenciosa presencia de la historia en *Memorias de Leticia Valle* de Rosa Chacel." *Estudios en honor de Janet Pérez: El sujeto femenino en escritoras hispánicas*," eds. Susana Cavallo, Luis A. Jiménez, and Oralia Preble-Niemi. Potomac, MD: Scripta Humanistica, 1998.

Gullón, Germán. "La (cambiante) representación de la mujer en la narrativa española contemporánea: *Chamábase Luise*, de Marian Mayoral." *Discurso Femenino Actual*, ed. Adelaida López de Martínez. San Juan: U de Puerto Rico, 1995.

Hirsch, Marianne. *The Mother/Daughter Plot. Narrative, Psychoanalysis, Feminism.* Bloomington: Indiana UP, 1989.

Jiménez, Francisco Chacón, ed. *Historia social de la familia en España.* Alicante: Instituto de Cultura ‹‹Juan Gil-Albert››, 1990.

Mangini, Shirley. "Woman, Eros, and Culture: The Essays of Rosa Chacel." *Spanish Women Writers and the Essay. Gender, Politics, and the Self*, eds. Kathleen M. Glenn and Mercedes Mazquiarán de Rodríguez. Columbia: U of Missouri P, 1998.

Martín Gaite, Carmen. *Desde la ventana.* Madrid: Austral, 1992.

---. *Usos amorosos de la postguerra española.* Barcelona: Anagrama, 1990.

Moix, Ana María. *Julia.* Barcelona: Lumen, 1991.

Nichols, Geraldine C. *Escribir, espacio propio: Laforet, Matute, Moix, Tusquets, Riera y Roig por sí mismas.* Minneapolis: Institute for the Study of Ideologies and Literature, 1989.

---. *"Julia.* 'This is the Way the World Ends....*" Novelistas femeninas de la postguerra española.* ed. Janet W. Pérez. Madrid: Porrúa, 1983.

Oliver, Kelly. *Family Values. Subjects between Nature and Culture.* New York: Routledge, 1997.

Papero, David V. *Bowen Family Systems Theory.* Boston: Allyn and Bacon, 1990.

Rehrer, David S. *Perspectives on the Family in Spain, Past and Present.* Oxford: Clarendon, 1997.

Scarlett, Elizabeth. "Retrato de la joven Rosa Chacel." *Bazar: Revista de Literatura.* 4: La narrativa del 27 y de la vanguardia. (Fall 1997): 110-15.

Schumm, Sandra J. "Progressive Schizophrenia in Ana María Moix's *Julia.*" *Revista Canadiense de Estudios Hispánicos* 19. 1 (Fall 1994): 149-71.

Schyfter, Sara E. "The Fragmented Family in the Novels of Contemporary Spanish Women." *Perspectives on Contemporary Literature* 3.1 (May 1977): 23-29.

Thompson, Peter. *"Bajarse al moro*: A Socio-political Examination of the 'Family' and Contemporary Spain." *Anales de la Literatura Española Contemporánea* 23.3 (1998): 811-19.

Turner, Harriet S. "Family Ties and Tyrannies: A Reassessment of Jacinta." *Hispanic Review* 51.1 (Winter 1983): 1-22.

3

Dysfunction, Discord, and Wedded Bliss: Baroque Families in *Don Quixote*

Donald D. Miller

Marriage as a religious sacrament legitimized by the Church and supported by emerging European legal systems has its beginnings in the late Middle Ages. This emphasis was due principally to questions of inheritance and the perception of the family unit as a foundation upon which modern societies and nations were built. During the Medieval Period and the Renaissance a variety of prescriptive texts appeared which attempted to guide families on a quest for stability and bourgeois perfection. These works ranged from Alfonsinian law, to instruction manuals for young nobles, and included the ubiquitous manuals of feminine comportment. Although not directly tied to *El ingenioso hidalgo don Quixote de la Mancha*, these Medieval, Counter-reformationist, and Humanist manuals, and the concept of marriage that they propose, indirectly influence and inform Cervantes's masterpiece. Even though the author occasionally refers to the steps needed to achieve wedded bliss, we find that Cervantes focuses his discussion of marriage and family on a Baroque deconstruction of Renaissance ideologies. Cervantes employs elements of satire and comedy to create dysfunctional, yet realistic families that could never achieve the behavioral perfection suggested by Fray Luis de León, Pedro de Luján, Juan de Molina, Juan Luis Vives and others. Through his critical observations on the realities of family life, Cervantes shows the complexities of conflictive familial interaction apparently ignored or glossed over by Renaissance clerics and scholars.

Recent trends in family psychology provide useful theoretical terminology that permit the investigator to comprehend the concepts of dysfunction and discord as they relate to nuclear families in *Don Quixote*. Specifically, the basic tenets of systemic family theory proposed by Salvador Minuchin, Murray Bowen and others, allow for an analysis of the patterns of familial interaction that affect erratic, violent and dysfunctional individual behavior.

In his foundational study *Families and Family Therapy*, Salvador Minuchin proposes that Structural Family Therapy (a subset of Family Systems Theory), "is one of many responses to the concept of man as part of his environment," or as he paraphrases José Ortega y Gasset, "a man is not himself without his circumstances" (4-5). Minuchin hypothesizes that the human mind and individual self-consciousness is directly connected to both internal and external stimuli and shows the connection between environment, family life and the individual. Hence, the human psyche must be studied within its complete social and familial context in order to gain a full understanding thereof. Family Systems Theory proposes that dysfunction can only be overcome by concrete changes in the environment and familial interaction.

According to Murray Bowen and Michael E. Kerr, "Three categories of dysfunction occur in nuclear families: (1) illness in a spouse; (2) marital conflict; and (3) impairment of one or more of the children" (163). Dysfunction within the family system, especially in interpersonal relationships, leads frequently to conflict and verbal or physical aggression. In analyzing the dysfunctionality of families in the *Quixote*, it becomes evident that the first two categories apply in the familial relationships of Don Quixote, Anselmo and Camila, Sancho Panza, and the Dukes, to cite a few examples. For purposes of this essay we will distinguish between clinical dysfunction, as described above and social dysfunction. Social dysfunction will refer to all interactions that break with societal norms established in the Golden Age for families and interpersonal relationships. In the *Quixote*, social dysfunction is by far the most prevalent. Cervantes's focus on the realities of inharmonious and conflictive family life clearly satirizes the marital bliss and familial symmetry proposed by his ecclesiastical and philosophical predecessors. Through satire and comedy, Cervantes shows both the positive and negative aspects of family life, and demonstrates that even in dysfunction some families can still hold together.

Understanding the basic social and religious philosophies relating to families in the Middle Ages and Renaissance is imperative to recognizing Cervantes's support and subversion of social norms. As far back as the Thirteenth Century, in his *Siete partidas*, King Alfonso X proclaims that marriage is the most important social contract of a modern society. He dedicates twenty-six titles and more than 200 laws to the subject, and as he himself notes, the fourth *partida* forms the perfect center of his book and the legal code of Castile and León. In the subsequent three centuries theologians publish a variety of texts concerning marriage such as *Coloquios matrimoniales* by Pedro de Luján, and *Sermón en loor del matrimonio* by Juan de Molina that emphasize the religious importance of the sacrament of marriage. During the Renaissance, other Spanish writers, such as Juan Luis Vives and Fray Luis de León, influenced by Erasmian thought, produce decidedly humanistic manuals of female comportment that address the subject of perfect married life. The most pervasive of these texts that could have influenced Cervantes's discussions on the state of matrimony would be Fray Luis de León's *La perfecta casada* (1583). León's instructions for bourgeois women utilize the biblical text in Proverbs 31:10-31 to comment on the role of a woman in her home and at the same time the role of her husband as governor of his wife, children and possessions. In both volumes of the *Quixote*, Cervantes presents and deconstructs the discourses created by these earlier texts, first commenting on the "blessed state of matrimony," then subverting and criticizing the humanist discourse on marital perfection and functionality.

More than three decades ago, Robert V. Piluso carried out an in-depth study of theme of marriage in Cervantes in *Amor, matrimonio y honra en Cervantes*. With soberness he analyzes the choice of state: singleness, matrimony, widowhood, or religion; the election of a spouse; and the reciprocal duties of the couple according to the socio-cultural context in which Cervantes's writings were created. However, Piluso overlooks the dynamic and humoristic approach that Cervantes takes to families and the idyllic family systems created in the Renaissance. In his recent book *Grotesque Purgatory*, Henry W. Sullivan includes an appendix titled, "A Checklist of Theological Impediments to Matrimony in *Don Quixote, Part I*." He compares the articles of the Council of Trent with the first tome of the Quixote, explaining which marriages presented therein are valid or not, according to the norms prescribed by the doctors of the Church. Apart from this, critical attention over the past twenty years has focused more on courtship, weddings, symbols and deceit involved in marriage in Cervantes's *Novelas ejemplares*.

Simultaneously there has been a shift in Cervantine criticism towards comedy, irony, parody and satire as motivating forces in the *Quixote*, leaving behind previous work that focused on the alienation, temporal angst, and disorientation of the Manchegan hidalgo (El Saffar xi). Among the recent investigations on irony and satire, the works of Eduardo Urbina stand out. In *Principios y fines del Quijote* and *El sin par Sancho Panza: parodia y creación*, Urbina demonstrates the prevalence of satirical/burlesque elements throughout both volumes of the *Quixote*.

Taking into account the concepts of familial dysfunction proposed by Family Systems theorists, and the recent critical focus on satire and comedy in the *Quixote*, we will analyze the manner in which Cervantes uses satire and comedy to present a variety of families that do not function according to the norms created for Spanish society during the Medieval Period and Renaissance.

The first clinically dysfunctional family in the *Quixote* includes Don Quixote, his housekeeper and his niece. Although they are not connected directly as a stereotypical nuclear family, these three characters clearly operate as a family unit. They suffer from the first Bowenian category of dysfunction, illness of a spouse, or in this case the supposed psychosis of the family patriarch. Don Quixote's illness and the severe lack of education of the housekeeper and niece create a family incapable of functioning as a healthy unit. In fact they suffer from the maladies linked to morphostasis. Simon, Stierlin and Wynne explain that families in morphostasis "tend predominantly to maintain a status quo, and whose structural adaptability [is] limited. This structural rigidity went hand in hand with a high level of pathology and symptomatic behavior in individual family members" (229). Don Quixote's family is unable to adapt to his perceived illness, and all their attempts to "cure" him eventually fail. They cannot even convince him to leave his obsession in order to eat; unusually lean features characterize every image of this knight-errant. In his condition, Don Quixote does not provide logical guidance and adequate leadership that would allow his family to change. For their part, the housekeeper and niece refuse all blame for the family's ills, instead they point at the man of the house as the origin and center of their problems. The women spend most of their time trying to convince Don Quixote to lead the peaceful life of a country gentleman, while the hidalgo fantasizes about adventures with castles, dragons and maidens in distress. Don Quixote's obsession with chivalry goes to the extent that he expresses his willingness to give away his family for the chance to fight characters from epic poetry. Early in the novel, the narrator explains that Don Quixote "Diera él por dar una mano de coces al traidor de Galalón, al ama que tenía y aun a su sobrina de añadidura" (36).[1] Don Quixote's family expresses concern over his apparent mental illness upon his return from his first adventure. The housekeeper feels compassion for the ailing hidalgo, and the niece blames herself for letting his condition get so bad before notifying the village priest and barber (65). The women seek for sources external to the sick paternal figure instead of focusing on his individual psychological problems. Any physical violence (typical of a dysfunctional family) in reaction to Don Quixote's illness is turned away from the family members and towards the chivalric novels, the supposed source of his affliction. The morning following Don Quixote's return, the women, the priest and the barber scrutinize the hidalgo's library and condemn his books to the fire. In this manner they defer their anger to the "innocent" books (71). This coping strategy functions well until Don Quixote discovers his loss and searches for the library, which the priest has walled up. Instead of helping the situation, the niece exacerbates the problem by suggesting that an evil enchanter has carried away all his books (84).

In Chapter 2 of *Don Quixote II*, the housekeeper and niece's aggression, caused by Don Quixote's behavior, focuses on Sancho Panza, the perceived agitator of their uncle and master's "locura." Two weeks after the adventures of the *Don Quixote I*, Sancho returns to his master's house and engages in a scandalous argument with the women. The three engage in a barrage of verbal abuse and vituperation, typical of the violence found in dysfunctional families. Cervantes satirizes the communication skills of the members of the lower class as they attempt to discuss their differences:

> -¿Qué quiere este mostrenco en esta casa? Idos a la vuestra, hermano, que vos sois, y no otro, el que destrae y sonsaca a mi señor, y le lleva por esos andurriales. A lo que Sancho respondió: -Ama de Satanás, el sonsacado, y el destraído y el llevado por esos andurriales soy yo, que no tu amo... él me sacó de mi casa con engañifas, prometiéndome una ínsula... -Con todo eso —dijo el ama— no entraréis acá, saco de maldades y costal de malicias. Id a gobernar vuestra casa y a labrar vuestros pegujares y dejaos de pretender ínsulas ni ínsulos. (574-75)

This comical interchange emphasizes the disintegration of the Quijano family and provides entertainment for the priest and barber, who are attempting to assess Don Quixote's sanity. Later in this section Cervantes satirizes the gestures of admiration and familial love that the niece shows towards Don Quixote. After listening to a short discourse on nobility and the benefits of arms over letters the niece exclaims, "¡Válame Dios!...¡Que sepa tanta vuestra merced tanto, señor tío, que, si fuese menester en una necesidad, podría subir en un púlpito e irse a predicar por esas calles...," and later "¡Ay, desdichada de mí...que también mi señor es poeta! Todo lo sabe, todo lo alcanza: yo apostaré que si quisiera ser albañil, que supiera fabricar una casa como una jaula" (605). In her uneducated way, she attempts to praise Don Quixote by suggesting that if he gives up chivalry he can take a job as a preacher or bricklayer. In spite of their problems, this dysfunctional family is capable of showing sincere concern and affection for the afflicted Manchegan hidalgo; their problems are abated with Don Quixote's death.

A discussion of familial social dysfunction in the Quixote must also include Anselmo and Camila as well as the Dukes and the Panzas, who clearly break with nearly every norm prescribed by Golden Age treatises and manuals on family behavior. Due to the fact that the majority of the self-help books of the Sixteenth Century concentrate on suggestions for improving the imperfections of women instead of those of men, Teresa Panza and the Duchess play a key role in Cervantes's Baroque deconstruction of Renaissance norms. The author uses these women to criticize the unrealistic expectations of family ideologists and show that the vast majority of the Spanish population could not fit the mold. Camila on the other hand appears as the perfect wife, whose virtue is destroyed by an unwitting husband.

According to his guidebook for married women, Fray Luis de León's perfect woman should be honorable, virtuous, withdrawn from public life, enclosed in her home, maintaining pleasant silence and agreement with her husband's desires and counsel. The key to understanding Cervantes's deconstruction of the norms lies in the fact these concepts were taken socially as appropriate suggestions for all females, ignoring the fact that the majority of women could never fit León's mold. Fray Luis presents a bourgeois woman, generally the wife of a rich landowner. Neither the female villager, who lacked the economic means, nor the duchess, with tendencies toward idleness and mischief, fit within the standards created by Fray Luis. In her Marxist-Feminist analysis of *La perfecta casada*, María Ángeles Durán explains that León's text is very problematic because it presents an idealized woman, outside of time, space, and any economic reality. She notes that León's work suffers from a reduction of the real complexity of concrete situations to the simplified schematization of his model (260). By comparing his female characters and married couples to the imagined perfect married woman, we see Cervantes's ability to force the humanist discourse espoused by León and others to face a social reality.

Cervantes's closest study of gender stereotypes and social mores occurs during the intercalated novel *El curioso impertinente*. Through this piece the author discusses the nature of the "perfect" woman, foolish husbands who tempt their spouses, and disloyal friends who give in to their passions. Although the perfect women should do all that her husband requires of her, he must in turn trust her and teach her. By means of Lotario, Camila and Anselmo, Cervantes shows a preference for describing dysfunctional families at length. This ménage a trois exemplifies the second Bowenian principle of dysfunction, marital conflict. Anselmo, in his attempts to discover impropriety in his wife's behavior, causes dysfunction in his marriage and breaches the principle of trust (349). Anselmo is obsessed with ascertaining the virtue of his new wife and Lotario attempts to dissuade him from his plan to test her (351). He explains:

> Mira, amigo, que la mujer es animal imperfecto, y que no se le han de poner embarazos donde tropiece y caiga, sino quitárselos y despejalle el camino de cualquier inconveniente, para que sin pesadumbre corra ligera a alcanzar la perfección que le falta, que consiste en el ser virtuosa... La honesta y casta mujer es arminio, y es más que nieve blanca y limpia la virtud de la honestidad; y el que quisiere que no la pierda, antes la guarde y conserve... (354)

Lotario warns that although a woman might be virtuous and honest, she is weak and incapable of resisting temptation. Cervantes, through Anselmo the curious and impertinent spouse, creates a discourse on gender ideologies that mimics the commentary of Fray Luis de León, and even quotes the same biblical text from Proverbs 31 "Mujer virtuosa, ¿quien la hallará?" However, the discourse on virtue and male/female relationships shows dysfunction in a young, socially advanced couple. In the final analysis, the husband causes the marital distress and provokes the disloyalty and moral deviance of his wife.

During the second book of the novel, we encounter a different discourse on family relationships that breaks with early modern familial

standards. Through humor and satire Cervantes challenges the tenets of
Renaissance discourse on family life.   If Cervantes were to follow these
principles, one would suppose that the nobles in the *Quixote* would be
exemplary of proper marital conduct and that they would engage in the
just use of their power over the rustic, uneducated masses.

However, the Duke and Duchess break nearly as many social regulations as do
the Panzas in their confrontation with the ideals of behavior; their
marriage is socially dysfunctional, breaching all prescribed boundaries.

By Renaissance standards, the Duke fails in his duties to
maintain his wife quiet, secluded and engaged in worthwhile pursuits.
In fact, he recklessly disregards León's standards by allowing his
spouse to read chivalric novels.   According to these norms the Duke
creates social dysfunction in his marriage by allowing his wife too
many liberties.   In *Sermón en loor del matrimonio*, Juan de Molina
comments that a man must not be too fierce with his wife, but he must
not be "demasiado manso y no mostrarse varón en mirar por su casa"
(526).   The Duke's manliness is at stake if he is too soft on his wife
when she does not fulfill her obligations, an obvious condition that he
suffers.   León's directives in this matter indicate that a husband should
excuse his wife, "de leer en los libros de caballerías y del traer el soneto
y la canción en el seno, y del billete y del donaire de los recaudos, y del
terreno y del sarao, y de otras cien cosas de este hacer..." (270).   The
duchess evades these norms, holding parties and staging burlesque
dramatic performances aimed at humiliating Don Quixote and Sancho.
She becomes what Fray Luis calls a "ventanera, visitadora, callejera,
amiga de fiestas, enemiga de su rincón..." (72).   As enemy of home
and hearth, she flaunts her power and the liberty that her social position
affords her.

The duchess also fails to complete her maximum duties of
watching over her house, her family and servants.   On her social status,
Fray Luis comments:

> Traten las duquesas y las reinas el lino, y labren la seda,
> y den tarea a sus damas, y pruébense con ellas estos oficios, y
> pongan en estado y honra aquesta virtud... Tomen la rueca, y
> armen los dedos con la aguja y el dedal, y cercadas de sus
> damas, y en medio dellas, hagan labores ricas con ellas, y
> engañen algo de la noche con este ejercicio, y húrtense al
> vicioso sueño para entender en él, y ocupen los pensamientos
> mozos de sus doncellas en estas haciendas, y hagan que,
> animadas con el ejemplo de la señora contienden todas entre sí,
> procurando de aventajarse en el ser hacendosas. (54)

In his *Formación de la mujer cristiana*, Juan Luis Vives adds, "Salomón enumera como uno de los loores de la perfecta casada el haber buscado lana y lino y haberla trabajado con la industria y diligencia de sus manos" (1133). The comedy and satire in Cervantes' interpretation of these ideologies are obvious. The duchess does nothing to better the status of her husband and his holdings, nor does she teach her servants to carry out "proper" female activities. Vives warns against this, suggesting that the female servants should be:

> enseñadas y amonestadas porque se acuerden del mandato, no de un mortal cualquiera, sino nada menos que del Apóstol San Pablo, porque con toda diligencia y mansedumbre y bondad, y aun con alegría y con sabor, desempeñan su cometido, no gruñendo, no devolviendo respuestas, no murmurando entre dientes, no mustias, ni desabridas, ni encopetadas, porque no pierdan el agradecimiento de su trabajo ante Dios y ante los hombres; guarden sus manos puras de toda sisa y rapacidad. En este punto, las bestias muestran un ánimo más agradecido que muchos hombres." (1130)

The duchess fails in the charge to teach her female servants properly and carefully to fulfill their tasks with meekness and kindness. In fact, instead of guiding the minds of her damsels and maidservants in charitable good works, she induces them to commit comical but nevertheless cruel acts against her guests. In chapter thirty-three of Book II, the duchess invites Sancho to her room so that she and her ladies-in-waiting may laugh at his odd behavior, speech, and stories instead of enclosing herself in her chambers with the other women to rest, sew and embroider. Idleness leads her to seek entertainment at the expense of the lower classes.

On the subject of female servants, Vives also suggests that she should read the Bible and other good books and if she is unable to read, her companions should read to her from the holy writ (1132). The reading of these texts should set the moral tone and spirit of the home. The Duke and Duchess obviously fail in this commission because they teach their servants to read chivalric novels and stage comical, but cruel tests of Don Quixote's supposed craziness and Sancho's simplicity.

Early on during their visit to the Duke and Duchesses' country estate, Sancho finds himself being attacked by servants who want to clean his beard with filthy water and dirty towels. Instead of chastising the servants for mistreating her guests, we read, "perecida de la risa estaba la duquesa viendo la cólera y oyendo las razones de Sancho"

(806). Sancho does not know what to do and finally cries out "vosotros ministros de la limpieza, habéis andado demasiadamente de remisos y descuidados, y no sé si diga atrevidos... Pero, en fin, sois malos y mal nacidos, y no podéis dejar, como malandrines que sois, de mostrar la ojeriza que tenéis con los escuderos de los andantes caballeros" (807). According Vives, the married woman should guide and direct her home, in accordance with her husband's wishes and according to the rules of etiquette and good behavior. She should be kind and benevolent with her servants and guests and yet she is cruel and causes public scandal through the activities of her servants. Vives tells us:

> Adminístrelo todo la mujer a voluntad o mandato de su marido, o sino, de tal manera que sepa anticipadamente que su marido no se lo ha de desaprobar. No sea desabrida con la servidumbre ni dura, sino benévola y afable, de suerte que antes conozcan tener en ella madre que señora, según dice San Jerónimo; más con su dulzura que con su aspereza, gánese el respeto, cuyo atajo más breve es el camino de la virtud; nada añaden a su autoridad y respeto, antes bien los merman, las riñas, las villanías los denuestos, las voces no los golpes. Con discreción, con seso, con reposo y gravedad de costumbres, de palabras, de avisos, cualquiera cosa se hace más de prisa y muy mejor que no con ímpetus y violencia; más respeto nos merecen los prudentes que no los airados; más obliga el mando quieto que no el arrebatado; la calma impone más que el atropello" (1129-30).

Instead of focusing on virtue, discretion and tranquility, the duchess is the first to chase down boars in the hunt and encourage her servants in the mistreatment of her newest *servidores* Don Quixote and Sancho. Together the Duke and Duchess plot to play a joke on Don Quixote and Sancho due their mental conditions and simplicity.

> Las razones de Sancho renovaron en la duquesa la risa y el contento; y eviándole a reposar, ella fue a dar cuenta al duque de lo que con él había pasado, y entre los dos dieron traza y orden de hacer una burla a don Quijote, que fuese famosa y viniese bien con el estilo caballeresco. (815-16)

During the hunt, the multitude of servants stage a fantastical play to force Sancho to disenchant Dulcinea. The duchess encourages the cruelty of Sancho's task of disenchantment by self-flagellation through 3,300 lashes (823-26). At other moments Don Quixote suffers a severe scratching by a cat in a bag, which the servants lower to his window. Rather than severe reprobation, this act receives approval from the duchess.

The Duke and Duchess display two final elements of social deviance. According to Juan de Molina's interpretation of the Bible, those who have no children are cursed and do not fulfill their responsibilities as a couple (518). Also, living off the men and women working their lands, they fall into the idleness that creates what Fray Luis de León calls "most grave and damaging ills" (112).

Moving away from the idle nobility, we perceive a further deviance from Renaissance marital ideologies through the Panza's. The clearest example of social errancy and the second category of Bowenian familial dysfunction occurs within this lower-class family. Marital conflict is a constant in the relationship between Sancho and his wife. Cervantes uses Sancho, Teresa and their children to show the inability of Medieval and Renaissance family ideologies to cope with the lives of common people. Although the Panza's have a tendency to argue, verbally abuse one other, and show evident symptoms of dysfunction, Cervantes proves them capable of morphogenesis. Fritz B. Simon, et.al., explain that "the long-term functionality of a family depends, as does every system, on the extent to which the system's structures are capable of change (adaptability). Without the ability to change, the potentiality for the development of individuals and families is limited" (228-29). The Panza's, though uneducated and poor, show the greatest ability to adapt to their surrounding and make changes in their family life and structure according to their fluctuating social roles. We see evidence of this as Sancho changes from peasant to squire to governor and back again.

Although Teresa initially ignores Sancho's fantasies, and refuses Sancho's suggestion that they will marry Sanchica outside her social station, she eventually comes around. When the duchess sends her a coral necklace and explains Sancho's new governorship of the Ínsula Barataria, Teresa immediately embraces the idea. She goes to town, explains her new social situation to the priest and barber, and asks where she can buy new dresses and hire a coach to take her and Sanchica to their new residence. However, when Sancho returns without the power of government, she is happy to accept the money he has brought with him. This adaptability to the ups and downs of the family's social station clearly displays morphogenesis.

A more complete understanding of the dysfunctionality of the Panza family comes from analyzing the relationship between Sancho and Teresa and their individual behaviors. A certain ambiguity exists

in Sancho's personality.   He plays alternate roles as good
husband/loving father and rustic villager who verbally abuses his mate.
Panza clearly states his love for his family on several occasions during
the course of Cervantes's metanovel (78, 143, 181, 202, 306, 362, 375).
If he feels pride in his accomplishments, he wishes his wife and
children were there to see him (306).   When his situation with Don
Quixote becomes difficult, even grave, Sancho comically expresses a
desire to be with his family, carrying out his daily rituals (139, 143,
400, 476).   On other occasions Sancho denigrates his wife while
conversing with Don Quixote.   Instead of calling her blessed as Fray
Luis de León suggests, Sancho shows little confidence in her abilities
to adapt to changes in her life.   When Don Quixote offers him a
kingdom for his services, he states, "aunque lloviese Dios reinos sobre
la tierra, ninguno asentaría bien sobre la cabeza de Mari Gutiérrez,
Sepa señor, que no vale dos maravedís para reina; condesa le caerá
mejor, y aun Dios y ayuda" (88).   Sancho suggests that Teresa would
be of little use as a queen and even as a duchess she would need divine
intervention.   In spite of the defects and wanderings of Sancho,
Cervantes portrays him as a family man.

The words and deeds of Teresa Panza figure into the novel as a
humorous criticism of the feminine ideals portrayed in texts like those
written by León and Vives.   To begin with, the perfect married woman
should know how to manage the affairs of her house and create
confidence in her husband (*La perfecta* 93).   However, Cervantes
subverts the idyllic marriage on Sancho's return after several
adventures.   As he rides into town, Teresa shows more concern for the
family property than for her missing husband.   Teresa first inquires
how the ass is doing. The comical double entendre is obvious although
she does praise God for his return.   The next obvious questions she asks
are "What have you gained as a squire? What dress have you brought
me? What shoes for your children?" (538).   The combative banter the
pair exchanges continues when Teresa asks what the *ínsula* is that
Sancho might govern:

> No es la miel para la boca del asno –respondió Sancho-;
> a su tiempo lo verás, mujer, y aun te admirarás de oírte llamar
> señoría de todos tus vasallos.—¿Qué es lo que decís, Sancho, de
> señorías, ínsulas y vasallos?...No te acucies, Juana por saber
> todo esto tan apriesa; basta que te diga la verdad y cose la boca.
> (539)

Sancho returns the previous insult and tells her to be patient and shut her mouth until she understands better. Later, when Sancho swears that he will become a governor, Teresa replies:

> Eso no, marido mío ... viva la gallina, aunque sea con su pepita; vivid vos, *y llévese el diablo cuantos gobiernos hay en el mundo*; sin gobierno salistes del vientre de vuestra madre, sin gobierno os iréis, o os llevarán, a la sepultura cuando Dios fuere servido. (594-95; my emphasis)

On the one hand, Teresa Panza ironically and aptly refers to the man-made institution of government, which has little or no power over major life events. On the other hand, these insults are evident in the verbal abusiveness that hinders a dysfunctional family's progress towards normalcy.

According to Fray Luis, Juana should be of discreet reasoning and sweet speech, including staying at home and keeping quiet (153). However, instead of holding her tongue and agreeing with everything her husband says, Teresa shares her opinions freely. María Ángeles Durán comments that:

> en el ininterrumpido cuidado de su casa por la casada, el silencio se convierte en una obsesión para el predicador [Fray Luis de León]. El silencio es la garantía de que la desobediencia y la rebeldía se mantienen contenidas en niveles no peligrosos, que no arriesgan la pervivencia del sistema productivo defendido. (272)

According to León, "Cuenta Plutarco, que Fidias, escultor noble hizo a los elienses una imagen de Venus que afirmaba los pies sobre una tortuga, que es animal mudo y que nunca desampara su concha; dando a entender que las mujeres, por la misma manera, han de *guardar siempre la casa y el silencio*" (155: my emphasis).

Cervantes subverts the sweet speech and silence of the perfect wife through Teresa, who always says and does as she pleases, even to the point of criticizing her husband. In her letter to the duchess, she says "en este pueblo todos tienen a mi marido por un porro, y que sacado de gobernar un hato de cabras, no pueden imaginar para qué gobierno pueda ser bueno" (947). Instead of silencing Sancho's defects, Teresa points them out frequently. The subject of reclusion in the home is a moot point. In her life as a poor villager, Teresa is socially and publicly open. Paradoxically, while this behavior would have been interpreted as social dysfunction according to Vives and

León, her tendency to speak plainly and reveal family strife would today be viewed as a positive indicator of family health. She does not have the liberty to remain enclosed in her home to govern the servants and children. She must cook, farm, wash at the river, and go to market as any woman of her social class while her husband gallivants around the countryside. She cannot remain enclosed within the four walls of her home.

In spite of the fact that verbal confrontation and abusiveness are signs of dysfunction in a relationship, the Panza's repartee reflects the typical Golden Age portrayal of their social class. Their insults are rarely, if ever, malicious. Along the same lines, Teresa's daily routines reflect the only possibility for a woman of her status. Cervantes uses the Panza's to show the inadequacies of family and marital ideologies as they relate to the lower class.

The Panza's, Duke and Duchess, Anselmo and Camila, and Don Quixote's family all represent different aspects of psychological and social dysfunction in early Baroque families. Cervantes clearly proves that human nature does not concord with Renaissance manuals of comportment. Whether for their lack of comical importance or the surreal nature of their relationships, the few "perfect" families in the *Quixote* are underdeveloped. Cervantes briefly pays homage to the mother of Marcela, a charitable woman, and her father a man who dies of sorrow over his wife's death (62). While their economic status has elevated their morality, their lack of a title of nobility, prevents their fall into opulence. Other exemplary families include the good wife of an innkeeper (81) and the Miranda family (413). Cervantes chooses not to develop in depth these families that actually succeed in following Renaissance norms.

Cervantes uses comedy and satire to comment on, and then dissect the Renaissance norms of family behavior. He deconstructs the arguments of Fray Luis de León, Juan Luis Vives, Pedro de Luján, and other similar writers in order to show the realities of life in the Golden Age. This typical Baroque reaction to Renaissance ideologies shows Cervantes's understanding of marriage and family relationships in the Seventeenth Century. The dysfunctional families that Cervantes portrays allow the observer an in-depth look into family psychology as portrayed in Spanish literature. Through satire Cervantes encourages his readers to take a serious look at their own relationships and laugh at their own imperfections. A final note on the subject of marital relations may be found in the words of our hidalgo. As they gain the helmet of Mambrino, Don Quixote explains how he might move up the social ladder and gain himself a royal wife:

> De manera que está la diferencia en que unos fueron
> [altos nobles], que ya no son, y otros son, que ya no fueron; y
> podría ser yo déstos, que, después de averiguado, hubiese sido
> mi principio grande y famoso, con lo cual se debía de contentar
> el rey mi suegro, que hubiere de ser; y cuando no, la infanta me
> ha de querer de manera, que a pesar de su padre, aunque
> claramente sepa que soy hijo de un azacán, me ha de admitir por
> señor y por esposo; y si no, aquí entra el roballa y llevalla donde
> más gusto me diere; que el tiempo o la muerte ha de acabar el
> enojo de sus padres. (214-15)

The comical-quixotic discourse on dysfunctional marriage could end on
this note.   If you cannot find a perfect wife, steal a princess.

NOTES

[11] In the *Chançon de Roland*, the evil Guenelon betrays Roland to the
Serracens.

Works Cited

Bowen, Murray and Michael E. Kerr. *Family Evaluation: An Approach Based on Bowen Theory.* New York: W.W. Norton, 1988.

Cervantes, Miguel de. *El ingenioso hidalgo don Quijote de la Mancha.* Barcelona: Planeta, 1992.

Durán, María Ángeles. "Lectura económica de fray Luis de León." *Nuevas perspectivas sbore la mujer.   Actas de las primeras jornadas de investigación interdisciplinaria organizadas por el Seminario de estudios de la mujer de la Universidad Autónoma de Madrid.* 2 vols. Madrid: Universidad Autónoma, 1982, 2:257-73.

León, Luis de. *La perfecta casada.* Madrid: Taurus, 1989.

Luján, Pedro de. *Coloquios Matrimoniales.* Madrid: Aguirre, 1990.

Minuchin, Salvador. *Families and Family Therapy.* Cambridge, MA: Harvard UP, 1974.

Molina, Juan de. "Sermón en loor del matrimonio" Ed. Francisco López Estrada. *NRFH* 34 (1985-86): 741-68.

Simon, Fritz B., Helm Stierlin and Lyman C. Wynne. *The Language of Family Therapy: A Systemic Vocabulary and Sourcebook.* New York: Family Process P, 1985.

Stone, Marilyn. *Marriage and Friendship in Medieval Spain: Social Relations According to the Fourth Partida of Alfonso X.* New York: Peter Lang, 1990.

Sullivan, Henry. *Grotesque Purgatory: A Study of Cervantes's Don Quixote, Part II.* University Park, PA: Pennsylvania State UP, 1996.

Urbina, Eduardo. *El sin par Sancho Panza : parodia y creación.* Barcelona: Anthropos, 1991.

---. *Principios y fines del Quijote.* Potomac, MD: Scripta Humanistica, 1990.

Vives, Juan Luis. *Formación de la mujer cristiana.* In *Obras Completas I.* 3 vols. Madrid: Aguilar, 1947.

4

Matrofobia y matrilinealidad en *Un aire de familia* de Silvia Italiano

Miryam Criado

Pocas relaciones humanas alcanzan tal grado de intensidad y al mismo tiempo de contradicción como la relación madre/hija, en donde el amor y el odio, la obsesión y la indiferencia, la admiración y el desprecio se funden y conjugan de tal modo que es casi imposible saber dónde termina un sentimiento y dónde comienza otro. Sin embargo, este tema tan cercano y conflictivo para cualquier mujer apenas ha sido tratado dentro de la narrativa femenina hispánica hasta estos últimos años. En la mayoría de las novelas del siglo XX la protagonista o es huérfana de madre o la figura materna aparece meramente esbozada en un segundo plano. María Inés Lagos señala:

> El tema de la relación entre madre e hija que domine el relato es infrecuente en la literatura hispanoamericana. En general, las escritoras han evitado este tema tabú debido probablemente a un mecanismo de autocensura, ya que usualmente la exploración del tema madre-hija produce una imagen negativa, o al menos crítica, de la madre (...) Sólo a la muerte de la madre, la autora [puede] verbalizar la frustración de no haber tenido una relación más abierta e íntima con su madre. (137)

Únicamente tras su muerte, la figura materna es presentada de forma positiva. En las novelas donde la protagonista es huérfana, la madre simboliza un elemento imprescindible para el paso de la infancia a la adolescencia o a la madurez. Esta ausencia funciona como símbolo del desarraigo de la protagonista y de su alienación. Es esta carencia la que contribuye a crear la sicología de las protagonistas presentándolas frágiles y solitarias, sin un modelo con el cual poder identificarse y que les sirva de guía. Estas mujeres crecen confusas, aisladas e impotentes en una sociedad patriarcal cuyas reglas no comprenden. Por lo tanto, bajo el argumento superficial subyace la búsqueda de una madre sustituta, una figura materna que las ayude a encontrar su lugar en el mundo[1].

Sin embargo, en aquellas novelas donde la madre aparece, su presencia provoca una distorsión radical en cuanto a la manera en la que es construida. La figura materna, en vez de simbolizar el pilar necesario para dar estabilidad a sus hijas en el proceso de adquisición de identidad, es generalmente caracterizada como una caricatura, como un estereotipo ridículo. Se la convierte en un estorbo, en una fuerza opresora que estrangula cualquier intento de independencia por parte de sus hijas. En numerosos casos, además, la figura materna es presentada como un rígido estereotipo de una clase social y, en ese sentido, simboliza los valores y tradiciones que su hija rechaza[2]. Así pues, la madre pasa de ser un ideal para convertirse en la personificación de la presión social que sirve para perpetuar la reproducción de los roles sexuales[3].

La naturaleza conflictiva de la figura materna como construcción imaginaria[4] y de la maternidad como experiencia han llevado a una abierta matrofobia en todos los campos del fenómeno literario, incluyendo la crítica y la teoría literaria. Por regla general, las mujeres que son madres no son caracterizadas como seres individuales sino que son juzgadas y condenadas por su fracaso en la representación de su papel. Marianne Hirsch en *The Mother/Daughter Plot* considera que el hijacentrismo es el mayor problema que se plantea al analizar la relación madre-hija en la narrativa escrita por mujeres; es decir, la ausencia de la voz de la madre y el predominio de la voz o perspectiva de la hija, incluso cuando la misma protagonista es, a su vez, madre.

Las obras que basan su discurso en el hijacentrismo participan activamente en la represión de la voz materna. Esta represión se basa no sólo en el rechazo de los valores que consideran que las madres representan, es decir, la reproducción de la economía patriarcal, sino en menospreciar la capacidad intelectual misma de las madres. La narrativa construye a la figura materna como ignorante, supersticiosa, preocupada únicamente por las apariencias mientras que el padre es quien representa el verdadero conocimiento. De este modo, las hijas parten del principio, propuesto por el mismo patriarcado, por el cual se considera que de una madre no se puede aprender nada: su voz, su palabra, su experiencia y su modo de entender el mundo que la rodea son inferiores a los del padre. Por otro lado, las hijas contribuyen al silenciamiento de sus propias madres al aceptar inconscientemente la supuesta necesidad de la ruptura con la madre para poder desarrollar su individualidad.

Según Luce Irigaray, en nuestra sociedad, el sentimiento de unión con la madre está prohibido. La cultura patriarcal promueve el rechazo y la negación de la madre. Deshacerse de la dependencia emocional que le une a ésta e identificarse con la figura del padre se consideran imprescindibles para poder desarrollarse y madurar adecuadamente. La neurosis nace, por tanto, de la negación del vínculo con la madre, con su matriz, con su útero. Y el repetido temor a la castración no es el de la posibilidad sino el de la certeza del corte del cordón umbilical ("Bodily" 42). En el fondo, esta negación de la madre es un reflejo de la ruptura del vínculo con la naturaleza al pretender olvidar y negar lo que representa su propio origen y, sobre todo, su primera dependencia. Los niños tienen la posibilidad de recuperarse de parte de esa neurosis provocada por este matricidio simbólico porque tienen la figura del padre en la que se reconocen a sí mismos. Al igual que Orestes, pueden recobrar la razón. Sin embargo, la hijas, como Electra, nunca podrán aliviar esa neurosis porque se encuentran doblemente alienadas: de sí mismas, es decir, del mundo femenino, y por el mundo masculino que deben aceptar.

Irigaray propone que para conseguir la realización de este matricidio simbólico, el lenguaje falogocéntrico patriarcal ha convertido a la figura materna en un "símbolo reverso" al que se le han atribuido características opuestas a las que en la realidad tiene. En vez de representar el ser que da la vida se la ha convertido en símbolo de muerte; en vez de representar a quien nutre de alimento a su criatura se la ha descrito como devoradora; en vez de dar placer y vida el sexo femenino es representado como castrador ("Bodily" 41).

En la novela *Un aire de familia* (1995) la argentina Silvia Italiano, partiendo del hijacentrismo que reprime la voz materna y desautoriza su discurso y conocimiento —estrategias que refuerzan las estructuras del patriarcado—, consigue desarticular el entramado ideológico que destruye la matrilinealidad. De este modo, crea un espacio alternativo para expresar la voz materna y para que ésta recobre su autoridad y prestigio. Esta novela comienza mostrando a su protagonista, Cecilia, tras un momento de crisis familiar. Desde las primeras páginas, Italiano reproduce el esquema familiar de madre tiránica que impide desarrollarse a su hija y un padre que, pese a su debilidad de carácter frente a su esposa, intenta protegerla con cariño y apoyo. Durante doscientas sesenta y seis páginas se nos muestra una estereotipada relación entre madre e hija, en la cual esta última siente que debe desembarazarse de la dependencia emocional que las une para poder desarrollarse e independizarse. Pese a ello, la fuerza del vínculo materno es tan enorme que Cecilia se siente devorada por los recuerdos que tiene de su madre. Sin embargo, al final de la novela, toda esta construcción se desmorona al otorgarle voz a la madre durante cinco páginas. Sólo cinco páginas convierten a Cecilia en una narradora no fiable, todos sus recuerdos son cuestionados, y la voz de su madre, que aparecía anteriormente bajo la perspectiva de Cecilia, se descubre ser la ventriloquía de la voz del padre poniendo en boca de su mujer frases y sentimientos jamás expresados realmente por ella.

Italiano parte de los típicos esquemas de la relación problemática entre madre e hija pero ofrece una nueva perspectiva. *Un aire de familia*, al permitir que el discurso materno se contraste con el de la hija, desconstruye todo el montaje ideológico que la lectora había asumido como válido hasta ese momento. De este modo, se pone de manifiesto la contradicción que existe en la mente de Cecilia entre la madre real y la madre ficticia construida mediante la manipulación de sus recuerdos y la importancia que esta doble figura materna tiene en la interpretación de su propio pasado y su personalidad. Italiano cuestiona, por tanto, el hijacentrismo, y denuncia las consecuencias nefastas que la represión y desautorización de la voz materna tienen sobre la hija.

Linda Schierce Leonard propone en *Meeting the Madwoman* que existen dos madres para cada hija. Una, la mujer real, atrapada bajo el rol de madre, y otra, la que esta autora denomina la Madre Loca, que es la construcción mental que la hija ha creado de su madre y que ha interiorizado. Esta Madre Loca no es un espejo de la real, sino que se trata de una creación mental basada en la interpretación de palabras y acciones de su madre y su comparación con el mito de la madre ideal que nuestra sociedad propone como natural. Este proceso se corresponde con el acuñado por Freud como el "inconsciente dinámico", el que Thurer, en *The Myths of Motherhood*, resume de la siguiente manera:

> The mechanism for distorting reality (...) was probably Freud's most brilliant contribution to our understanding of human behavior. The working of the unconscious, the ever-present, very human tendency to remove disturbing ideas by means of rationalization, compromise, and repression, is known to us all, and helps to explain not only neurotic symptoms, dreams, art, literature, but even something so mundane as why our children may hate us when we are behaving perfectly decently. What they actually hate is their psychic representation of us, not the real thing. (243)

El objeto de *Un aire de familia* es lograr, por un lado, desvincular la madre real de la imagen ficticia creada a través de la manipulación de recuerdos por parte de Cecilia y, por otro, desligar a la madre del ser monstruoso o del ser demente, destruir la identificación entre los términos madre y locura. La novela de Silvia Italiano consigue minar las estructuras patriarcales en las que la protagonista se basa para cimentar la re-creación monstruosa de su madre y, así, la novela adquiere un sentido completamente diferente al de las novelas hijacentristas de cuyos modelos parte.

El argumento de la novela es el siguiente. Cecilia, una profesora de arte de la Universidad de Buenos Aires, encuentra la foto de una mujer con la que su marido reconoce tener relaciones. Este descubrimiento provocará una crisis en ella, no porque destruye un matrimonio ya percibido como vacío por ambos, sino porque en la mujer de la foto reconoce los rasgos de su hermana Amanda, quien desapareció a los doce años. La desaparición de Amanda marcó la vida de Cecilia completamente, no sólo porque su madre nunca pudo superarla sino porque Cecilia, desde los seis años, empezó a sentirse culpable. Cecilia abandona a su marido, su casa y su trabajo, y viaja a la Patagonia donde permanece un mes y medio en casa de los tíos de su amiga Julia. Al empeorar su estado, su amiga se lleva a Cecilia a Nueva York para pasar dos semanas en un intento de ayudarla a superar su depresión. Una vez allí, el día siguiente de su llegada, al perseguir a un ladrón que de un tirón le roba la cadena que lleva al cuello, Cecilia se pierde por las calles y no logra encontrar a su amiga ni recordar la dirección de la casa donde se alojan. Pasados unos breves momentos de ligera angustia se descubre a sí misma sintiéndose liberada. No intenta ni contactar a Julia ni volver a la Argentina. Por el contrario, Cecilia siente que este nuevo espacio geográfico le dará la fortaleza para rehacer su vida.

Con el tiempo, Cecilia hace nuevos amigos, encuentra trabajo, se tiñe el pelo de rubio, pierde diez kilos, se opera los pechos y asume otro nombre. Estos cambios, que la protagonista interpreta como liberadores, son cuestionados por la lectora al percibir que todos ellos conducen a que Cecilia se convierta en una doble de la mujer de la foto —la cual lleva consigo, como un amuleto, desde que abandonó su casa en Buenos Aires—, a la que tanto su marido como su madre, Dora, parecen desear por encima de ella. Cuando después de todas las alteraciones físicas decide borrar su antigua identidad adquiriendo un nuevo nombre elige llamarse como su hermana desaparecida: Amanda. Este nuevo nombre y apariencia, pese a que en un principio le dan seguridad en sí misma, poco a poco comienzan a producirle innumerables fobias. Su terror más intenso es el que desarrolla hacia los espejos, hasta el punto de no soportar ver su imagen reflejada. A esta especulofobia se añade el miedo a la soledad, a los recuerdos, e incluso al propio miedo. Todas estas fobias y su gradual intensificación la van llevando a un claro desequilibrio. Al cabo de los meses descubre, por casualidad, que en la Argentina todos creen que murió en Nueva York en el incendio de una discoteca, porque allí encontraron la cadena con sus iniciales. Es entonces cuando decide asumir completamente la personalidad de Amanda y consigue, mediante un entramado de nuevas mentiras, que su madre vaya a Nueva York para encontrarse con ella. A su llegada, es cuando la narración permite a la madre hablar por sí misma en vez de a través de la ventriloquía de Cecilia[5]. En este momento todos los recuerdos de su hija se insertan como piezas de un rompecabezas diferente al que ella había creado, dando un nuevo significado a su vida y a su pasado. Sin embargo, este descubrir una realidad alternativa a la que ella había construido no la lleva a la liberación sino a la pérdida total de su cordura, a la demencia. Cecilia termina viviendo en una bruma en la que el futuro no existe y el presente y el pasado se encuentran fundidos; en la que ya no puede distinguir quién es ella misma, si Amanda o Cecilia.

La mayor parte de los recuerdos de Cecilia relacionados con su madre y su padre van desde los seis a los diez años, después aparecen los recuerdos de su madre en relación a conflictos de la adolescencia. En ningún momento la figura de la madre sale bien parada; por el contrario, se la construye como un personaje completamente histérico obsesionado por la desaparición de su hija Amanda e incapaz de querer a su hija menor. Poco a poco, intercalados en el texto y entremezclados con la narración del presente, van apareciendo todos aquellos recuerdos de la relación con su madre que más la han afectado. Todos los recuerdos de Cecilia tienen como objeto re-crear la figura de su madre como una Madre Loca, un ser monstruoso que esgrime como amor maternal una crueldad que raya en el sadismo. Cecilia describe su comportamiento histérico en las continuas peleas a gritos con el padre (53); la imposición de una educación tradicional basada en la inferioridad física y mental de la mujer: "¿Dónde viste vos una mujer filósofa? No hay ninguna mujer filósofa (...) Hijita, el pensamiento abstracto no es para las mujeres, las mujeres somos materialistas, una mujer no puede desvincularse del cuerpo e interesarse por el espíritu" (56); la idealización de Amanda en detrimento de su hermana menor (54); el hacerla sentir culpable por la desaparición de su hermana (35, 68); sus continuos intentos de separarla de su padre, de impedir que hicieran cosas juntos (36); su falta de apoyo ante la separación de su marido al tomar el lado de éste (69); e incluso, la represión de su sexualidad: "¿Acaso no había sacrificado su propia realidad carnal?¿Y a qué divinidad? A una mala madre, una divinidad que no concede ningún favor a cambio de los sacrificios en su altar?" (57).

Sin embargo, los hechos que más marcaron a Cecilia y de los

que se responsabiliza a la madre por el posterior comportamiento de su hija están relacionados con su deseo de convertir a su hija menor en una doble de Amanda, deseo llevado a cabo en los "juegos" que Dora inventó tras su desaparición. Cuando se encontraban solas, la madre vestía a Cecilia con las ropas de Amanda mientras pretendía que hablaba y abrazaba a la hija desaparecida, como si Cecilia hubiera dejado de existir.

La caracterización monstruosa de esta Madre Loca se contrapone con la figura del padre quien desde el principio se construye como la única persona en quien Cecilia parece encontrar apoyo y comprensión. El padre de Cecilia se presenta ajeno a la locura de la madre y a la educación represiva que su hija menor recibe:

> Recordó lo ineficaz de la intercesión de su padre y los ataques de llanto incontrolable que desataba en su madre la simple sugerencia de que Ceci y papá saldrían solos, sin que ella estuviera presente para oficiar de cancerbero. Y eso le parecía lo más imperdonable, la barrera que su madre trató de levantar entre ella y el padre, su papi querido, el mejor de todos, el más cariñoso, el más divertido, que no hubiera dejado disfrutar de ese padre extraordinario que perdería a los diez años, y cuyo único defecto había sido el no tener suficiente carácter para hacerle frente a su mujer. (36-7)

El padre es descrito como un ser impotente ante la autoridad y tiranía maternas. Sin embargo, pese a no poder evitar el comportamiento sádico de su esposa, Cecilia le atribuye en sus recuerdos el papel de figura protectora. Además, le convierte en el intercesor entre madre e hija, pues repetidamente intenta que no se rompa el vínculo de amor que debe existir entre ambas. En otras palabras, el padre es quien es presentado luchando por salvaguardar la matrilinealidad que parece no existir, de hecho, en ningún momento. Como si esta matrilinealidad en realidad fuera antinatural en esta relación entre madre e hija y, por tanto, él se empeñara en un imposible.

En *Un aire de familia* se contrapone el tiempo presente con los recuerdos de la protagonista para marcar la relación causa y efecto que existe entre el modo de ser y el comportamiento actuales de Cecilia y su pasado. A pesar de ello, los recuerdos no se suceden con facilidad porque, desde el principio, la protagonista intenta reprimirlos.

> No quería recuerdos. Sus recuerdos sólo podían reavivar rencores y a una madre no se la puede acusar. Las madres son seres abnegados que aman sin condición a la sangre de su sangre. Las madres, todo el mundo lo sabe, aman

a los hijos idiotas y criminales con la misma generosidad. La
falla está siempre en el hijo, en su ingratitud, en su egoísmo.
No, a una madre no se la puede acusar. Cecilia se sentía
infame con su dolor y sus recuerdos inculpatorios. Por nada
del mundo quería recuerdos, por nada del mundo. (39)

En estas líneas quedan vinculados estrechamente el hecho de
recordar con la figura materna. Como si el mero hecho de recordar sólo
pudiera traer consigo la presencia monstruosa de la madre. Sin
embargo, hay algo aquí que no funciona. Cecilia se dice a sí misma
que "a una madre no se la puede acusar" después de que ya ha dado a la
lectora numerosas muestras de la supuesta crueldad de su madre. En
esta cita se declara infame, ingrata y egoísta por acusar y recriminar el
comportamiento inhumano de su madre. Cecilia se monstruiza para
afirmarse aún más como víctima. Como sugiere Gallop al comentar
sobre la descripción de una misma como un ser monstruoso: "once the
ironic reversal is decoded, the self-portrait is revealed as immodest
boasting. The image of the monster thinly disguises a monstrous
narcissism" (13). Otro aspecto interesante es que esta cita incide una
vez más sobre el aspecto antinatural de la matrilinealidad, de la
artificialidad de forzar el amor entre madre e hija por tratarse de dos
personas completamente incompatibles para dar y recibir amor, dado
que el primero es un ser devorador y el segundo necesita libertad e
independencia para desarrollarse. Estas palabras son uno de los
primeros indicios para cuestionar la fiabilidad de la perspectiva de
Cecilia y su modo de interpretar sus recuerdos.

En varias ocasiones la protagonista se reconoce como una
persona sin recuerdos. No sólo es incapaz de recordar su pasado sino
que, además, apenas una persona desaparece de su vida, con ella
desaparecen todas las imágenes que posee de ésta. Es como si el
pasado, su niñez, nunca hubiera existido. En su mente sólo caben las
imágenes del presente. Sin embargo, al alejarse físicamente de la
presencia de la madre es cuando los recuerdos empiezan a brotar sin
control, como piezas sueltas de un rompecabezas.

A Cecilia le sorprendió ese recuerdo. No su contenido,
sino el hecho mismo de recordar, de llevar dentro una imagen
de Cecilia niña, porque se creía sin recuerdos, vivía en un
presente absoluto y no recordaba nada de su infancia, casi
nada de su adolescencia. Su pasado estaba constituido por
los recuerdos que tenían de ella los demás miembros de la
familia (...) Los momentos de su vida que no existían para los
demás y los demás no nombraban, habían dejado de existir
para ella. (29)

Cuando Cecilia viaja a la Patagonia los recuerdos empiezan a surgir inesperadamente, sin que ella los busque. Para que Cecilia pueda recordar necesita que la madre se convierta en ausencia. Su constante presencia le impide poder pensar por sí misma. Todos sus recuerdos, además, están relacionados con ella. De hecho, en todos ellos el sujeto de la acción es su madre. La madre es quien actúa y la hija la que sufre pasivamente las acciones de su madre.

En la novela de Silvia Italiano el proceso de monstruización de la madre está intrínsecamente unido a la capacidad de Cecilia para interpretar de forma verbal las imágenes del pasado que se agolpan en su mente. La ausencia de la madre es lo que permite que Cecilia desarrolle un lenguaje que explique su pasado. Es decir, es necesario el silencio materno para que la hija adquiera una voz propia. Sólo la lejanía materna crea un espacio vital para que Cecilia pueda atribuirles forma lingüística, significantes, a los referentes, a las imágenes que como piezas inconexas de un rompecabezas van brotando sin control en su mente. Por lo tanto, *Un aire de familia* plantea el proceso de adquisición de lenguaje de una hija en relación con la necesidad de la represión de la voz materna.

Margaret Homans considera que, en nuestra cultura, la relación entre la necesidad de la ausencia materna y el proceso de adquisición del lenguaje se encuentran estrechamente vinculados. Es más, se ha convertido en un mito que subyace en gran parte de la literatura occidental: "the death or absence of the mother sorrowfully but fortunately makes possible the construction of language and culture" (2). La madre debe desaparecer para que pueda surgir la palabra. En este mismo mito se basa uno de los grandes principios del sicoanálisis. La palabra surge del deseo y el deseo surge por la ausencia. El llanto del bebé, ese primer significante usado por el ser humano, está denunciando la ausencia materna y su significado es el deseo que se quiere satisfacer, la necesidad de cubrir esa carencia. Es la no-presencia de la madre lo que impulsa al ser humano a ese intento primario de comunicación a través del grito. A su vez, este grito está conectado con la reaparición de la madre, de modo que el bebé toma conciencia del poder del lenguaje, del poder para re-crear, re-animar, traer de vuelta al ser que estaba ausente[6].

Un aire de familia parte de este mismo principio. Es la ausencia de la madre, su lejanía espacial, lo que permite a Cecilia recordar y crear verbalmente una imagen de su madre a través de la interpretación de las imágenes del pasado que van surgiendo en su mente. Esta especul(ariz)ación destinada a re-crear a su madre está, sin embargo, destinada al fracaso. Cecilia no puede verbalmente dar una representación veraz de la madre real sino que lo que construye es la imagen ficticia que lleva interiorizada de la Madre Loca, un ser monstruoso que no se corresponde en absoluto con su madre —como se demuestra al final de la novela cuando ésta se apropia del discurso. Es el clásico conflicto de la palabra intentando no sólo representar, dar forma verbal al referente, sino suplirlo, creando un nuevo referente imaginario. Barbara Johnson observa la conexión que existe entre el apóstrofe y el grito primario del bebé y apunta:

> There may be a deeper link between motherhood and apostrophe that we have hitherto suspected. The verbal development of the infant, according to Lacan, begins as a demand addressed to the mother, out of which the entire verbal universe is spun. Yet the mother addressed is somehow a personification, not a person (...) If demand is the originary vocative, which assures life even as it inaugurates alienation, then it is not surprising that questions of animation inhere in the rhetorical figure of apostrophe (...) If apostrophe is structured like demand, and if demand articulates the primal relation to the mother as a relation to the Other, then [the figure of apostrophe] comes to look like the fantastically intricate history of endless elaborations and displacements of the single cry, "Mama!". (38)

En la novela de Silvia Italiano todos los recuerdos de Cecilia están directamente vinculados a la relación con su madre. Sin embargo lo esencial de estos recuerdos es que funcionan como apóstrofes porque se suceden unos a otros reprochando, increpando, acusando a la madre de su crueldad, indiferencia y ceguera ante los sentimientos de su propia hija. Pese a que por la distancia Cecilia afirma que se había olvidado de que tenía una madre, sus recuerdos son apóstrofes en el sentido de que al recordar, "hacen presente, animan y dan cuerpo humano" a la figura de la madre, no a su madre real, hay que recordar, sino a la imagen ficticia de la Madre Loca/Monstruo.

El lenguaje nace como demanda; es un apóstrofe requiriendo ser escuchado por la madre. El bebé tras el grito-lenguaje anima o crea la aparición de la madre que cubre sus necesidades y asegura su vida. Así Cecilia vuelve a ese grito inicial del bebé para ser escuchada, para asegurar su subsistencia. Necesita que su madre la oiga, la escuche y se haga presente para poder alimentarla emocionalmente con su cariño, o con su sentimiento de culpabilidad. Cecilia desea que escuche para poder castigarla; ver sufrir a la madre es lo único que ella cree puede ayudarle a superar la opresión de todos esos recuerdos terribles y dolorosos.

Porque en su adolescencia Cecilia había pensado en el

suicidio, y no sólo para liberarse de una vida que a los
dieciocho años se le había hecho insoportable, sino también
para castigar a su madre (...) Porque habiéndola hecho
comparecer ante un tribunal en el cual ella, Cecilia, era al
mismo tiempo víctima, fiscal, defensor y juez, y habiéndola
declarado culpable de los cargos de incomprensión,
frustración, represión, opresión y desamor, decidió
imponerle una pena sin precedentes: la condena a muerte de
la víctima. Como para ejecutar esa condena no le quedaba
más remedio que constituirse también en verdugo, tendría
que suicidarse (...) La razón por la que no lo hizo, (...) fue que
suicidarse la dejaba a ella, la víctima, sin su merecida
compensación, es decir, la privaba de la satisfacción de ser
testigo del sufrimiento del reo. Pero ahora sí podía espiar el
sufrimiento de su madre. (146)

El comprobar que todos en la Argentina la creen muerta la sitúa
en una nueva posición. Ahora es Cecilia quien ha desaparecido
trágicamente dejando a la nueva Amanda con el papel de la
superviviente. Cecilia espera ver en su madre la misma desesperación
ante su muerte que la que sintió ante la desaparición de su hermana.
El texto, ya citado, en donde se muestra a la madre disfrazando a
Cecilia niña con las ropas de Amanda, sirve para construir la
monstruosidad de la figura materna y, además, plantea de manera
directa otra invocación a un ser ausente. La madre abraza a Cecilia
como si Amanda hubiera vuelto a casa, como si Cecilia hubiera
desaparecido y en su lugar estuviera su hermana mayor. Dora elige entre
sus hijas, abrazando la ficción de su hija mayor y dejando a la pequeña
Cecilia como alienada protagonista y testigo de este deseo:

Recordó que algunos días su madre, con la misma
sagrada solemnidad con que el sacerdote toma la hostia para
darla a un comulgante, sacaba un vestido del ropero y se lo
ponía a ella y después la miraba y la besaba, frenética,
mojándole las mejillas con sus lágrimas, y la llamaba
¡Amanda, mi tesoro!, y ella, con las mejillas mojadas por las
lágrimas de su madre y por las suyas, gritaba ¡soy Cecilia,
mamá!, ¡soy Cecilia! (36)

En esta cita se puede comprobar lo que se repite en la mayoría de
los recuerdos de Cecilia. Pese a que no tengamos una primera persona
como narradora y un tú al que se dirija el apóstrofe, la narración en
tercera persona, al incorporar el estilo directo en un diálogo sin
receptores, está planteando una doble invocación. La madre al exclamar:
"¡Amanda, mi tesoro!" está invocando a su hija muerta en la visión
grotesca de su hija disfrazada y Cecilia gritando "¡soy Cecilia, mamá!,

¡soy Cecilia!" invoca a una madre ausente que no escucha, que se dirige a otra persona. Toda la novela plantea la repetición de estas dos invocaciones: la madre pretendiendo resucitar a su hija desaparecida a través de la continua mención de su nombre y sus recuerdos, y Cecilia exigiendo que su madre olvide por un momento a esa hermana ausente y la escuche a ella, a la sobreviviente.

Estas dos invocaciones —la de la madre hacia Amanda y la de Cecilia a su madre—, estos deseos de atraer la presencia del ser ausente, consiguen su objetivo de una manera no esperada. La invocación constante de la madre anima a un ser monstruoso, a una Cecilia completamente fragmentada mentalmente pero con un físico diseñado como réplica del de su hermana. Así el ser deseado se convierte en un ser doble monstruoso: "Amanda por fuera, Cecilia por dentro" como el mismo texto repite en varias ocasiones. Por otro lado, la invocación de Cecilia para que su madre la escuche no se produce como ella desea, ya que re-crea a un ser también monstruoso. El invocante, o las invocantes en este caso, dejan de tener el poder y dominio sobre la presencia y ausencia del ser invocado y, por tanto, se convierten en víctimas de su propia creación.

En su análisis del poema de Shelley "Ode to the West Wind" Barbara Johnson explica: "The poet addresses, gives animation, gives the capacity of responsiveness, to the wind, not in order to make it speak but in order to make it listen to him— in order to make it listen to him doing nothing but address *it*" (31). De la misma manera, Cecilia no pide respuesta o explicaciones a su madre, no la quiere escuchar; lo que quiere es que su madre la escuche a ella, oiga el rencor que durante tantos años ha ido acumulando contra ella. De hecho, la materialización del deseo de la invocación destruye el apóstrofe, desconstruye la creación literaria. Sale a la luz lo ficticio de lo creado por el lenguaje frente a la veracidad de lo real.

En la novela de Silvia Italiano, al convertirse en una realidad tangible el deseo implícito de la figura retórica se destruye al invocante. La materialización del deseo implícito del apóstrofe, es decir, el que el receptor escuche al emisor, se lleva al extremo de la animación, es decir, la presencia de la madre dispuesta no a escuchar sino a hablar. Es como si al final del poema de Shelley apareciera el viento contestando y corrigiendo las metáforas usadas. Nos encontramos frente a la desconstrucción, la desfamiliarización del funcionamiento tradicional del apóstrofe. Cuando aparece Dora, la madre, se distorsiona el lenguaje, los significantes y significados dejan de ser fiables, dejan de tener una correspondencia natural y se denuncia su arbitrariedad. Cecilia vuelve a quedar muda ante la voz de su madre.

Cecilia se encuentra con una madre que no sólo no la escucha sino que se apropia del relato, del discurso del pasado y le ofrece una nueva versión de los acontecimientos que desata otros recuerdos y la obliga a enfrentarse con el recuerdo del abuso sexual de su padre. La voz que durante meses la torturaba y a la que ella no podía atribuir un rostro es ahora identificada con la voz de su padre.

> Otra voz, que no era la suya, ni tenía sexo, ni timbre, ni tono identificables y decía: *mamá siempre prefirió a Amanda... mamá hubiera querido que desaparecieras vos no Amanda... durante todo el embarazo mamá sentía que le quitabas hasta las ganas de vivir... que eras un vampiro chupasangre.* (175)

Estas ideas que durante años la mortificaron y que ella creía recuerdos de cosas vividas no eran más que las palabras del padre construyendo una imagen monstruosa de la madre para evitar que la niña chillara mientras él la abusaba sexualmente. Cuando tras las palabras de la madre, Cecilia recuerda el abuso sexual también sufrido por su hermana mayor, esa voz anónima encuentra su contexto y, por consiguiente, identifica a su padre como el origen de las palabras y sentimientos que hasta ahora había atribuido a su madre. De este modo todos los recuerdos de Cecilia pasan a cobrar un nuevo sentido:

> *Me dice no tengas miedo, Ceci, papá está aquí para proteger a su regalona, a su reina, y se sienta en la cama y me besa el pelo (...) mamá sufre mucho porque mamá quería a Amanda más que a nada en el mundo, más que a vos y más que a mí, pero nosotros dos también nos queremos mucho, ¿no es cierto?, y si mamá no nos quiere no nos importa ¿no es cierto? No, papi, digo yo, pero sí que me importa, yo quiero que mamá me quiera. Papá me desabrocha el saco del piyama primero y después me baja el pantalón. Me da vergüenza y me da miedo(...)Es nuestro secreto, Ceci, me dice papá, no se lo tenés que decir a nadie (...) Ceci, cuando mamá te tenía en la panza decía que eras muy mala y le hacías mal, que eras como un vampiro, y por eso no te quiere, pero yo siempre te quise, más que a nadie, no me tenés que traicionar, Ceci. No, papi. Nunca, Ceci. Nunca, papi.*(274-5) [Cursiva en el original]

En *Un aire de familia* este abuso sexual se complica más al convertir a la madre en inusitado cómplice de este acto. La madre conoce el abuso sexual sufrido por su hija mayor, Amanda, porque ésta vino a pedirle ayuda acusando al padre, pero ella no la creyó: "al principio no te creí pero después vi que era verdad, lo que me decías era cierto, y yo, en vez de protegerte y hacerle frente a tu padre, me dije ya va a pasar, no es nada, si pienso que es un sueño, será un sueño" (268).

Dora se siente doblemente responsable por la desaparición de su hija: por el abuso sexual sufrido y por no haber hecho nada para evitarlo. A partir de ese momento su obsesión será proteger a su hija menor de la posibilidad de este abuso. Cuando Dora llega a Nueva York y cree hablar con Amanda le explica el extraño comportamiento de Cecilia. Al apropiarse del discurso la madre ofrece un nuevo significado a las imágenes del pasado de su hija. No sólo Dora nunca rechazó a Cecilia y siempre la quiso sino que era Cecilia precisamente quien se autoaniquilaba pretendiendo ser su hermana desaparecida:

> Pero tu hermana fue ingrata y nunca me agradeció lo que hice por ella, cómo me sacrifiqué viviendo aún años con tu padre para salvarla, por supuesto no sabía lo que pasaba, ni lo que ya había pasado, pero veía bien que yo seguía en la casa por ella (...) quería ser como su hermanita, era una obsesión, me pedía siempre que le pusiera tus vestidos, yo los tenía guardados porque no me podía deshacer de ellos, y Cecilia me imploraba cuando estábamos solas que le pusiera tus vestidos y miráramos el álbum con tus fotos, quería ser como vos. (269-70)

Dora nunca llegó a comprender las extrañas reacciones de Cecilia porque ignoraba la manipulación a la que su marido la tenía sometida. No sospechó siquiera que su esposo estaba repitiendo el abuso sexual con su hija menor.

Un aire de familia presenta grandes similitudes con la novela de Toni Morrison *Beloved* en la construcción de la relación madre e hija. En estas dos obras se muestra a una madre que provoca la destrucción de su propia hija: la muerte física de Beloved y síquica de Cecilia/Amanda —nótese el parecido entre los nombres de las hijas: Beloved y Amanda. Sethe, la protagonista de Morrison, degolla a su hija Beloved para evitar que sufra la misma esclavitud de la que ella acaba de escapar. Dora al negar la pedofilia de su marido provoca la huida de Amanda. Las dos hijas sufren la amenaza de la agresión masculina —por el amo blanco en *Beloved* y por el padre en la novela de Italiano—, pero se deposita en manos de las madres la responsabilidad de protegerlas por más indefensas que ellas mismas se sientan a su vez. Así se desplaza la culpa del verdadero agresor situándola sobre la madre quien se encuentra en una situación de obvia desventaja en cuanto a su poder real para poder proteger a sus hijas.

Lo más notable en cuanto a la relación entre ambas novelas es que a ambas madres, Dora y Sethe, se les ofrece la oportunidad de hablar, de explicarse ante la hija a la que victimizaron. Marianne Hirsch comenta:

Sethe's story, like Yocasta's is, as Morrison insists, 'not a story to pass on,' yet this novel does allow the mother to speak for herself, to speak her own name and the daughter's, to speak, after eighteen years, her unspeakable crime to her daughter. It allows Beloved to return, like Persephone, so that mother and daughter can speak to each other. (7-8)

En *Beloved* y *Un aire de familia* se nos presentan argumentos hasta ahora inenarrables donde se alternan la autoridad patriarcal, la relación sexual incestuosa y el horror ante las consecuencias presentes que las decisiones y acciones del pasado han provocado. Es precisamente la narración de lo inenarrable lo que ha permitido la creación de un espacio alternativo en el cual las madres pueden hablar, explicar, dar su versión de los hechos para poder intentar reconstruir la matrilinealidad que la ley patriarcal destruyó.

Sin embargo, el encuentro entre madre e hija tiene consecuencias devastadoras para la primera en vez de provocar un alivio terapéutico. La hija que destruyeron reaparece como un ser monstruoso: Beloved tiene el comportamiento de un bebé de año y medio —cuando fue asesinada— y el físico de una joven de 18 años —el tiempo que ha transcurrido desde el infanticidio. A su candor, deseo de ser amada y estar junto a su madre se unen un rencor y deseo de destrucción igualmente intensos. Algo semejante se produce entre Dora y su hija. En vez de encontrarse con su idealizada Amanda, la madre se enfrenta con la simbiosis física y mental de sus dos hijas en un solo cuerpo y una sola mente. Es un ser que la necesita con la misma intensidad que la odia.

Este encuentro deja a ambas madres consumidas por el dolor y por la presencia insaciable de sus hijas. El proceso devorador de las hijas queda reflejado en el deterioro de la salud de las madres a partir de este encuentro: Sethe enferma de tal manera que apenas tiene fuerzas para moverse o respirar y Dora desarrolla una depresión nerviosa y no puede dejar de llorar. Finalmente, a Sethe se le otorga la oportunidad de salvarse cuando al revivir alucinatoriamente la escena que la llevó al infanticidio —la llegada a la puerta de su casa de un hombre blanco en un carro— decide esta vez asesinar al hombre blanco causante del mal en vez de dirigir la agresión hacia su hija. En ese momento Beloved desaparece y a Sethe se le concede una segunda oportunidad para recuperarse y vivir. Sin embargo, Dora nunca podrá recobrarse porque por segunda vez no pudo evitar el abuso de su marido hacia su hija. En vez de dirigir su agresividad hacia su marido, en ambos casos, la dirigió hacia sus hijas ignorando la llamada de auxilio de ambas. Este segundo fracaso la encadena a vivir desesperada, atada a una hija cuyo cuerpo es el de una mujer de treinta y dos años pero cuya mente se quedó anclada en el momento de sufrir la agresión paterna a los seis años.

Pese a mostrar a la madre como cómplice, *Un aire de familia* deja claro el hecho de que el verdadero culpable de la demencia de Cecilia es el padre no sólo por la violación física sino como responsable de la ruptura de la relación matrilineal. Pese a simular ser su protector, el intermediario entre ambas, el padre es la causa del silencio que las separa. Con sus sutiles amenazas el padre silencia primero a Cecilia y luego a la madre a través de la ventriloquía, al atribuír a esta última palabras y sentimientos que consiguen alienar a la una de la otra. Cuando ambas mujeres rompen el silencio impuesto por el padre se descubre su manipulación.

El abuso sexual sufrido por Cecilia es una clara metáfora de la violación mental a la que la sociedad homocéntrica somete a la mujer, alienándola de sí misma y provocando la destrucción de la matrilinealidad. La figura paterna se convierte en símbolo de la economía patriarcal en su deseo de controlar y silenciar a las mujeres. De hecho, el mismo discurso de la novela hace obvio que la violación paterna es tanto física como mental. En una de las descripciones del abuso sexual que sufre Cecilia se asocia claramente el ahogo de su voz con el sexo masculino: "Bésame, Ceci, bésame, me dice papá y yo me asfixio, no puedo respirar, no puedo gritar, no puedo hacer nada y me dan arcadas y papá me empuja la cabeza hacia atrás y hacia delante" (275). Con su pene, el padre viola la boca de la niña silenciándola, acallando sus gritos, y con sus palabras viola su mente.

El funcionamiento de estas estrategias de represión de la mujer sólo puede ser garantizado mediante la colaboración de las mismas mujeres en este proceso. Se necesita la supresión de la voz de ambas, madre e hija, para que la manipulación del padre siga siendo invisible. De este modo, el silencio en el que Cecilia basa la relación con su padre es lo que produce su autodestrucción. Lo mismo se puede decir de la madre: silenciada por el padre a través de la ventriloquía; por la sociedad, por el tabú sobre la sexualidad que le impide hablar y prevenir a su hija; y finalmente, por las leyes, ya que como Dora misma explica a su hija, hablar y denunciar la agresión paterna, la convierten en una loca para la sociedad y la podían haber llevado a perder la custodia de su hija (269).

La complicidad de Cecilia con su propia destrucción la lleva a una locura que la silencia, aun más que antes. El silencio exigido por su padre para ocultar su violación, el silencio que el deseo ajeno impone a su persona y que la llevan a querer convertirse en un reflejo que la aliena, el silencio de la locura consiguen poco a poco hacerla invisible, hacerla desaparecer para la sociedad.

> *Aunque no le conté nunca mi secreto. No le dije nunca*
> *que soy Amanda, por afuera soy Amanda y por dentro soy*
> *Cecilia, pero ella se dio cuenta sola. Es de Amanda el cuerpo*
> *que papá encuentra en la cama por la noche. Por fuera soy*
> *Amanda y por dentro soy Cecilia. (...) Mamá está triste y*
> *llora otra vez. ¿Por qué llora? Si no sabe que fue tan*
> *incapaz de proteger a Cecilia como a Amanda. Yo no se lo*
> *dije. Entonces, ¿por qué llora? Debe ser porque Cecilia*
> *murió pensando que ella no la quería... Pero no, ¿qué estoy*
> *diciendo?...* (275-6)[Cursiva en el original]

En el flujo de conciencia de Cecilia los tiempos verbales ya no representan una concepción lineal cronológica sino que sus fronteras se han borrado completamente. El futuro ha dejado de existir y el presente actual —Cecilia en la habitación de un manicomio—, el pasado cercano —el momento en que la madre le re-descubre el abuso sexual de su hermana Amanda— y el pasado lejano—cuando ella misma es víctima del abuso paterno— se encuentran completamente fundidos.

A esta fusión temporal se une la fluidez del concepto de identidad. No sólo Cecilia ya no puede separar su identidad de la de su hermana sino que la percepción de la habitación que la rodea, los muebles, los sonidos muestran su fusión con el espacio que la rodea[7]:

> *Todo parece un sueño. También parece real. Si*
> *pudiera elegir elegiría estar soñando (...) Sigo en esta pieza*
> *triste de esta casa triste y desconocida, sentada en el borde*
> *de la única silla. La ventana que tengo delante me parece*
> *ahora una boca grande y negra con colmillos amarillentos.*
> *(...) Sólo sé que las cosas no son siempre como a uno le*
> *parecen, ni como uno cree, ni como uno dice, ni como uno*
> *recuerda, ni como uno quiere.* (276)

Cecilia vuelve a una etapa pre-edípica, intenta la fusión con la madre en una imperfecta regresión al pasado que la aísla. Encerrada en la habitación de un hospital siquiátrico, Cecilia personifica la vuelta al útero materno en el que el tiempo y la separación de identidades todavía no existen. La ventana, esa vagina metafórica que establece el umbral de unión entre este útero y el espacio exterior, es presentada como una boca monstruosa y la realidad externa como una espesura negra y amenazante.

El final de la novela parece plantear la imposibilidad de renacimiento o cambio. Se presenta a Cecilia sumida en la demencia y a Dora, su madre, en la depresión. Aunque para algunos la locura es una forma de rebeldía, realmente, no es más que un proceso de autodestrucción que no promueve el cambio. Señala Shoshana Feldman en "Women and Madness":

> Depressed and terrified women are not about to seize the means of production and reproduction: quite the opposite of rebellion, madness is the impasse confronting whom cultural conditioning has deprived the very means of protest and self-affirmation. Far from being a form of contestation, "mental illness" is a *request for help*, a manifestation both of cultural impotence and of political castration. This socially defined help-needing and help-seeking behavior is itself part of female conditioning, ideologically inherent in the behavioral pattern and in the dependent and helpless role assigned to women as such. (7)

Llama la atención el gran número de novelas escritas por mujeres que al tratar la ruptura de la matrilinealidad desarrollan el tema de las enfermedades cuyo origen es sicosomático. Existe una clara relación proporcional entre la inestabilidad emocional y fragilidad física de las hijas protagonistas de estas obras y el nivel de locura o monstruosidad con que la figura de la madre es construida. La relación de odio/amor con la madre, el deseo de negar el lazo biológico y psicológico que le une a ella se manifiesta en una agresión síquica hacia el propio cuerpo. Recuérdense las migrañas, depresiones, insomnio y vómitos de la protagonista de *Julia* de Ana María Moix (España), la asfixia en *La raíz del sueño* de Marta Brunet (Chile), la agorafobia en *Desde el mirador* de Clara Sánchez (España), la depresión nerviosa en *El mismo mar de todos los veranos* de Esther Tusquets (España), embarazo psicológico y depresión en *Como agua para chocolate* de Laura Esquivel (México), la bulimia en *Beatriz y los cuerpos celestes* de Lucía Etxebarría (España), o el desequilibrio psicológico anunciado en las últimas páginas de *Balún Canán* de Rosario Castellanos (México). Estas enfermedades sicosomáticas vienen a reflejar la agresión de estas mujeres hacia sí mismas[8]. Su malestar sicológico no se manifiesta en rabia o ira hacia afuera; todas las protagonistas callan ante la agresión que consideran que su madre está ejerciendo sobre ellas. Ninguna se revela. La protagonista de *Un aire de familia* explica:

> En treinta años [su madre] no había escuchado jamás su voz por encima del tono que conviene a una niña educada y luego a una joven respetuosa y luego a una mujer discreta, salvo por los gritos involuntarios que le arrancaban las pesadillas. Nunca había expresado rabia ni odio. Y no soportaba más ser esa Cecilia obediente, mesurada, austera,

mansa (...) Casi podría decirse que en todos esos años lo
único que había hecho para llamar la atención había sido
engordar, ocupar un poco más de espacio. (57)

Los deseos insatisfechos, la ira, la angustia se revierten sobre
ellas mismas y las convierten doblemente en víctimas: de la supuesta
tiranía de su madre y de su debilidad física. Esta actitud victimizante,
lejos de provocar la lucha o el cambio, deja a estas protagonistas
inmovilizadas en su rencor, les impide luchar contra las estructuras
patriarcales que provocan su opresión porque todo su odio y
agresividad la dirigen hacia sí mismas y hacia sus madres. De este
modo, las hijas se convierten en partícipes involuntarias del sistema
represivo que las subyuga.

Sin embargo, en todas las novelas de mujeres que rezuman
rencor y desprecio hacia la madre subyace al mismo tiempo un enorme
deseo de unión, de reconciliación. Judith Herman señala: "Women's
literature of the past ten years is filled with the voices of daughters
seeking their mothers. The quest generally begins from a point of
estrangement, anger, and reproach and moves toward solidarity. One
can detect the longing for closeness behind the anger" (140). El
problema yace en que la reconciliación entre madre e hija es imposible
mientras se privilegie la voz de esta última. Únicamente mediante la
creación de espacios en los que la madre pueda apropiarse del discurso
y recuperar la autoridad de su voz se puede conseguir la regeneración de
los lazos afectivos matrilineales. Al otorgar a la madre la posibilidad de
recuperar su voz, hablar, explicarse y dialogar con su hija, se consigue
desmonstruizar a la figura materna y destruir la ficción de la Madre
Loca. Sólo la autorización de su palabra puede devolverle la
humanidad, la individualidad que la sociedad patriarcal le robó desde el
momento que impuso sobre ellas el rol de la "madre ideal". Como
asegura Irigaray: "if mothers could be women, there would be a whole
mode of a relationship of desiring speech between daughter and
mother" ("Women-Mothers" 52).

Aunque Silvia Italiano cierra las puertas de la recuperación y
superación a sus personajes, las abre para sus lectoras. Partiendo de la
tradición hijacentrista falogocéntrica que silencia la voz materna, esta
autora consigue subvertir las estructuras patriarcales en las que este
hijacentrismo está basado para crear un espacio alternativo en el que la
madre puede apropiarse de la palabra y recobrar su autoridad discursiva.
Al mismo tiempo, su novela consigue plantear problemas tan
esenciales para el feminismo como son las destrucción de la
matrilinealidad como estrategia patriarcal para aislar y controlar a la
mujer y el desarrollo de la identidad femenina basado en el deseo
masculino.

La lectora al poder escuchar la voz de la madre en las últimas páginas ha podido separar la fusión entre el ser que es Dora y la Madre Loca interiorizada de Cecilia. Las cinco páginas en las que Dora se apropia del discurso permiten la destrucción de la ley del silencio impuesta por el padre y denuncian el verdadero origen de la agresión sufrida por ambas, madre e hija. Las palabras de la madre surgen de las físuras del entramado ideológico patriarcal amenazando con su mera existencia la estabilidad de dicho sistema. Es más, al comprobar que la imagen fícticia de la Madre Loca es una construcción paterna cuyo móvil es controlar, abusar y manipular a su hija le permite llevar esta novela a otro nivel, a reconocer como válido lo que sugiere Susan Caplan: "las hijas odian a sus madres porque eso es lo que se les ha enseñado"(2). Es la sociedad patriarcal la que utiliza a la mujer para reproducir su sistema ideológico y luego la repudia, hace que las nuevas generaciones la vean como un monstruo, como a una loca que no debe ser escuchada porque su voz es irracional y su comportamiento aberrante. La economía patriarcal ha utilizado y manipulado la relación entre madre e hija para asegurarse su propia reproducción. La destrucción del vínculo matrilineal es un elemento clave para garantizar el mantenimiento del estatus quo, de la opresión femenina, porque consigue no sólo victimizar a las mujeres sino que incluso ellas mismas —tanto madres como hijas— participen activamente en su proceso de subyugación. Novelas como *Un aire de familia* de Silvia Italiano subvierten las estrategias del patriarcado consiguiendo hacer evidente la importancia y la necesidad del restablecimiento de los lazos matrilineales para romper con el ciclo de victimización que las mujeres sufren y del que, desgraciadamente, son partícipes.[9]

NOTAS

[1] Ejemplos de este tipo de protagonistas se encuentran en *Ifigenia* de Teresa de la Parra (Venezuela), *Memorias de Leticia Valle* de Rosa Chacel (España) y *Nada* de Carmen Laforet (España).

[2] Así, las madres que aparecen en *La mujer habitada* de Giconda Belli (Nicaragua), *Balún Canán* de Rosario Castellanos (México), *Estaba la pájara pinta sentada en el verde limón* de Albalucía Angel (Colombia), por citar unas cuantas, no son caracterizadas como seres individuales sino como caricaturas sociales. Por un lado se las acusa por no haberse comportado de acuerdo a la construción imaginaria de la madre ideal mientras que, al mismo tiempo, son rechazadas por representar el rol materno en su papel reproductor de la economía patriarcal.

[3] No es frecuente encontrar novelas en las que la protagonista sufra la experiencia del embarazo y la maternidad. Sin embargo, hay algunos ejemplos interesantes de novelas que no sólo tratan la maternidad sino que,

además, subvierten este mismo concepto a través de asociarlo con temas hasta ahora silenciados o excluidos de la literatura, como son los sentimientos de horror de una mujer ante los cambios que un embarazo produce en su cuerpo, como expresa el personaje de Agnes en *La hora violeta* de Montserrat Roig (España); el embarazo debido a la violación que Isabel Allende (Chile) narra en *La casa de los espíritus*, Sara Gallardo (Argentina) en *Enero*, o Rosario Ferré (Puerto Rico) en su cuento "La bella durmiente"; y el aborto como elección en *La nave de los locos* de Cristina Peri Rossi (Uruguay).

[4] El concepto madre es una construcción ficticia porque parte del presupuesto de que cuando una mujer se queda embarazada, así como su cuerpo cambia para adaptarse al nuevo ser, su propia mente sufre una trasformación que la convierte en un ser diferente: generoso, sacrificado y sin más deseo que el de satisfacer las necesidades de su criatura. Esta falacia ha sido tan asimilada por nuestra cultura que ha pasado a considerarse como una verdad natural. De este modo, las mujeres que no se comportan de acuerdo a este modelo materno, impuesto por la economía patriarcal, son consideradas aberrantes, monstruos egoístas o locas. Son las mujeres a las que se imputa su antinaturalidad no a la construcción imaginaria de madre ideal.

[5] En esta novela aparecen dos tipos de ventriloquías superpuestas. Por un lado se encuentra la ventriloquía del padre al atribuir a su mujer sentimientos y frases nunca expresados por ella y, por otro, la ventriloquía de la misma Cecilia al asociar con su madre experiencias tergiversadas que nunca ocurrieron tal y como ella afirma recordar.

[6] Esto implica, además, la asociación que el bebé establece en la que cualquier carencia, dolor, hambre o molestia puede ser resuelta con la presencia de la madre. Esto lleva a atribuirle una omnipotencia que, al descubrir falsa años más tarde, al comprobar la humanidad y la imperfección de su madre, le hace degradarla por debajo de la categoría de los demás miembros de la familia que no fueron objeto de tal idealización.

[7] Waugh señala: "Schizophrenic experience is an experience of isolated, disconnected, discontinuous material signifiers which fail to link up into a coherent sequence. The schizophrenic thus does not know personal identity in our sense, since our feeling of identity depends on our sense of the persistence of the 'I' and the 'me' over time (...) The fragmentation of subjectivity (conceived as ego) is the final defense against the fear of annihilation by the object and the *desire*, therefore, to destroy the object oneself" (9).

[8] Elizabeth Spellman (Hirsch 166) relaciona la somatofobia , es decir, la ansiedad y la negación que el propio cuerpo provoca, con la represión materna, no sólo en cuanto a la madre sino en cuanto a la maternidad misma. En la mayoría de las obras en donde aparece la represión materna, la maternidad de la protagonista está fuera de cuestión. Existe, además, un claro rechazo hacia los niños que se extrema en la obra de Silvia Italiano al llevar a la protagonista a sentir repulsión por éstos y a maltratar físicamente al bebé que cuida a diario sin que sienta ningún remordimiento

por ello. En las otras dos ocasiones en que se menciona la capacidad
reproductora de Cecilia es para provocar el extrañamiento sobre la
maternidad tradicionalmente concebida al describir su aborto (65) y la
venta de un óvulo, no con fines altruístas, sino con el objeto de comprar
muebles para su apartamento (173).

Obras Citadas

Allende, Isabel. *La casa de los espíritus*. Barcelona: Plaza y Janés, 1982.
Angel, Albalucía. *Estaba la pájara pinta sentada en el verde limón*.
      Barcelona: Argos Vergara, 1984.
Belli, Gioconda. *La mujer habitada*. Barcelona: Emecé, 1996.
Brunet, Marta. *La raíz del sueño*. Santiago: Zig-zag, 1949.
Caplan, Susan. *Don't Blame Mother. Mending the Mother-Daughter
      Relationship*. New York: Harper & Row, 1989.
Castellanos, Rosario. *Balún-Canán*. México: Fondo de Cultura Económica,
      1957.
Chacel, Rosa. *Memorias de Leticia Valle*. Barcelona: Plaza y Janés, 1986.
Esquivel, Laura. *Como agua para chocolate. Novela de entregas mensuales
      con recetas, amores y remedios caseros*. México: Planeta, 1989.
Etxebarría, Lucía. *Beatriz y los cuerpos celestes*. Barcelona: Destino, 1998.
Feldman, Shoshana. "Women and Madness: The Critical Phalacy."
      Diacritics 5 (Winter 1975): 2-10.
Ferré, Rosario. *Papeles de Pandora*. México: Joaquín Mortiz, 1976.
Gallardo, Sara. *Enero*. Buenos Aires: Editorial Sudamericana, 1958.
Gallop, Jane. "The Monster in the Mirror: The Feminist Critic's
      Psychoanalysis." *Feminisms and Psychoanalysis*. Ed. Richard
      Feldstein and Judith Roof. Ithaca: Cornel UP, 1989. 13-24.
Herman, Judith & Helen B. Lewis. "Anger in the Mother-Daughter
      Relationship." *The Psychology of Today's Woman. New
      Psychoanalytic Visions*. Ed. Tony Bernay. Cambridge, Mass:
      Harvard UP, 1989. 139-63.
Hirsh, Marianne. *The Mother/Daughter Plot. Narrative, Psychoanalysis
      and Feminism*. Bloomington: Indiana UP, 1989.
Homans, Margaret. *Bearing the Word. Language and Female Experience in
      Nineteenth-Century Women's Writing*. Chicago: Chicago UP, 1986.
Irigaray, Luce. "The Bodily Encounter with the Mother." *The Irigaray
      Reader*. Ed. Margaret Whitford. Cambridge: Basil Blackwell, 1991.
      34-46.
---. "Women-Mothers, the Silente Substratum." *The Irigaray Reader*. Ed.
      Margaret Whitford. Cambridge: Basil Blackwell, 1991. 47-52.
Italiano, Silvia. *Un aire de familia*. Barcelona: Seix Barral, 1995.
Laforet, Carmen. *Nada*. Madrid: Destino, 1983.
Johnson, Barbara. "Apostrophe, Animation, Abortion." *Diacritics* 16.1
      (1986): 29-47.
Lagos, María Inés. *Escritoras de Hispanoamerica*. Ed. Diane Marting.

México: Siglo XXI, 1990.

Leonard, Linda S. *Meeting the Madwoman.* New York: Bantam, 1993.

Moix, Ana María. *Julia.* Barcelona: Seix Barral, 1970.

Morrison, Toni. *Beloved.* London: Vintage, 1997.

Parra, Teresa de la. *Ifigenia.* Caracas: Monte Avila Editores, 1990.

Peri Rossi, Cristina. *La nave de los locos.* Barcelona: Seix Barral, 1989.

Rich, Adrienne. "Notes Toward a Politics of Location." *Women, Feminist Identity, and Society in the 1980's.* Ed Myriam Diaz-Diocraretz. Amsterdam: Benjamins, 1985.

Roig, Montserrat. *La hora violeta.* Barcelona: Plaza y Janés, 1991.

Sánchez, Clara. *Desde el mirador.* Madrid: Alfaguara, 1996.

Thurer, Shari. *The Myths of Motherhood. How Culture Reinvents the Good Mother.* Boston: Houghton Mifflin Co, 1994.

Tusquets, Esther. *El mismo mar de todos los veranos.* Barcelona: Lumen, 1978.

Waugh, Patricia. *Feminine Fictions. Revisiting the Postmodern.* New York, Routledge, 1989.

5

Dysfunctional Family, Dysfunctional Nation: *El cuarto mundo* by Diamela Eltit

Lea Ramsdell

Drawing the comparison of a nation to a family is a rhetorical device that has been used to drum up popular support for politicians and regimes of force throughout the history of the modern nation-state. In the twentieth century, for example, Hitler stands out as a master at manipulating his public image as "father" of the nation. Bill and Hillary Clinton also referred to the "national family" during the 1996 presidential campaign. In Latin America, a string of paternalistic leaders availed themselves of the nation/family metaphor, including Lázaro Cárdenas in Mexico, Getúlio Vargas in Brazil, Juan Perón in Argentina and Augusto Pinochet in Chile.

Pinochet's nationalistic discourse, in which he unabashedly held his wife and himself up as the mother and father figures of Chile, is laid bare by the writer Diamela Eltit. In her novel *El cuarto mundo* (1988), she deconstructs the family imagery rooted in the *machismo/marianismo* opposition that was appropriated by the ruling elite for the purpose of galvanizing its control. She reverses the nation/family metaphor by creating a fictional family/nation that mirrors the violence and psychosis of power relations in the dictatorship.

The complex interconnectedness of the individual, family and nation in Eltit's novel can be illuminated by family systems theory. This psychological approach views the family as an organism, as a system of parts acting both together and autonomously as it strives to integrate its separate members into a solid unit without forcing them to give up their independence or individuality (Knapp 226). But each family system in turn belongs to a larger organism, the sociocultural system, within whose confines it must operate. Though the individual, family and social environment exhibit different qualities as systems, the feature that they all have in common is their interdependence: any change initiated at any level will have repercussions for all the other constituents of the organism (Knapp 227). A functional system is open to change and tolerant of diversity. A dysfunctional organism, however, is closed to the possibility of difference. The family systems therapist Virginia Satir describes dysfunction in the following manner:

> Dysfunctional families constitute a "closed system": closed systems are those in which every participating member must be very cautious about what he or she says. The principal rule seems to be that everyone is supposed to have the same feelings, opinions and desires, whether or not this is true. In closed systems, honest self expression is impossible and if it does occur, the expression is viewed as deviant, or "sick" or "crazy" by the . . . family. Differences are treated as dangerous, a situation that results in one of more members having to figuratively "be dead to themselves" if they are to remain in the system. (185)

Eltit's novel *El cuarto mundo* probes the implications of dysfunction for the individual, the family and the nation in the particular case of Chile. It is imperative to review the sociohistorical context out of which this text emerged in order to grasp its critique of closed systems. In 1973, a bloody military coup d'état replaced the Chilean socialist president Salvador Allende with General Augusto Pinochet. In an attempt to legitimize his regime and its systematic violence, Pinochet announced that he would "rescue" Chile from its chaotic past by instituting a set of policies designed to bring about national unity. His rhetoric frequently resorted to the "family of Chile" metaphor. The cornerstone of Pinochet's performance as father of the nation was *marianismo*, a gender ideology exalting women's role as mothers. He targeted women as the "pillars" of the family, addressing them on numerous occasions in order to praise them for their key role in the family and, by extension, in the nation. By invading the domestic sphere with his nationalist discourse, Pinochet politicized the notion of family and justified public scrutiny of private relationships. In *Mensaje a la mujer chilena: texto del discurso*, a speech delivered one month after the military overthrow, Pinochet codified *marianismo* into offical discourse. Beginning with the premise that women are morally superior to men, the speech emphasized their especially important task as mothers:

> La labor anónima de las mujeres que trabajan en el laboratorio silencioso del hogar, velando por resguardar el más precioso capital de la Nación: el cuidado de sus hijos, esperanza futura de la Patria. (10)

Pinochet had no room for subtleties in his melding of the public and private as he brashly applied cold metaphors of capitalist economics to women's labor in the home, drawing the connection between capitalist production and reproduction. He continued to uphold the ideal of *la madre sacrificada* by assuring women that he, and therefore the whole nation, recognized and appreciated the mother's sacrifice: "Tenemos que comprender la grandeza de las funciones del hogar y, al mismo tiempo, entender que la espiritualidad de esa misión está en el hecho de servir en la humilde función de la cocina, de la mujer que cambia los pañales al niño" (14). In this way, Pinochet exhorted women to take stock in their maternal roles, which served both private and public ends. His aim was to convince them that they already exercised public power and should not seek out other avenues of political action (Marcy 16).

This official endorsement of the cult of motherhood, then, became the linchpin not only for subduing female unrest in the domestic realm, but also for consolidating Pinochet's absolute power as the father figure who had his "children's" best interests in mind. Anyone who challenged the state therefore evoked the father's wrath and was punished accordingly. Pinochet's national family, then, was built on the "threat and reward" model that has been elaborated by family systems therapists. Under this rubric, the individuals of a family system are assumed to be morally weak and in need of an authority to threaten punishment in order to maintain an orderly unit (Knapp 229). In Chile, the threat of having a family member "disappeared" was enough to persuade even recalcitrant members of society to pay lip service to the national "family." These nationalist ideologies were designed to maintain stability by quelling resistance, thereby making Chile an attractive market for international capitalism.

The official performances of political and economic might by the Pinochet administration and big business crowded others out of the public sphere. Diamela Eltit was a spectator of these performances as she formed part of the larger audience of Chile. She recognized the frightening power of the dictatorship's drama, with all its trappings and theatricality, to effect troubling changes in society and in the lives of individuals. She decided to turn the tables by staging her own counter-performances, which included her participation in activities sponsored by underground resistance movements.

The novel *El cuarto mundo* is core to Eltit's repertoire of defiant acts. Written in 1988, it resists the hegemonic discourse coming out of the alliance between Pinochet and international capitalism by exposing the violence and trauma generated by the nuclear family unit as a result of its struggle to conform to sociocultural paradigms. Eltit's reappropriation of the family narrative rejects the patriarchal manipulation of notions such as maternal bliss, heterosexual romance and traditional gender roles for the purpose of "nation-building." The fictional family that she presents is composed of a father, mother, a twin brother and sister, and a younger sister.

As seen through the lens of Judith Butler's theoretical framework in *Gender Trouble*, the genders of these anguished characters are nothing more than performance. While Eltit's characters hopelessly attempt to carry out their functions in accordance with the official model of the family, they repeatedly find themselves subverting their narrowly defined roles. This is inevitable, given Butler's definition of gender as arbitrary and learned: "Gender is the repeated stylization of the body, a set of repeated acts with a highly rigid regulatory frame that congeal over time to produce the appearance of substance, of a natural sort of being" (33).

In other words, gender is a performance, and the cultural parameters of that performance become so ingrained in a society that they are considered to be the only ones that are normal or natural. Butler argues throughout her study that there are no "natural," or inherent gender characteristics or behaviors; rather, the attributes that come to be associated with masculine or feminine in any given culture are the result of social conditioning underpinned by the political objectives of those in power. It is to the advantage of dominant institutions that individuals believe that gender identity is immutable so that they will conform to the appropriate set of gender-tagged gestures for fear of being labeled "abnormal," an aberration of nature.   As Butler explains, the critical examination of gender as performance becomes a subversive act in that it shakes up the binary categories of identity on which Western culture has come to depend for ordering society through uneven power relations. The implications of this analysis to family systems theory are significant, especially in a closed system where authentic self-expression is considered dangerous.   If an individual fails to fulfill society's expectations of him or her as a gendered being, the effect ripples through the family and sociocultural organisms eliciting admonishment and punishment.

In *El cuarto mundo*, Eltit resorts to the narrative act itself as a means of deconstructing the binary gender categories to which Butler refers by placing a male-narrated text alongside a female-narrated one within the space of the same novel. The terms "male" and "female" in this context, however, end up having less to do with socialization or biological make-up, which are shown to be ambiguous, than they do with political affiliations and relationships within the power structure. For example, the masculine voice of the male twin that dominates the first part of the novel mimics the voice of patriarchal authority, although there are lapses in his narration that give glimpses into his alternative gender orientations. The direct transgression of this authoritarian discourse becomes the radical project of the second part of the novel when the female, who is the male's twin, assumes the role of narrator. Speaking from the margins, her text is permeated with unconventional narrative techniques and cutting orality. She openly reveals the androgynous identity of her brother who is a transvestite, an aspect of his behavior that his narration intends to mask. The ordering of the narratives, which leaves the female voice with the final word, is key to the novel's political impact.   Therefore, the conventional narration by the male twin will be examined first and will serve as a counterpoint to the analysis of the female twin's narration, which defies conformity from every angle.

In an interview with Julio Ortega, Eltit claims with characteristic irony that she wrote the first, male-narrated part of the novel "como una señorita" ("Resistencia" 236), a reference to her conscious use of non-confrontational, traditional narrative techniques to communicate a masculine perspective. As in the Bible, the male twin's narration begins with the beginning, the story of his own and his twin sister's genesis in their mother's womb. As Butler points out, such a story of origins is "a strategic tactic within a narrative that, by telling a single, authoritative account about an irrecoverable past, makes the constitution of the law appear as a historical inevitability" (36). By laying claim to knowledge of his and his sister's origins, the male voice establishes its authority and thus sets up his monolithic discourse as a reliable, objective description of events as they occurred in the "natural" course of things, much in the fashion of political leaders who exploit myths surrounding the "birth" of nations for the purpose of increasing their credibility.

The narration recounts a strict chronology of important events in the development of the twin fetuses, their birth, and their growth into adolescence. Aside from a few references to prophetic dreams that vaguely foreshadow future strife in the family unit, the narration is linear in the scientific tradition of cause and effect. For readers trained to read and think in this fashion, the male twin's narration is accessible and deceptively coherent, even as it evades issues of power with verbal meanders. As noted by Dick Gerdes, "The male's discourse can be seen as indirect, winding, nonconfrontational, thoughtful, connoting superiority . . ." (x), all qualities that might be used to describe the discourse of power that perpetuates the image of the national "family" living together in harmony. Guillermo García-Corales offers a similar assessment as he comments on the parodic nature of the male-produced discourse in the novel: "La precisión con que el hermano expone estas percepciones funciona como una parodia del discurso que busca un verosímil lineal con la 'realidad'" (96). The precision with which the male twin relates his version of events is intended to cover up the subjectivity of his account, which is the conventional rhetorical strategy used by writers and politicians alike to ward off skepticism on the part of their audience.

Also in the vein of nationalistic rhetoric is the male twin's refusal to let other voices be heard as he relates the development of dynamics within his family. Dialogue is noticeably, and oppressively, absent from the male narration with the result that the thoughts, feelings and actions of others reach the reader only after being filtered through the narrator's perspective. Moreover, Barbara Loach observes that the twin brother's narration "conveys a feeling of dominance and control (also seen in the absence of dialogue) that interprets every outward event as menacing" (163), indicating that not only is this account clinical, it tends to be paranoic as well, an underlying feature common to discourses of power.

In spite of his authoritarian narrative style, the male twin does provide insightful information about family members. In essence, he can not escape reflecting that he is a cog in a more complex system. Though the thoughts, feelings and acts of the other characters are related completely from the male twin's perspective, there are cracks in his authoritarian narrative techniques that allow ambiguities to surface, especially in relation to gender roles in his family and how these affect his own gender identity. In fact, García-Corales notes that the male narration pokes holes in the ideal of woman as self-sacrificing mother:

> . . . emerge una burla velada con respecto al modelo conservador que boga por un rol casi mítico de la mujer limitada en especial a las funciones reproductivas, mujer que no desea ni necesita nada, que vive por y para los demás, sin ofrecer ninguna resistencia a su condición subordinada. (103)

The veiled criticism to which he refers can be seen as the deconstruction of myths surrounding what Adrienne Rich, in *Of Woman Born*, refers to as "institutional motherhood."

This deconstruction begins in the first paragraph of *El cuarto mundo*, which presents the reader with the scene of a sick, feverish woman whose husband, instead of offering assistance, rapes her. This violent act results in the conception of the narrator, a male embryo speaking from the womb. He comments that, as a physical part of his mother's organism, he is also obligated to share in her dreams, dreams of "terrores femeninos" (11) in the aftermath of the violation done to her body. The next day, the woman's condition has visibly worsened, yet her husband, who is unable to cope with his wife's sickness, rapes her again and a twin, female embryo is introduced into the already occupied uterine space. The fact that this family finds its origins in the masculine violence of its patriarch shatters the myth of the family being built on heterosexual desire and love, as the long tradition of foundational fictions in Latin America would have its readers believe (Sommer 2).

Eltit directly challenges the basic tenets of the gender ideology of Pinochet's discourse as the male twin *in utero* observes the actions and motivations of his mother from the inside out. At first, he expresses his irritation at his mother's docile nature and his curiosity about her obsession with her body:

> A decir verdad, mi madre tenía escasas ideas y, lo más irritante, una carencia absoluta de originalidad. Se limitaba a realizar las ideas que mi padre le imponía, diluyendo todas sus dudas por temor a incomodarlo. Curiosamente, demostraba gran interés y preocupación por su cuerpo.

Constantemente afloraban sus deseos de obtener algún vestido, un perfume exclusivo e incluso un adorno demasiado audaz. (13)

As the weeks of gestation wear on, the male fetus comes to realize that his mother's behavior as he describes it above is not authentic: "Atento al afuera, supe que mi madre le mentía a mi padre y que su estudiado comportamiento no era más que una medida estratégica para perpetuar su ilusión de poder" (16). Here the ideology of *marianismo* is revealed as artifice, as a deception acted out by a woman who has no natural inclinations toward the behaviors enshrined in such an ideology. The mother conforms to the official code of femininity by suppressing her own feelings so that her husband retain his illusion of power. Bolstered by social gender norms, the family system remains intact and unthreatened. The narrator also discovers that guilt, and not love, motivates his mother's performance of gender. In this way, Eltit decenters the primary role assigned to women by revealing the non-substantive nature of gender, which Butler describes as follows: "There is no gender identity behind the expressions of gender; that identity is performatively constituted by the very 'expressions' that are said to be its results" (25).

While maintaining the outward appearance of conforming to the dictates of society's expectations of her, internally the woman suffers another "feminine terror," namely that of maternity. Instead of experiencing the "maternal bliss" exalted by institutional motherhood, Eltit's character is anguished by having her body usurped by twin fetuses. The emotional strain and physical ailments that accompany the pregnancy compel her to believe that she will die because of her progeny. She feels incapable of fighting off these anti-maternal instincts: "Sentía que su propia creación gestante la estaba devorando" (21). The association of rivalry and violence, rather than peace and love, with maternity is not only a realistic depiction of the contradictory nature of creative processes, it is also a powerful indictment of the male glorification of motherhood, especially for the purposes of nation-building.

Though in the end the woman survives pregnancy and child birth, her rage against what masculine society has obliged her to endure is passed on to her offspring through her breast milk: "Mi madre y su leche continuaban transmitiendo la hostilidad en medio de un frío irreconciliable" (22). This first corporeal rebellion will prove key as a destabilizer of the family. Rather than assume her maternal role as nurturer and emotional support of her children, she chooses to rebel against her own body as an instrument that is ultimately expected to provide productive members of the national family. The resentment against her forced performance of "femininity" accumulates through the years as the woman puts up with the endless obligations of being a mother.

In addition to having her energies sapped by motherhood, the woman is tormented by her performance as dutiful wife. She faces personal degradation on a daily basis as her husband belittles her and betrays her with his mistress. The male twin alludes to the dysfunctional aspects of the gender performance that is expected of his mother when he describes one of her dreams: "Pude sentir el último sueño de mi madre, en el que se postraba a los pies de un hombre pidiéndole ser la primera elegida para el sacrificio" (71). This dream reflects the ambivalence experienced by women living with the gender categories regulated by the *machismo/marianismo* dichotomy. On the one hand, the woman feels guilty for her unwillingness to completely give up the self for the sake of family while, on the other hand, she experiences such rage that she offers herself to be sacrificed in order to escape society's unrealistic expectations of her.

In the end, the woman does sacrifice herself, but not to the whims of societal pressures to achieve the feminine ideal. Acting on her own sexual desires, she commits adultery, the ultimate act of female resistance to social codes of femininity as well as the sure way to obliterate one's position in the family unit and in the community according to the laws of *marianismo*. By transgressing the ideal of female fidelity touted by official discourse, the woman enacts a counter-performance of gender by becoming an agent of her own desire, a prerogative deemed appropriate only to masculine gender performance.

As a consequence of her rejection of her pact with family and society, the gradual breakdown of the family unit, which has been in progress for years, is then conveniently blamed on the mother. She becomes a scapegoat for the dysfunctional family, much as those who resisted inclusion in Pinochet's national family were identified as the root of the country's woes. Under the "threat and reward" model of this particular family system as well as that of the larger social organism, "events are linear and blame may be readily assigned" (Knapp 230), as evidenced by the male twin's indictment of his mother:

> Mi madre precipitó el encierro. Desplomó el universo,
> confundió el curso de las aguas, desenterró ruinas milenarias y

atrajo cantos de guerra y podredumbre.   Mi madre cometió
adulterio.

El adulterio de mi madre derribó con un empujón brutal a
toda la familia. El intenso dolor de mi padre ante la actividad en el
sexo de mi madre nos llevó desde el asombro hasta una vergüenza
más crítica que todas las anteriores. (75)

The male twin draws the parallel between his mother's "crime" and
the reversal of natural phenomena, thus expressing in exaggerated form
the belief that his mother's adultery goes against nature and is catastrophic
for the family. Once again, gender behavior that is judged proper by
society is made to appear to be natural whereas deviations from that
behavior, such as female adultery, are considered severe aberrations of
what nature intends. Furthermore, the family's honor is dependent on the
"honor" (in other words, acceptable gender performance) of the woman.
The mother's action and its overarching affect on the family reflect the
basic tenet of family systems theory that "in the family, everyone and
everything impacts and is impacted by every other person, event and
thing" (Satir and Baldwin 191).

Eltit thus employs the authoritarian masculine voice of the male
twin to expose the artifice of female fidelity and motherhood, two
fundamentals of Pinochet's gender ideology, through exposing the
ambiguities and psychosis of the mother and her role in the family. Yet,
as is the case with all the family members, the mother is incapable of
completely breaking away from norms of gender identity upheld by
dominant culture. Her affiliations with and resistance to power are in
constant tension and she passes this same conflictive state on to her
children.

The fruit of the abusive relationship between the mother and father
consists of a twin son and daughter and a younger daughter, all of whom
develop multiple sexual identities that refuse to fit nicely into established
paradigms. The male and female twins take turns at assuming both
conventionally feminine and masculine traits and behavior, while the
youngest sister is strangely attached to her father and attempts to emulate
his performance of masculinity. The relationships between the male twin
and his parents and siblings, particularly his twin sister, fuel his struggle
with sexual identities as he is seduced by masculine power even as he is
drawn to the feminine because of its marginalization from that same
power.

As a fetus privy to the subconscious of his mother and sharing the
uterine space with his female twin, the male twin's gender conditioning

begins. In family systems theory, the two parents and the child typically form what is known as the "primary triad." In this case, however, it is the mother and her twin fetuses that make up this triangular relationship, which Satir describes as the "essential source of identity of the self." She continues: "On the basis of his learning experience in the primary triad, the child determines how he fits into the world and how much trust he can put in his relationships with other people" (Satir and Baldwin 170). As a result of his place in the primary triad, the male twin becomes conscious of the inauthenticity of his mother, of her passivity as a tactic of survival, and this breeds both his distrust of and fascination with female gender performances. Furthermore, the male twin concedes that it is impossible for him to avoid completely the female influence that envelopes him in his doubly feminine environs: "Las formas femeninas, dominantes en la escena, lanzaban mensajes incesantes. Preservarme de su desesperanza era impensable; más bien debía dejar móviles y abiertas mis marcas masculinas" (20). Here the male twin hints at the origins of his fluid gender orientations, having experienced a female-dominated internal world that clashes with the patriarchal external environment that he is destined to inhabit. Aware of the uselessness of trying to fight off feminine influences, the male twin decides to cultivate flexibility as a strategy for negotiating the arbitrary distinctions that he has begun to perceive between the feminine and masculine spheres.

The mixed messages of gender identification that began in the womb continue throughout the infancy of the twins. The male twin is officially given his father's name, but the mother tells him "Tú eres María Chipia" (23). Janet Lüttecke sees this act as the mother's appropriation of the male prerogative to name things, which she undertakes as vengeance against her husband who raped her and is responsible for her present maternal state. Moreover, Lüttecke upholds that: "El nombre bautismal del mellizo, que es el paterno, el patriarcal si se quiere, el sancionado por la ley, se esfuma detrás del nombre matriarcal, y es este último que lo define" (1083). The male twin senses the weight of his two names as sites of gender conflict and their repeated use as labels to refer to him are a constant reminder of his split gender orientation.

As the twins grow and develop, they undergo social conditioning designed to reinforce the notions of superiority in the male term of the gender opposition and to mold them into creatures of conformity to the dominant gender ideologies. When the male twin suffers a severe fever, the mother becomes hysterical and turns her complete attention to making him well, while his twin sister is shoved to a remote corner of the room and ignored. The twin sister's attempts to ensnare some of the mother's attention by babbling endearingly or learning to crawl only aggravate the mother, who resents being distracted from preserving the life of her son. When he does recover, the mother is overcome with happiness and pride. Yet the female twin, again in an effort to assert her worth, overshadows the focus on her brother by choosing the moment of his recuperation to enunciate her first word (30).

Rather than garnering parental attention for herself, the female twin's more advanced behavior deeply disappoints the father, who expects the male twin to be the leader in cognitive development. Gisela Norat observes that the female twin is denied recognition of her feats because her precociousness defies the norms of the *machismo/marianismo* codes: "En fin, a pesar de su desarrollo lingüístico la niña no recibe el merecido reconocimiento porque, simbólicamente, con el dominio de la palabra, ésta le ha usurpado la supremacía al varón" (79). The mother, aware of the growing disgust of the father toward his son because of his failure to keep up with his twin sister developmentally, lavishes more attention on the male twin by constantly praising him and exaggerating his accomplishments in the father's presence. The son eventually satisfies his parents' expectations by walking across the room when not yet one year old.

The affect of this experience on the male twin is that he begins to perceive the benefit of conforming to his father's notions of gender relations, in which the masculine is clearly considered superior and worthy of special treatment:

> Tomé alegremente el nombre de mi padre y llegué a la tan ansiada armonía con el exterior . . . Entendí la vida como una forma de placeres alternos que venían suministrados por mi madre, quien se esforzaba por crear para nosotros una atmósfera de gran comodidad. (31-32)

In the act of gladly taking on his father's name, the male twin submits to his family's conditioning of gender identity and aligns himself with masculine authority. As a natural consequence, he sees the advantage of supporting the dominant code for female behavior and no longer questions the authenticity of his mother's actions.

Nevertheless, his gender boundaries remain fluid. A significant moment in the narration that highlights a gap in masculine performance consists of a rare scene in which son and father are alone together buying clothes. While the male twin had made it an issue to reveal that his mother's concern for fashion was artificial, by contrast he describes his father's penchant for clothing as genuine. As it turns out, both father and son share a particular liking for silk and, in a reversal of gender-specific behavior, it is the father, and not the mother, who lingers over the task of shopping for clothes for his son:

> Yo compartía con él el placer por la seda, que me cubría de agradables escalofríos cuando se deslizaba por mi carne desnuda. Mi padre tardaba horas en tomar una decisión. Extendía sobre el largo mesón dos o tres camisas, comparándolas o examinando la calidad y nitidez de los brillos. Extasiado por los pliegues, las yemas de sus dedos recorrían la superficie de las prendas con la precisión de una caricia íntima y con el temblor de una pertinaz impotencia. (44)

This description of the father's interaction with clothing, which purposely resorts to sensual words such as "extasiado," "caricia íntima," and "temblar," could easily be read as a sexual encounter. Here the father demonstrates a sensitivity sadly lacking from the violent penetration of his wife that was presented in the initial scene of the novel. Nevertheless, this sensual obsession on the part of the father is not quite appropriate to the guidelines of male behavior. His deviation from proper gender performance makes an impression on the male twin, who feels that he shares in the "excentricidad" (44) of his father. The son perceives, then, that the fascination that they both have for silk is "off-center" or not quite "normal" for them as males. Shopping and clothing, along with cosmetics and jewelry, are tagged as feminine obsessions. The transgression of these gender borders by the father and his son, the primary representatives of patriarchal power, insinuates that regimes of power may also break their own rules regarding appropriate gender behavior in secret.

In his interactions with his twin sister, on the other hand, the male twin experiments more freely with a range of gender performances. From a young age he and his twin sister engage in play in which they are capable of acting out the gender-specific behaviors that they have learned through observation of the dynamics in their family:

> El ancestral pacto se estrechó definitivamente, ampliándonos a todos los roles posibles: esposo y esposa, amigo y amiga, padre e hija, madre e hijo, hermano y hermana. Ensayamos en el terreno mismo todos los papeles que debíamos cumplir,

perfectos y culpables, hostiles y amorosos . . . Jugábamos, también,
al intercambio. Si yo era la esposa, mi hermana era el esposo, y
felices, nos mirábamos volar sobre nuestra suprema condición. (34)

The implication that the twins were happy performing the "opposite"
gender role undermines the dominant belief that nature, and not cultural
practices, determines gender categories. The reference to flying reinforces
the message that breaking away from the strict boundaries of the binary
gender distinction brings with it a sense of liberation.

The male twin's gender identifications are further complicated as
he approaches puberty and becomes aware of his own desire. At the age
of twelve, his first sexual encounter is with someone who is intentionally
described as a figure of unknown sex:

> Ondulaciones, persecuciones y aguijonazos imprimían un
> ritmo jadeante a mi respiración, que se elevaba nasalmente vulgar.
> En el límite de mis fuerzas, busqué decididamente la consumación,
> pero la figura huyó, dejándome ardido contra las piedras. (47)

This figure's performance as the initiator of the encounter places the male
twin, who is not in control, in the traditionally feminine position as
passive receiver (Lüttecke 1084). Later, when thinking back on the
moment, the male twin realizes that, though the identity of the figure was
fuzzy, he was unquestionably aroused, communicating that gender is
irrelevant when it comes to sexual desire:

> No pude precisar quién ni qué me sedujo ese anochecer.
> En ninguna de mis constantes reconstrucciones pude afirmarlo con
> certeza, aunque estoy seguro de haberme encontrado con la
> plenitud de la juventud encarnada en una muchacha mendicante o
> en un muchacho vagabundo que, cerca de la noche, se convirtió en
> una limosna para mí. (48)

The fact that the male twin's sexual awakening takes place with a person
of unknown gender underlines the ambiguity already present in his own
self-image and influences the development of his gender orientations into
adolescence.

Furthermore, the incident brings to the twins' consciousness the
sexual desire that permeates their relationship. Upon learning about the
male twin's erotic experience, the female twin falls into a delirious fever.
Feeling that her brother has violated their male-female bond in the family

organism, she wishes death upon herself in order to punish him. She is only cured when the male twin assures her that, in his imagination, the person with whom he experienced desire was her, his twin sister, and that, as far as he was concerned, she was present during his encounter in the street. This admission stands in defiance to the patriarchal code for properly channeled heterosexual desire and marks the twins as outcasts for their failure to suppress their incestual attraction.

While the male twin fluctuates between gender roles and tries to smooth over the fact with typically masculine performances, the twins' younger sister, María de Alava, insists on affiliating herself with patriarchal power, exuding masculinity in her appearance and attitudes. Though she has a limited role in the events recounted in the male twin's narration, the reader is made aware of the close, perhaps even incestual, relationship between María de Alava and the father. Because of her special bond with the family patriarch, she holds a certain power within the family and stalks their common domain authoritatively. In addition, María de Alava emulates the father's world vision, which in effect is that of modern Western patriarchy, by categorizing everything in terms of binomial opposites:

> Mi hermana menor portaba la muerte anhelada por mi padre y eso la obligaba a reducirse a dos polos: el éxito o el fracaso, el bien o el mal, la vida o la muerte. Exactamente en esa pobreza convencional mi padre había arraigado en ella con mayor profundidad. Sólo en ocasiones mostraba rasgos diferentes que coincidían con su enfrentamiento al núcleo femenino. (63)

María de Alava, then, rarely identifies with traditionally feminine features of herself. Moreover, she fails to demonstrate solidarity with her mother and sister, which is a source of constant friction within the family. Significantly, María de Alava's doting father always rescues the miniature female patriarch from the conflicts that her pro-*machismo* stance generates.

In spite of the male twin's efforts to represent the logic and values of the masculine power structure in both his narrative style and his interpretation of events, the ambivalence surrounding gender-tagged behaviors on the part of all the family members, even the father, shows through. A dysfunctional family that revolves around animosity and violence emerges from just below the surface of the text. Family systems theory explains that "in dysfunctional families, fear and anxiety usually force members to create a *pseudo self*, so that one's inner feelings and

outer behavior are *not congruent*" (Knapp 226).   Eltit uses the pseudo
selves of her characters to turn the tables on the dictatorship's myth of
unity, for if the nation can be compared to a family, so too can the story of
a dysfunctional family implicate the national family as a fabrication, a
performance riddled with flaws.

Though the deconstruction of gender ideologies continues into the
second part of the novel, the form and content of the narrative take an
abrupt turn as the female twin's voice takes over the story of the family's
disintegration.   To symbolize this turn Eltit resorts to the term *sudaca*, a
pejorative (similar to "wetback") used in Spain to refer to Latin Americans
(Ortega, "Diamela Eltit" 78), almost as an organizing principle to an
otherwise unwieldy text.   The word is charged with political force in the
female twin's narration.   *Sudaca* connotes that which is south, below,
inferior, distasteful, backward, left open to exploitation.   In this radical
context, however, it also signifies the subversively marginal, the female,
the agitator, and the active agent of change.

In this sense, *sudaca*, becomes an apt adjective to describe both the
form and content of the female narration.   Whereas the male twin attempts
to cover up or rationalize certain actions and behaviors in the family
within a conventional narrative framework, the female twin unwinds the
fall of the family in a stream-of-consciousness form that pushes the limits
of literary language.   In her narration, there is no doubt about the gender
ambiguity of both the male twin, who is consistently referred to as María
Chipia, and María de Alava in her role as the representative of patriarchy.

Moreover, the second part of the novel makes explicit the
connections among this nuclear family, the dysfunctional national family,
and international capitalism with the repeated use of the word *sudaca*.
The deployment of the term points to the subtext of Pinochet's discourse
and actions regarding foreign investment.   While pumping up the image
of the Chilean family through nationalistic rhetoric, he simultaneously
sponsored economists from the University of Chicago to re-structure
Chile's economy through austerity measures.   In so doing, his subliminal
message to the national family was that he also considered them a horde
of *sudacas* incapable of determining their own economic destiny.   But in
the novel, the female twin's narration develops a new spin on the term by
using it against the oppressor.   *Sudaca* comes to be associated with the
feminine, the marginalized who are left not only to destabilize the national
sell-out to foreign interests, but also to conceptualize an alternative model
of family and of nationhood.

The adjective *sudaca* with its layered meanings is the most appropriate to describe the introductory fragment to the second section of the novel, which recounts a sexual encounter between the twins in a manner in a manner markedly different than that of the male twin:

> Mi hermano mellizo adoptó el nombre de María Chipia y se travistió en virgen. Como una virgen me anunció la escena del parto. Me la anunció. Me la anunció. La proclamó.
> Ocurrió una extraña fecundación en la pieza cuando el resto seminal escurrió fuera del borde y sentí como látigo el desecho. "¡Oh, no! ¡oh, no!", dijimos a coro al percibir la catástrofe que se avecinaba. Evolucionábamos a un compromiso híbrido, antiguo y asfixiante que nos sumergió en una inclemente duda.
> Decidí entregar a María de Alava la custodia del niño que acabamos de gestar. Lo decidí en ese mismo instante original como ofrenda y perdón para las culpas familiares.
> (El niño venía ya horriblemente herido.)
> María de Alava, que había presenciado toda la escena, hizo un canto mímico que alababa nuestra unión y dijo:
> -La familia sudaca necesita mi ayuda. Este niño sudaca necesitará más que nadie mi ayuda. (83)

Read side by side with the masculine account of the family, the female twin's text jolts the reader's sensibilities by describing the conception of a child resulting from incest with narrative techniques that emulate those of oral storytelling. One of the most striking contrasts with her twin brother's narration is the inclusion of quotes that allow for the expression of voices other than that of a monolithic narrator (Loach 163). The use of verbs such as "anunciar," "proclamar," "hacer un canto," and "alabar," as well as the inclusion of exclamation points also appeals to the auditory sense. Moreover, the female twin's narration is laced with parallelism, another feature typical of oral performance (Briggs 9). In the first paragraph, both the verb "anunciar" and a parallel syntactical structure are repeated three times: "Como una virgen me anunció la escena del parto. Me la anunció. Me la anunció. La proclamó" (83). The female twin's more orally-based style of creative expression becomes a means of resisting the hegemony of the male twin's narration, which conforms to the paradigms of official discourse.

The entire narration in this second part of the novel is cast as performance not only by the incorporation of oral storytelling techniques, but also by direct and repeated references to theatrical terms and imagery, the rehearsals and playing of roles, and the constant feeling that the narrator is being watched as she expresses herself. For example, in the initial fragment of the female twin's narration quoted above, the very first sentence openly refers to gender as a role to be performed when the narrator blurts out that her brother decided to take on his feminine name and cross-dress as a virgin. The male twin consciously prepares to perform the feminine gender while simultaneously fulfilling a masculine role by engaging in sex with his twin sister and fathering the life that begins to grow in her.

Interestingly, this act of incest is itself presented as a performance, similar to a Greek tragedy, in that an audience, consisting of María de Alava and the parents, is present to observe the spectacle. The panopticon effect created by the narration clearly reflects the sensation experienced as the public sphere under the totalitarian government successfully invaded the private sphere, laying it open for the eyes of the nation to observe and judge. When the parents burst into the scene of the incestual encounter, both twins are struck with terror by their father's rage. Yelling rhetorically "¡Qué hicieron!" (85), the father does not solicit a reply; rather he levels judgment on them.

This narrative form grounded in performance effectively expresses the contradictions inherent in the characters' relative affiliations with the powerful and the powerless, and with what it means to be *sudaca*. As a case in point, María Chipia blames his twin sister for the family catastrophe that they have wrought, accusing her of infecting him with "un rencor orgánico y venéreo" (85). He falls into an epileptic fit, but in the middle of his convulsions manages to echo his father's accusation by repeating "¡Qué hicimos!" (86). María Chipia caves in to masculine authority in an attempt to renew his association with paternal power and avert the consequences of having defied the law of the father. By repeating "Yo soy un digno sudaca," an oxymoron given the inherently derogatory sense of the word *sudaca*, María Chipia hopes in vain to convince himself of his self-worth, that he belongs to the nation of *sudacas* despite his fractured and insincere performance of male gender. Yet, to be part of the national family is in fact to be inferior given the status of Latin American countries in the world order.

Likewise, the female twin, in her guilt and shame, hopes to align herself with masculine authority by turning to her sister María de Alava, the female representative of patriarchy in the family, for assistance. María de Alava has assumed control over the family situation as the parents have turned into permanent voyeurs who are immobilized by the sight of their children's forbidden behavior. At the moment that the twin realizes that she has conceived, she decides that she will give the baby to her sister when it is born as an offering, a sacrifice to erase the family's sins. María de Alava responds by emphasizing the *sudaca* nature of the impending family and marks the offspring as an aberration, not only as the fruit of an incestual relationship, but also as the product of a backward society. As the child of a *sudaca* family, he or she will have little chance of survival without assistance from a power source.

The remainder of the female twin's narration is a dizzying description of eroticism, betrayal, deprivation and shame that the family experiences as her pregnancy progresses. María de Alava plays a central role during the gestation period as an agent of patriarchal authority, particularly in her role as the confessor of the female twin. Out of desperation, the female twin seeks out her sister to absolve her of her transgressions and give her some guidance. Taking the attitude of a grand inquisitor, María de Alava condemns her sister's actions and demands that she articulate, in hierarchical order, all her sins. But as the female twin attempts to do so, the image of her brother dancing enters her thoughts and she realizes the uselessness of the confession. The female twin's effort to be accepted back into the fold of the national family via María de Alava, its representative, fails.

In fact, the female twin reveals that her true desire is to undermine official performances of family harmony. María Chipia succeeds in pressing his twin sister to confess this secret to him in one of their moments of physical intimacy: "Quiero hacer una obra sudaca terrible y molesta" (88). With this declaration of defiance, the female twin drops the pretense of female performance to state straight-forwardly her mission to agitate dominant patterns of thought.

As it turns out, this mission will be fought on two fronts as the work she envisions must resist both the national family and "the most powerful nation in the world." María de Alava is the one to deliver the message that this nation has cursed their country of *sudacas* and is making them suffer, a thinly veiled reference to the United States and its economic hegemony in Latin America: "Mi hermana ocultó su cara entre las manos y dijo que un homenaje nos podría liberar definitivamente de la nación más poderosa del mundo, que nos había lanzado el maleficio" (97). As is to be expected, the younger sister, aligned with dominant forces of the *sudaca* family, advocates that a homage be paid to this nation in order to ward off its advances.

But the female twin, as a marginal *sudaca*, takes action by writing a letter to María Chipia in an effort to have him join forces with her in the creation of the child growing inside her, their symbol of resistance. In the letter, she uncovers the espionage and intrigue on the part of the family members who are cooperating with this most powerful nation: "Soy víctima de un turbulento complot político en contra de nuestra raza. Persiguen aislarnos con la fuerza del desprecio" (103). She and her mother have discussed this plot and believe that both the father and María de Alava have already sold out to the most powerful nation. The female twin also implicates her brother in this conspiracy because of his continued association with their father:

> No te perdono, pues aún temes a mi anciano padre, que no ha derrotado a su virilidad. Tú temes aún a la suavidad de la seda. Temes a mi hermana y a mi madre, que parece que la multiplicidad de tus sueños te acercará a la nación más famosa y poderosa del mundo. (103-104)

The female twin's accusation that María Chipia is ruled by fear of both feminine and masculine gender performances points to his inability to distance himself from masculine power in order to take a stand against the most powerful nation.

In the meantime, the female twin moves forward with ambivalence in the development of her *sudaca* work, her imperfect fetus, as a means of undermining the collusion between her family and foreign powers. Repeated references to the likely defects of this progeny due to its genetic weakness are sprinkled throughout her narration, often as parenthetical asides such as "(El niño venía ya horriblemente herido)" (83), "(Supe que el niño venía con el cráneo hundido)" (85), and "(Canto, también, por el niño que ya sufre un proceso irreversible)" (100). The female twin knows that the product of this gestation period will not be easily palatable to society. The concentration of *sudaca* characteristics that it embodies will repulse the national family and "the most powerful nation in the world." This deformed being, this "obra sudaca terrible y molesta," when it leaves her womb to enter the world will be a thorn in the side of dominant cultural and economic models as its presence bears testimony to their malevolence.

As the female twin's pregnancy progresses, economic necessity and sickness begin to overtake the house, an allusion perhaps to the affects of austerity policies implemented by the "Chicago Boys" under the Pinochet regime. During this period, the parents have faded into the background and the twins gradually become "parental children." They are now the couple that dominates the household.   In an effort to ward off their hunger as the scarcity of food in the household becomes intense, the twins give themselves over to their sexual desires under the watchful eyes of their parents.   Hunger drives the family to desperation and María de Alava, who is no longer concerned with the *sudaca* child to be born to her sister, announces to the twins that she and her parents will abandon the house. This abandonment reflects the actions of the dictatorship that, despite its nationalist rhetoric, deserted the "family of Chile" as it courted foreign interests in order to insure that the ruling class would have its appetite satisfied.

When the female twin hears her sister's announcement, she is taken aback by the news:

> Todavía incrédula, entiendo que María de Alava, después de todos estos años, ha hablado la verdad. Pensar que sus palabras son sinceras, después de tantos años, me da fuerzas para resistir el abandono y el abandono de la fraternidad. (120)

Though the news of being abandoned by her family at this crucial moment when she is preparing to give birth is devastating to the female twin, her first glimpse of authenticity coming from María de Alava, the power source, gives her a certain hope that the hard-core exterior of the power structure can be cracked.   This hope is also expressed through the commitment of María Chipia, who finally does take a stand by remaining with his sister to bring forth the forbidden fruit of their relationship.

In the final paragraph of the novel, Eltit underlines the importance of this fraternal support by shockingly identifying herself as the female twin who is giving birth to the preceding novel: "Lejos, en una casa abandonada a la fraternidad, entre un 7 y un 8 de abril, diamela eltit, asistida por su hermano mellizo, da a luz una niña. La niña sudaca irá a la venta" (128).   The resultant creative work is therefore marked as *sudaca* and female, a doubly marginalized entity (Norat 82).   Like everything else in capitalist society, this progeny, this novel, is destined to make its way to the market and suffer its fate there.   Yet it comes into the world as the product of fraternity, of the collaboration of brother and sister, and it embodies the seed of hope that Eltit holds out for *sudacas* and other persons marginalized by dominant power structures to join together to formulate new paradigms that dash the hegemony of "the most powerful nation" with its overarching capitalist system.

And so the culmination of Eltit's family narrative, designed to counter that of the Pinochet regime, is the birth of an offspring that results from the incestual relationship between the twins. This act of resistance strikes at the core of Pinochet's pseudo family by violating the sanctity of heterosexual romance, which is meant to reproduce productive citizens loyal to the state, not deformed beings of questionable value. The breaking of the incest taboo ruptures the conventional family structure, opening a space for multiple familial configurations. In the novel, a new kind of couple, a fraternal couple of mixed gender roles and affinities, displaces the traditional couple governed by the *machismo/marianismo* opposition. The prototype of the nuclear family based on a sharp division of labor between the sexes is dispersed and is replaced by an "androgynous" family in which masculine and feminine are irrelevant terms.

As a constituent of the larger sociocultural organism, the fictional family both bears the brunt of the dysfunctional nation and becomes a site of activity for opening the closed system. In the context of dictatorial Chile, the union between the twins, which leads to the creation of a *sudaca* work, indicates their ability to overcome the tactic of "divide and conquer" and is a call to solidarity. On a figurative level, their incest points to the interchange of ideas, emotions and strategies among those united in opposing the dictatorship and its collusion with the forces of globalization. It is a step toward an open system in which diversity is valued and authenticity is encouraged. Thus, Eltit's *El cuarto mundo* succeeds not only in deconstructing the nuclear family and its attendant "family values," it also offers an alternative construct of the family-read-nation that is built on the foundation of fraternal collaboration.

Works Cited

Briggs, Charles L. *Competence in Performance: The Creativity of Tradition in Mexicano Verbal Art.* Philadelphia: U of Pennsylavania P, 1988.

Butler, Judith. *Gender Trouble: Feminism and the Subversion of Identity.* New York: Routledge, 1990.

Eltit, Diamela. *El cuarto mundo.* Santiago: Planeta, 1988.

García Corales, Guillermo. *Relaciones de poder y carnavalización en la novela chilena contemporánea.* Santiago: Asterión, 1995.

Gerdes, Dick. Forward. *The Fourth World.* By Diamela Eltit. Trans. Gerdes. Lincoln: U of Nebraska P, 1995. vii-xi.

Knapp, John V.   "Family Systems Psychotherapy, Literary Character, and Literature: An Introduction."   *Style* 31.2 (1997): 223-254.

Loach, Barbara Lee.   "Power and Women's Writing in Chile: 1973-1988."   Diss. Ohio State U, 1991.

Lüttecke. Janet A.   *"El cuarto mundo* de Diamela Eltit."   *Revista Iberoamericana* 60.8 (1994): 1081-1088.

Marcy, Anne.   "Female Discourses in Authoritarian Chile: The Transgressive Voices of Diamela Eltit and Pia Barros."   Masters Thesis.   U of New Mexico, 1994.

Norat, Gisela.   "Diálogo fraternal: *El cuarto mundo* de Diamela Eltit y *Cristóbal Nonato* de Carlos Fuentes."   *Chasqui* 23.2 (1994): 74-85.

Ortega, Julio.   "Diamela Eltit y el imaginario de la virtualidad."   *Una poética de literatura menor: La narrativa de Diamela Eltit.*   Ed. Juan Carlos Lértora.   Santiago: Cuarto Propio, 1993. 53-81.

---.   "Resistencia y sujeto femenino: Entrevista con Diamela Eltit."   *La Torre: Revista de la Universidad de Puerto Rico* 4.14 (1990): 229-241.

Pinochet Ugarte, Augusto.   *Mensaje a la mujer chilena: Texto del discurso.*   Santiago: Editora Nacional Gabriela Mistral, 1976.

Rich, Adrienne.   *Of Woman Born.*   New York: Norton, 1976.

Satir, Virginia.   *Conjoint Family Therapy.*   Palo Alto, CA: Science and Behavior Books, 1967.

Satir, Virginia and M. Baldwin.   *Satir Step by Step.*   Palo Alto, CA: Science and Behavior Books, 1983.

Sommer, Doris.   *Foundational Fictions: The National Romances of Latin America.*   Berkeley: U of California P, 1991.

6

Familia y comunidad como bases del proceso de adaptación social en tres largometrajes chicanos :
...*y no se lo tragó la tierra,* *El Norte* y *My Family*

María Claudia André

Desde sus orígenes en 1895, el cine ha cumplido el múltiple propósito de entretener, informar y educar en forma masiva a los distintos segmentos sociales proyectando a través de la gran pantalla, experiencias, dilemas y conflictos comunes del hombre contemporáneo. D.W. Griffith, convencido de que la cinematografía eventualmente reemplazaría a la literatura y la historia escrita, se destaca entre los primeros interesados en desarrollar la capacidad de este medio con fines didácticos. *Birth of a Nation* (1915) es la primera superproducción fílmica en la cual se intenta reflejar una objetiva y singular versión de los sucesos históricos más relevantes de la Guerra Civil norteamericana. Griffith consideraba que dada su calidad visual, el cine sería un excelente instrumento, superior y de mayor alcance a todo texto narrativo, puesto que en el largometraje "There will be no opinions expressed. You will merely be present at the making of history. All the work of writing, revising, collating, and reproducing will have been carefully attended to by a corps of recognized experts, and you will have received a vivid and complete expression" (Stevens 2). Sin embargo y a pesar de que esta producción fue un rotundo éxito, el productor se dio cuenta de que lograr una versión comprehensiva y totalitaria de la historia era una tarea tan imposible como absurda y por ello, *"The Birth of a Nation"* was reedited many times over the years both by Griffith himself and by others who contested his version of the Civil War and Reconstruction" (Stevens 4). En la actualidad, la crítica contemporánea coincide en que en realidad, D.W.Griffith se veía más interesado en preservar el discurso hegemónico de la clase gobernante que en lograr una representación objetiva de la historia en la cual se describieran los hechos desde diferentes perspectivas sociales.

El desafío que encierra la representación visual de la historia ha cautivado tanto a cineastas como a documentaristas quienes, al igual que Griffith, han procurado captar a través del lente, los grandes eventos y los avatares de las figuras más prominentes del acontecer mundial. En particular, a partir de la década de los 40, al discurso reduccionista de las grandes narrativas que proponen una versión única y totalizante de la historia, comienza a sumársele el eco de los sectores populares, marginales y minoritarios, los cuales, interesados en incorporar sus propias experiencias y perspectivas dentro del contexto social, comienzan a explorar diversos medios de expresión artístico-cultural. Desgraciadamente, antes de que las voces de tales segmentos comenzaran a ocupar un cierto espacio dentro del medio visual, Hollywood ya se había encargado de incorporar y de pervertir su imagen mediante una amplia variedad de estereotipos que todavía se mantienen vigentes. Tal es así, que las superproducciones cinematográficas reflejan frecuentemente a los hombres latinos y a los afro-americanos en roles de pandilleros narcotraficantes o pobres campesinos y, a las mujeres, como voluptuosas prostitutas, ignorantes sirvientas o abnegadas madres y amas de casa. Aunque estos estereotipos todavía circulan dentro del medio visual, tales interpretaciones se han ido modificando gradualmente gracias a la activa participación de escritores, cineastas y artistas de ascendencia hispana quienes han trabajado arduamente para aumentar la difusión de las culturas minoritarias y subvertir los estereotipos originales. Durante los últimos 30 años, el "North American Latino Cinema" (Cine Latino de Norte América) y en particular, el "Chicano Cinema" (Cine Chicano) han producido obras fílmicas de alto valor estético y de profundo contenido social procurando concientizar a los espectadores sobre los problemas que confrontan diariamente las comunidades de inmigrantes mexicanos y chicanos (mexicano-americanos) residentes en los Estados Unidos (Maciel 312). La temática del cine documental mexicano-americano se ha centrado en recrear la historia del Movimiento Chicano iniciado por César Chávez en la década de los 60 y ha intentado con ello, sustentar y promover las tradiciones culturales de las comunidades migrantes. En años más recientes, tanto la cinematografía como el arte documental se han interesado en informar al resto de la población sobre los problemas laborales, educacionales y de salubridad de la comunidad hispana dentro de las grandes urbes. A los problemas de adaptación se le suma en la actualidad, el difícil proceso de asimilación de las constantes olas de inmigrantes quienes, a su vez, se enfrentan - junto con el drama del exilio y la problemática del lenguaje - a una serie de conflictos externos (explotación, discriminación e injusticia social) e internos (fatalismo, resignación y sumisión con respecto a los grupos mayoritarios) que limitan su rápida adaptación a la sociedad norteamericana.

La literatura y el arte chicano han desempeñado un papel crítico-didáctico como firme salvaguardas del sistema de valores tradicionales de la cultura hispana, otorgándole particular relevancia a aquellos temas que mejor reflejan la integridad individual, familiar y social de dicha colectividad. Originalmente gran parte de la temática cinematográfica chicana se enfocaba en la superaración de una serie de pruebas ético–morales que el protagonista debía afrentar sin sacrificar ni autonomía ni su identidad. Más recientemente, e influenciados por los nuevos debates del discurso posmoderno, tanto el cine como la literatura chicana han sido prolíficos en la producción de obras de tinte político-social cuyos temas giran en torno a cuestiones de raza, de clase y de género. Para Jesús Salvador Treviño, "El arte fílmico chicano debe ser claro en sus denuncias contra brutalidades actuales y pasadas e ir más allá; atender las necesidades de la comunidad, reflejar la belleza de nuestra forma de vida, señalar nuestro camino para el futuro, unirse a la causa común. El nuestro debe ser un arte de defensa y de apoyo" (Maciel 317). Partiendo de este preciso comentario, me propongo en este ensayo analizar la relevancia y el papel fundamental que desempeñan la familia y la comunidad en este proceso de adaptación social, según lo reflejan las siguientes producciones cinematográficas: "*... y no se lo tragó la tierra/... And the Earth did not Part*" (*Tierra* 1971); "*El Norte*" (1983) y "*My Family, Mi Familia*" (1995). El ensayo examinará cómo los roles de la familia y de género se perpetúan de generación en generación respaldando el sistema patriarcal, religioso y moral que son la base de los valores tradicionales de la cultura hispana. Al enfocarnos en cada una de estas producciones, veremos cómo el discurso chicano incorpora la voz de protagonistas anónimos -aunque de gran relevancia dentro del ámbito familiar y social- para reflejar las experiencias vivenciales de diferentes individuos e incolectividades residentes en los Estados Unidos. Finalmente, tomando en consideración la crítica de una variedad de autores y críticos chicanos, se estudiarán dentro del contexto cinematográfico, los metadiscursos culturales que giran en torno a las relaciones de género, de clase y de raza dentro y fuera del ámbito social de la cultura norteamericana. Me interesa analizar estas producciones dentro de un marco crítico pertinente a esta cultura, por cuanto estimo acertado el siguiente comentario de Francisco A. Lomelí y Donaldo W. Urioste, "...the uniqueness of Chicano reality is such that non-Chicanos rarely capture it like it is." La percepción de autores no chicanos no puede considerarse del todo válida, puesto que se trata de una perspectiva externa, "This perspective loses the spontaniety of a natural outpouring of a people's subconscious through the writer's creativity; instead it becomes a calculated object of study which is valued from a relative distance, that is, not lived" (12).

"Y no se lo tragó la tierra"

"*Y no se lo tragó la tierra/...And the Earth Did not Devour Him*" es una adaptación de la famosa novela de Tomás Rivera basada en las experiencias de los trabajadores migrantes durante la década de los 50. Por su particular cosmovisión y su innovador estilo narrativo, el texto en sí no sólo marcó un hito importante en la historia de la literatura chicana, sino que además, sirvió para dar considerable ímpetu a las nuevas generaciones de escritores de esta cultura. El relato nos es referido por un joven, cuyo proceso de introspección va delineando su conflicto psicológico al ir recordando sus dramáticas experiencias de vida junto a los trabajadores migrantes en el sudoeste de los Estados Unidos. La edición original de la obra de Rivera, además de incluir una traducción al español, se compone de catorce cuentos breves y de trece viñetas que cumplen una doble función: logran dentro del plano narrativo introducir las voces de personajes anónimos de la colectividad migrante y, dentro del plano estructural, proporcionar coherencia y fluidez al argumento. Para Brooke Fredericksen,"Rivera's narrative can be called a "migratory" narrative, that is, a novel that is mobile in itself, moving from story to story, from consciousness to consciousness, never losing a sense of the personal and individual struggle while including a collective of voices and building a community" (143). Al igual que Juan Rulfo en *El llano en llamas*

(1953), Rivera intenta, a través de una voz colectiva, sentar un claro testimonio sobre un período determinado en la vida del pueblo mexicano, enfocándose en el microcosmos de las familias migrantes:

> In... *Tierra*... I wrote about the migrant worker in [the] ten year period [1945-1955]. I began to see that my role... would be to document that period of time, but giving some kind of spiritual strength or spiritual history... I felt that I had to document the migrant worker para siempre [forever], para que no se olvidara ese espíritu tan fuerte de resistir y continuar under the worst of conditions [so that their spirit of resistance and willingness to endure should not be forgotten], because they were worse than slaves. (Bruce-Novoa 150-151)

Tal como refleja Rivera, la base fundamental de la cual emana la fuerza interior de su gente y su familia es el producto de sólidos lazos afectivos y una firme raigambre cultural que, sin duda, conforman el elemento básico de subsistencia comunitaria que les permite sobrevivir al hambre, a la pobreza y a la falta de recursos mínimos de salubridad e higiene. Esta fuerza interior se manifiesta mediante las experiencias narradas por una serie de personajes anónimos miembros de la comunidad, por cuyo intermedio se efectiviza una clara denuncia sobre sus miserables condiciones de vida. A las dificultades intrínsecas del desarrollo psicológico del ser humano, los trabajadores migrantes confrontan a diario severas crisis económicas, infranqueables barreras raciales y, dado el constante desplazamiento del grupo, desarrollan un marcado sentimiento de alienación y distanciamiento del mundo real. Por ello, tal como lo proyecta la obra de Rivera, la gradual madurez emocional que finalmente alcanza el protagonista es producto de una favorable dinámica colectiva y familiar que le provee la estabilidad necesaria para subsistir dentro de este conflictivo ámbito social. El fluir de la conciencia del joven narrador nos revela un microcosmos en el cual, a pesar de la explotación, el racismo y el sufrimiento, la comunidad se las ingenia para generar la protección y el calor afectivo necesarios para el equilibrado desarrollo individual de cada uno de sus miembros.

En "El año perdido", el cuento que da inicio al relato, el joven protagonista se halla refugiado bajo los cimientos de una casa para recapacitar sobre los eventos más trascendentes del año ya transcurrido. Los doce cuentos subsiguientes conforman los doce meses que el joven recuperará, tejiendo del hilo del recuerdo y que a la vez, nos manifesta en esta obra narrativa. Según Rivera, el proceso recordatorio como

marco de la estructura narrativa es una de las características principales
de la literatura chicana:

> Through memory the Chicano recuperates the past, discovers his
> history and affirms his own singular being and his identity as a
> collective person [...] Within the mind of this confused boy, we
> perceive a struggle whose ultimate resolution depends on his
> capacity to discover and find form to his past by means of
> words. (Olivares 67).

Como un shamán, el joven narrador entra en un trance que lo transporta
más allá de sí mismo para conectarlo con los ecos de su inconciente
colectivo, del cual rescata, al final de su proceso recordatorio, su
identidad y su función como cronista de la experiencia migrante. Julián
Olivares evalúa que "By discovering who he is, the adolescent becomes
one with his people. Through his quest, he embodies and expresses the
collective conscious and experiences of his society" (13). Bajo la casa,
en posición fetal, analizando críticamente las experiencias de vida junto
a los suyos, se ha 'reparido' y ha reparado su conciencia comunal para
reingresar voluntariamente como activo participante. En el epílogo,
una vez concluída su introspección, el narrador no sólo ha madurado,
sino que se halla psicológicamente preparado para reincorporarse y
fundirse al seno familiar:

> Quisiera ver a toda esa gente junta. Y luego si tuviera unos
> brazos bien grandes los podría abrazar a todos. Quisiera poder
> platicar con todos otra vez, pero que todos estuvieran juntos.
> Pero eso apenas en un sueño. Aquí sí que se está suave porque
> puedo pensar en lo que yo quiera. Apenas estando uno solo se
> puede juntar a todos. Yo creo que es lo que necesitaba más que
> todo. Necesitaba esconderme para poder comprender muchas
> cosas. De aquí en adelante todo lo que tengo que hacer es
> venirme aquí en lo oscuro, y pensar en ellos. (117)

En la conciencia comunal de su inconciente colectivo, el
narrador reconoce que para poder interpretar a su comunidad y definir
su función dentro de ella, debe tomar distancia. Una vez totalmente
alienado del grupo, puede distinguir su propia voz y analizar
objetivamente su participación dentro del contexto familiar y social.
Este párrafo encierra una clara alegoría sobre el proceso de maduración
psicosocial del joven narrador, el cual, una vez que ha definido y
asimilado tantos los aspectos positivos como negativos de su

comunidad, reingresa no sólo como miembro independiente, sino también como activo participante. Maxine Baca Zinn define que, contrario con lo que ocurre con las familias norteamericanas, las familias de origen mexicano operan primordialmente como sistema de apoyo socio-económico y emocional, concluyendo que los grupos no-hispanos emigran y se distancian de su núcleo familiar, mientras que los hispanos buscan permanencia y relación constante con los miembros de su familia. "The Mexican-American system appears to be more socioemotional than instrumental with its emphasis on interaction with large numbers of kin" (Mindel 28-29). Efectivamente, según lo demuestra Rivera, el verdadero caos para el protagonista se encuentra afuera del núcleo familiar y lejos de la protección del ámbito comunitario, puesto que intercambiar actividades con el mundo exterior implica exponerse a la burla, la explotación y la injusticia no sólo por parte de los anglos sino también de los chicanos 'avivados' que se aprovechan de la inocencia de los migrantes. Por ejemplo, cuando el joven queda a cargo de Don Laíto y Doña Bone para poder completar el ciclo escolar, la pareja de patanes chicanos, además de explotarlo a diario, lo involucran en un crimen, amenazándolo con denunciarlo a la policía si se niega a cooperar con ellos. En otra oportunidad, el primer día en la escuela, el protagonista es racial y socialmente marginado por su color de piel y por los piojos que ha recogido de los gallineros de las granjas en donde duerme con su familia. Antes de terminar la jornada, el narrador es injustamente expulsado de la escuela por defenderse de una pandilla de muchachones que se mofa de él, acusándole de ladrón. Al recordar estas traumáticas experiencias, Rivera comenta que "el niño migratorio descubrió las estratas sociales. Descubre del no tener, del no deber ser, del no deber estar. El sistema educativo se le revela como una estructura en la cual el no debe estar, en la cual no debe ser pero en la cual se le obliga participar" (Olivares 362). Al contrario de lo que ocurre dentro de la dinámica comunitaria, en la escuela el narrador es discriminado por el resto de los estudiantes y por un sistema educativo que prejuzga su desenvolvimiento social y su nivel académico.

Varios sociólogos opinan que parte de la falta de motivación entre los niños hispanos se debe a que los padres reprimen la mobilidad social de sus hijos al acentuar la importancia de la familia, el honor, y la masculinidad, dejando de lado otros valores positivos como la independencia, la automotivación y gratificación posterior. Según David Gómez, la experiencia escolar es terriblemente conflictiva para la gran mayoría de migrantes y chicanos por cuanto les menoscaba su personalidad y les aliena de su grupo familiar:

My early schooling was a terribly desctructive
experience, for it stripped away my identity as a *Mexicano* and
alienated me from my own people, including my parents.
[...]Sometimes when the brown world intruded into the white, I
felt divided within myself, but usually, I ended up choosing the
white world. Most of the time, I was simply a displaced person
who, in his better moments, should have realized he was trying
to be someone or something that he actually was not. (5-9)

En sus esfuerzos por asimilar culturalmente los diversos
segmentos minoritarios, la sociedad norteamericana logra que las
generaciones más jóvenes renieguen de los valores constructivos y
experiencias positivas de su propia cultura. Este distanciamiento de la
familia y la colectividad produce sentimientos de alienación y un
profundo estado de apatía social que socava el desarrollo de sus
facultades de adaptación e identificación con ninguna de ambas
culturas (Buriel 125). Estudios recientes han demostrado que los hijos
de inmigrantes hispanos sufren de marginalización múltiple, la cual
compromete el desarrollo de su identidad. "Immigrant children may
suffer shame and doubt, which compromises and undermines their self
confidence and development. Feelings of inadequacy and inferiority
commonly lead to a loss in faith in the child's abilities to 'make it' in
the new setting" (Suárez-Orozco 134). Sin embargo, en la obra de
Rivera se enfatiza en lo positivo de este conflicto interno, puesto que la
discriminación induce al joven a que comprenda cuáles son sus
limitaciones sociales y raciales sin despersonalizarse ni tratar de
aculturarse a un sistema dentro el cual jamás será aceptado. Olivares
concluye que al final de su periplo introspectivo, "This protagonist
arrives at the realization of his own being by virtue of the experiences
that, little by little, he threads together. And with this thread, like that
of Daedalus, he emerges from the labyrinth with his being and identity.
He becomes one with his people"(69). Este proceso de asimilación del
protagonista es llevado a cabo mediante un profundo cuestionamiento
de los valores tradicionales e intrínsecos de la cultura hispana, los
cuales, según percibe el joven narrador, se hallan en conflicto con su
propia interpretación de la realidad. En *tierra*, dicho cuestionamiento
se centra básicamente en torno al culto espiritual y la devoción a la fe
católica que profesan su comunidad, su familia, y en particular, su
madre. Al joven le exaspera la postura determinista y fatalista de su
madre, quien gasta los pocos centavos ganados con gran esfuerzo en

velas para rezarle a la Virgen por la salud de su hija y su esposo enfermos de insolación. Frustrado le cuestiona:

> ¿Qué se gana, mamá con andar haciendo eso? Por qué es que nosotros estamos aquí como enterrados en la tierra. O los microbios nos comen o el sol nos asolea... Y todos los días trabaje y trabaje. ¿Para qué? N'ombre, a Dios le importa poco de uno de los de los nosotros nomás pobres. (19)

Evaluando la precariedad de la situación familiar y la falta de recursos para mejorar su futuro, el joven desesperado maldice a Dios varias veces, aún temiendo que la tierra se abra para tragárselo por su blasfemia. Su maldición resulta como un acto de rebeldía contra las creencias y supersticiones que mantienen el opresivo discurso hegemónico, el cual, según percibe el protagonista, ubica a su colectividad en una posición vulnerable y de desventaja con respecto a las otras comunidades. Desesperado ante la impotencia de ver a su padre y hermana postrados, el joven asume el papel de jefe de familia y como tal, se atreve por primera vez a cuestionar la fe de su madre al rezarle a un Dios que ni atiende, ni presta ayuda a los necesitados. El cuestionamiento y el rechazo de las normas impuestas por sus padres forman parte del proceso de maduración psico-social del protagonista, pero además, y tal como evalúa Ramón Saldívar, "His iconoclastic act, cursing God, speaking the unspeakeable, is motivated by a double urgency: to liquidate the opressive idols and to articulate the power of self-determination" (20). Si bien la dinámica familiar se estabiliza cuando el padre se recupera, resulta evidente que el protagonista, al desafiar las creencias religiosas y tradiciones que definen su núcleo familiar y su comunidad, toma conciencia de su capacidad de libre albedrío. Aislándose temporariamente del núcleo familiar y social como crítico objetivo de la situación, el joven se libera de los tabúes que limitan a su comunidad, ganando la confianza necesaria para confrontar el estoicismo y el determinismo que subyuga al resto del grupo. "In short, by liberating himself from the cloudy trascendental idealism of Catholicism, the protagonist is now able to continue on this lively road of reconstructing a holistic sense of self and group identity" (Saldívar 208). El hilo del recuerdo lo ha conducido hasta los confines de su individualidad y ha retornado libre e independiente al seno de su familia, listo para reintegrarse como agente narratario de su colectividad. Identificándose como *alter ego* del narrador, Rivera sostiene "Through memory we encounter our own salvation. We discover that "we are not alone," but that, rather, we carry in ourselves

the history of all our people, our collective experience" (Olivares 76).
A través del personaje protagónico, el escritor chicano sostiene que
para poder comprenderse mejor uno mismo, y a la vez, asimilar su
condición humana, el hombre busca el reconocimiento de su raza, en
sus orígenes y en el de sus semejantes. Al descubrir su lugar y su
futuro junto a los otros hombres de su colectividad, el narrador logra
definir su identidad tanto en el plano personal como colectivo. Su
función será la de preservar las experiencias de los migrantes dentro la
memoria histórica de su raza para las nuevas generaciones de chicanos,
sirviendo de nexo o eslabón coordinante entre su cultura y la cultura
norteamericana.

Concluido su periplo introspectivo, el protagonista (obviamente
Rivera), ha aprendido a canalizar, a través de la vía literaria, su enojo y
su frustración contra un sistema opresivo. De esta frustración ha
surgido, según define Lomelí, "a new wave of cultural nationalism and
resistance as epicenters for ethnic revival. In reevaluating past
misdeeds, Chicanos redefined themselves, their course in history and
their cultural endowment"(90). El gran valor de la obra de Rivera yace
en que no sólo nos sirve de paradigma de la experiencia migrante, sino
que simultáneamente, nos proyecta una perspectiva ontológica sobre
los conflictos internos y la fuerza intrínseca de la raza mejicana. Tanto
en texto narrativo como en la versión fílmica se enfatiza el gran apoyo
emocional que representa la familia y el grupo comunitario. Por
ejemplo, la crianza y cuidado de los niños es responsabilidad de todos,
y cuando los jóvenes tienen edad suficiente para trabajar pasan a formar
parte de la mano de obra. Las decisiones laborales y sociales son
efectuadas por cada uno de los miembros participantes, y sólo cuando
se llega a un acuerdo unánime se determina un plan de acción
colectivo. Padres e hijos comparten el trabajo, las responsabilidades y
los momentos de crisis, pero también celebran las tradiciones de sus
mayores en animadas comunales. Los parientes, en particular los
padrinos o compadres, entretienen y se relacionan a diario con sus
ahijados, ofreciéndoles protección y afecto. Robert Alvarez Jr. explica
que el compadrazgo es una relación fundamental dentro de los
segmentos inmigrantes: "*Compadres* are expected to provide each other
with mutual help, to care for one another at a time of need and to be
readily available in times of crisis. *Compadres*, as kin, have provided
shelter for newcomers, access to jobs and a bastion from which the
people can become acclimatized to the new environment" (150).
Tierra refleja claramente que, a pesar de las patéticas condiciones
económicas y la constante discriminación racial, la dinámica del grupo

migrante promueve la sincera unidad de sus miembros y la confianza necesaria para mantener su estabilidad. Según sostiene Alvarez Jr.:

> *Confianza* (trust) is of particular importance to both institutions of compadrazgo and parentesco among hispanics in the United States, and is the basis of the relationships between individuals in many spheres of social activity. To have *confianza* with an individual is not just to regard that person with trust, but it signifies a relationship of special sentiment and importance involving respect and intimacy" (151).

En la obra de Rivera, la familia y la comunidad se ubican como núcleo generador de una potente fuerza que de la cual emana el calor y de afecto indiscriminado para cada uno de sus miembros y como institución provee los mecanismos sociales para ayudar a la gente en el proceso de migración y radicación. Esta es la única institución que provee no sólo el parentesco y la amistad, sino también los contactos de empleo para los cientos de inmigrantes que llegan a los Estados Unidos (Alvarez Jr. 148)

El Norte

El Norte (The North) fue escrita y dirigida por Gregory Nava en co-producción con su esposa Anna Thomas. Esta excelente película de índole documental significó un paso importante en el desarrollo del cine chicano, puesto que gracias al reconocimiento recibido en el Festival de Cannes en 1984, varios productores de cine comercial a nivel internacional comenzaron a darse cuenta del potencial de las películas con temas relacionados con la comunidad hispana. Según Maciel, "In this manner, *El Norte* opened up avenues to cinematographic art that contain a social message and made a valuable contribution to counteracting the offical propaganda in the United States against further Latin American emigration" (Maciel 324). El largometraje refleja la dramática lucha de uno de los tantos grupos étnicos socialmente marginados compuestos en su mayoría por pobres inmigrantes y campesinos de ascendencia indígena. Los protagonistas son Enrique y Rosa, dos hermanos guatemaltecos, quienes se ven forzados a abandonar su pueblo natal por cuestiones políticas. En realidad, más que una simple narración sobre los problemas que confrontan los indígenas en Guatemala, el verdadero conflicto radica en el racismo de los mestizos (ladinos) hacia los indígenas, en las paupérrimas condiciones en las cuales viven los inmigrantes antes y después de cruzar la frontera y, sobre todo, en la crueldad de los mismos chicanos que se aprovechan de la ingenuidad e ignorancia de los campesinos recién llegados. La película en sí se encuentra dividida en tres partes. En la primera, se resaltan la belleza idílica de una aldea maya y la dinámica afectiva del núcleo familiar de Enrique y Rosa. En la simple pero cómoda casa, la madre prepara la cena y conversa animadamente con sus hijos, mientras que en la montaña, el padre organiza una junta de campesinos para protestar por los abusos y la explotación a la que se hallan sometidos. Esa misma noche, después de una amena cena entre amigos y parientes, el destino de esta familia cambiará para siempre. Un grupo de fuerzas paramilitares es alertado sobre la insurrección de los rebeldes, quienes son interceptados, secuestrados y asesinados indiscriminadamente, incluyendo los padres de los protagonistas. Si bien Rosa y Enrique logran escapar de la tragedia familiar, saben que la milicia no se detendrá hasta encontrarlos. Con los escasos fondos que provee su madrina y los datos de un 'coyote' que les proporciona un campesino amigo, deciden ir vía Mexico hacia los Estados Unidos. Ya en territorio mexicano, en donde transcurre la segunda parte, los jóvenes deben confrontarse con una serie de problemas para los cuales no se encuentran ni psicológica ni físicamente preparados: el hambre, la pobreza, la discriminación y la mala fe de un hombre, quien haciéndose pasar por su amigo trata de matarlos para robarles su dinero. A pesar de estas y otras vicisitudes, los protagonistas encuentran finalmente al 'coyote' amigo y con su ayuda logran cruzar la frontera gateando por millas a través de un sistema drenaje abandonado, pero infestado de ratas. En la tercera parte, los hermanos 'renacen' a la vista de un paradisíaco Los Angeles que los recibe iluminado y lleno de promesas. Gracias a la ayuda de Nacha, una mexicana que le enseña a cómo vestirse y cómo manejarse dentro de los Estados Unidos, Rosa se va adaptando rápidamente a la nueva cultura. Enseguida, la joven cambia su peinado y vestimenta indígena por ropa a la moda americana, comienza a estudiar inglés y evita recordar todo lo que tenga relación con su pasado, puesto que tal como le dice a su hermano, "Si piensas en eso, te volverás loco". Enrique no aprecia demasiado el dramático cambio de Rosa, pero dada la insistencia de su hermana, y su gran cariño por ella, él mismo tratra de adaptarse a la nueva cultura. Unidos en la lucha por la subsistencia en un país en el cual perciben con entusiasmo la posibilidad de progreso, los hermanos se dedican arduamente a construir un hogar. Al poco tiempo, todo parece estable. Rosa y Nacha trabajan de empleadas domésticas, mientras que Enrique es ayudante de cocina en un distinguido restaurante. No obstante, los cambios en la personalidad y la dinámica afectiva de ambos comienzan a hacerse aparentes. Rosa, notando las diferencias socio-económicas, se esfuerza día tras día por afianzarse al estilo de vida americano, y Enrique empieza a percibir que en esta cultura impera la ley del más fuerte y que todo es válido en la lucha por la supervivencia. El fin se acelera cuando Enrique, al perder su trabajo a causa de que un chicano envidioso que lo denuncia a inmigración, acepta marcharse a Chicago dejando a su hermana sola en Los Ángeles hasta que pueda conseguir la prometida visa de trabajo. A pesar de los inútiles esfuerzos, el sueño no se realiza. La misma noche en que Enrique debe partir hacia su nuevo trabajo, Rosa se enferma de fiebre tifoidea por las mordidas de las ratas y es internada de urgencia. Finalmente, Rosa muere y Enrique queda solo y desamparado en esta ciudad inhóspita, lejos de su aldea y completamente desarraigado de su cultura.

A pesar de que *El Norte* fue un gran éxito, y es hoy en día un clásico de la cinematografía chicana, la crítica estima que la película perpetúa ciertos estereotipos culturales previamente establecidos por las grandes superproducciones de Hollywood. Por ejemplo, los mexicanos y los chicanos son representados como aprovechadores, mentirosos e insensibles, mientras que los norteamericanos parecen ser más abiertos y receptivos a los problemas que confrontan los protagonistas. Aunque para Maciel, éstas y otras deficiencias "can only be explained as an attempt to have the film reach wide sectors of the North American public, the great mayority of whom are unaware of the personal history, the culture and the characteristics of the migratory experience of the undocumented workers in the United States" (324). En este sentido, la película cumple con los objetivos mencionados por Maciel, considerando que, además de los elogios y premios a nivel nacional e internacional, han sido varios los críticos cinematográficos que se han sentido conmovidos por los conflictos que presenta el largometraje. Entre ellos, Rogert Ebert sostiene que lo importante de la película es que "*El Norte* takes place in the present, when we who are already Americans are not so eager for others to share our dream. Enrique and Rosa are not brave immigrants who could have been our forefathers, but two young people alive now, who look through the tattered pages of an old Good Housekeeping for their images of America" (Microsoft Cinema 95). Este comentario de Ebert resulta válido puesto que dada su juventud e inocencia, Rosa y Enrique no se dan cuenta que el proceso de adaptación y asimilación cultural demanda mucho más que su esfuerzo personal y su buena voluntad. A diferencia de *Tierra*, los hermanos en *El Norte* carecen del respaldo emocional y económico que prestan la familia y la comunidad. Aún cuando éstos tratan de adaptarse y copiar el estilo de vida americano, la sociedad les refleja una realidad muy diferente. En sus estudios sobre este complejo proceso, Raymond Buriel estima:

> Assimilation is neither desirable nor even possible for most Mexican- Americans. Complete assimilation means that Mexican Americans have become indistinguishable members of Anglo-American society. However, this is impossible, for the most part, due to Mexican Americans' distinctive *mestizo* features and to the proximity of Mexico, which remind Anglo Americans of Mexican Americans' ethnicity. And, although some successful Mexican Americans may consider themselves assimilated, this does not necessarily mean that Anglo-American society unequivocally accepts them as being assimilated. Under such circumstances, delusions of assimilation are likely to be accompanied by anxiety and confusion over one's identity. (126)

Inconcientemente, al renegar de su raigambre cultural, su lenguaje y su sistema de valores heredado, los hermanos no hacen más que sacrificar su propia identidad a una sociedad que nunca les asimilará como nativos y sólo ante la inminencia de su muerte, Rosa recapacita, "No somos libres Enrique. En nuestra tierra no hay lugar para nosotros, en México sólo hay pobreza y tampoco hay lugar y aquí no somos aceptados. ¿Cuándo vamos a encontrar un lugar? Tal vez, sólo muertos encontremos un lugarcito." Según Carola y Marcelo Suárez Orozco, la segunda generación de hispanos tienen oportunidades muy diferentes que los recién llegados quienes deben adaptarse de inmediato para sobrevivir:

> Individuals who choose to measure their competency in terms of the wider society rather than in terms of local identity risk a loss of emotional support from peers and kin [...] The movement away from the traditional sources of support and the traditional basis of social relationships can create feelings of acute loneliness. (135)

Además, ya que Enrique y Rosa no están familiarizados con el concepto de discriminación racial, ni perciben las diferencias sociales, ni comprenden que el color de su piel indígena sea un factor fundamental. Es por ello que no logran interpretar el por qué de los comentarios ofensivos que escuchan de los mexicanos o las limitaciones culturales y laborales que les impone la sociedad norteamericana. No obstante, tal como evalúa el sociólogo José Montoya, aún cuando existe cierta resistencia popular a causa de antiguos prejuicios raciales, los mexicanos y los chicanos han comenzado a aceptar y a enorgullecerse de su herencia indígena, "As Chicano people we now accept the Indio side of our heritage. Somehow we never had too much of a problem with our Hispanitude one way or the other. But to be considered an Indio!"(25). Dicha percepción se ha ido modificando gracias al Movimiento Chicano (o La Causa) y a la creación de Aztlán, un territorio utópico neo-indigenista creado "In the literature written beginning in 1960, the search for a territory to which to belong, one which would serve as a substitute for the absent nation. Aztlán has a historical support base- a real tie with the ancestral past, of indigenous roots [...] a symbolic fabrication that appeals to the mobilizing force of myths (Anaya-Lomelí 339). Estos movimientos han logrado, a través de su lucha, despertar un deseo de renovación estética, política y social. El término 'chicano', originalmente considerado peyorativo, ya no se emplea para referirse a los mejicanos o indígenas inmigrantes, sino que denota el orgullo del legado hispano-mejicano de los grupos residentes en los Estados Unidos (Martín Rogríguez 110). Alfredo Mirandé y Evangelina Enríquez concuerdan que muchas de las características más favorables de la familia chicana contemporánea se fundamentan justamente en los valores tradicionales de la cultura azteca:

A number of characteristics of the contemporary Chicano family -- such as the emphasis on familism and the importance given to extended relatives, the expectation that the individual subordinate his needs to those of the collective, the concept of respect and obedience to elders, as well as cultural norms of feminine virtue -- had their counterparts in Aztec society. (98)

Es por ello que, respondiendo obediente al llamado de sus ancestros, Rosa regresa en su lecho de muerte al refugio del seno familiar. En su delirio a causa de la fiebre, la joven visualiza los espíritus de sus padres muertos, quienes vienen a buscarla. Rosa se alegra al ver a su madre en la cocina preparando tortillas para el almuerzo y luego corre a los brazos de su padre del cual recibe una canasta con flores blancas y un pescado muerto. Dos pavos reales blancos acompañan estas premonitorias escenas que se manifiestan en la apariencia de sueño febril produciendo un efecto de realismo mágico. Ante la proximidad de la muerte, Rosa tiene la oportunidad de reincorporarse a su cultura indígena mientras que Enrique, sólo,

frustrado y sin el apoyo de ninguna fuente de reconocimiento
individual o colectivo, pierde todo contacto con su identidad étnica,
alienándose definitivamente de su comunidad, de su familia y hasta de
sí mismo. Sin llorar siquiera por la muerte de Rosa, el joven marcha a
su casa y a la mañana siguiente, como un autómata, sale a buscar un
nuevo trabajo. La alienación de Enrique posiblemente sea el resultado
de un profundo sentimiento de culpa por su propia sobrevivencia.
Suárez-Orozco ha encontrado que:

> Among many immigrants, particularly those with close relatives
> remaining behind in the war-torn region, something akin to
> "survivor guilt" has appeared [...] Such awareness creates a
> ready propensity to intense guilt should they fail or become
> derelict in their duties. Should these feelings occur, they can
> only be assuaged by expiatory re-application of the task at hand.
> Feelings of desperation give way to a harsh sense of
> responsibility that they must now seize upon any opportunity in
> the affluent society. Working to ease familial hardships is
> intimately related to this psycho-social syndrome of proneness
> to guilt over one's selective survival. (138)

En este sentido, la película de Nava es un claro manifiesto sobre
el complejo proceso de adaptación que día a día sufren cientos de
inmigrantes fronterizos y de chicanos, los cuales, viven en condición de
exiliados en su propio territorio, siendo ciudadanos nativos pero a la
vez extranjeros. No todos ellos, al igual que Enrique y Rosa, se hallan
psicológica o socialmente preparados para sobrevivir el shock cultural.
La experiencia de estos hermanos refleja claramente los sacrificios y
vicisitudes que confrontan aquellos jóvenes inmigrantes que persiguen
su sueño de un futuro mejor y los beneficios de una vida decente. Cabe
esperar, que siguiendo el ejemplo de *El Norte*, en los próximos años,
los diversos medios de expresión artística y las diferentes comunidades
hispanas continúen analizando críticamente tanto la problemática de la
inmigración como los conflictos internos y externos que deben
enfrentar las nuevas generaciones de inmigrantes.

My Family/ Mi Familia

My Family/ Mi Familia, la más reciente producción de Gregory
Nava y Anna Thomas, cuenta con el auspicio de Francis Ford Coppola
y la participación de un importantísmo elenco de actores chicanos,
entre los cuales se destacan: Jennifer López (María), Jimmy Smiths
(Jimmy), Essai Morales (Chucho) y Edward James Olmos en el papel
del narrador (Paco). La saga de la familia Sánchez, también dividida

en tres partes, comienza en un pueblo mexicano, un día de 1914, cuando el joven José decide partir en busca de un futuro más prometedor a Nuestra Sra. Reina de los Ángeles. Según narra Paco, el hijo mayor, su padre tardó un año en llegar a la ciudad de Los Angeles, la cual era en aquél entonces poco más que un pueblo y su frontera, "just a line in the dirt". José se hospeda con su tío 'el Californio', y pronto se emplea como jardinero en el East Side en donde conoce a María, con quien se casa y tiene dos hijos: Paco e Irene. La narración se acelera hasta el momento de la 'anunciación' del tercer hijo, quien promete ser especial, porque el día de su concepción José vio la silueta de un angel entre las nubes. Esta escena premonitoria introduce una serie de eventos que comienzan a desencadenarse pocos días más tarde cuando los oficiales de inmigración deportan a María de vuelta a México, aún siendo ciudadana. Según explica Marisa Alicea, con la Gran Depresión se justificó el cierre de la frontera y la expatriación de cientos de mexicanos documentados e indocumentados (38). La primera parte de la película concluye con el arrivo de María con su hijo Chucho en brazos después de un periplo de cuatro años. Durante el viaje de retorno, el destino de Chucho queda fijado por el espíritu del río. En una dramática escena, madre e hijo caen al agua y los arrastra la corriente pero no se ahogan; sin embargo, tanto María como las curanderas de la aldea saben por cierto que el niño se ha salvado de milagro y que en cualquier momento, el espíritu del río volverá a buscarlo.

La segunda parte se inicia en 1959, precisamente el día que los Sánchez celebran la boda de su hija Irene. Aquí, el narrador, nos pone al tanto sobre lo que ha ocurrido con la familia durante los últimos años. Él mismo ha entrado en la marina; su hermana Irene está por casarse; Toni, aún siendo la más bonita de barrio, anuncia que se hará monja; Memo planea estudiar abogacía; Jimmy, el menor, es todavía un niño y Chucho, es 'la oveja negra' de familia porque es *pachuco*. Este segmento de la película, además de reflejar la dinámica afectiva entre los Sánchez y sus hijos, se enfoca a través del personaje de Chucho, en la psicología de los pachucos, la generación rebelde de la década de los 50. Según define Octavio Paz, el pachuco como una aberración, un híbrido sin raíces que resulta de lo foráneo, puesto que al rechazar las alternativas tradicionales socialmente establecidas, no sólo no se adapta a la sociedad norteamericana, sino que además niega de la autenticidad de lo mexicano. "Incapaces de asimilar una civilización que, por lo demás, los rechaza, los pachucos no han encontrado más respuesta a la hostilidad ambiente que esta exasperada afirmación de su personalidad [...] El pachuco ha perdido toda su herencia: lengua, religión,

costumbres, creencias" (13-14). En su estudio sobre adolescentes
chicanos, Joe Martínez expresa que esta postura es común en la
mayoría de los jóvenes quienes aspiran, al ser miembro de una banda,
probar su machismo y su mejicanismo: "Their participation in the gang
confers status, reinforces their identity, extends the longevity of the
group, provides a role model for other adolescents and lends spurious
validity to the claim that Mexican-American culture spawns
gangs"(125). Este personaje encarna a cientos de jóvenes chicanos, los
cuales sufren de lo que Suárez-Orozco considera un conflicto de
marginalidades múltiples que les menoscaba el desarrollo de su
identidad. Este es un fenómeno común de las segundas generaciones y
que surge entre muchos factores por el bajo estatus social, la mobilidad
limitada, la situación minoritaria de los padres y, sobre todo, por la falta
de educación y oportunidades de desarrollo individual. Es preciso tener
cuenta que a pesar de que las segundas generaciones de jóvenes buscan
refugio emocional en las pandillas, la gran mayoría de ellos
permanecen en la periferia y superan la mística de la pandilla una vez
que han completado su adolescencia (Suárez-Orozco 135). Sin
embargo, Chucho no llega a superar esta etapa; durante una terrible
discusión José expulsa a su hijo de la casa. Días más tarde, Chucho
mata sin querer al jefe de la pandilla rival. Con la ayuda de Jimmy, su
hermano menor, logra mantenerse prófugo de la justicia hasta que la
noche en que soplan los vientos de Santa Ana, el espíritu del río regresa
para llevárselo consigo. Después de chistar la lechuza, Chucho es
baleado por la policía frente a los aterrados ojos de Jimmy.

En la tercera parte, los jóvenes ya se han transformado en
adultos. Paco es escritor, pero trabaja en el restaurante que Irene
comparte con su esposo; Toni ha dejado los hábitos para casarse con un
misionero americano; y Jimmy, al igual que su hermano Chucho, es un
"vato-loco", un pachuco moderno lleno de hostilidad y resentimiento
contra una sociedad que considera injusta. La drástica muerte de su
hermano lo ha marcado profundamente y, desde entonces, reniega no
sólo del núcleo familiar, sino también del sistema legal que rige la
sociedad norteamericana. En general, los Sánchez se mantienen unidos
y nunca intervienen en la vida de sus hijos, aún a pesar de no
comprender del todo por qué éstos se empeñan en renegar de las
tradiciones familiares, religiosas y culturales que son el fundamento
básico y núcleo de su propia identidad. Bruce-Novoa estima que
algunos mexicanos no perciben las diferencias entre su cultura y la
chicana, mientras que otros rechazan radicalmente la simbiosis cultural:

Why are Chicanos so repulsive and despicable to Mexicans? Why, despite a few exceptions, do Mexican writers tend to view us negatively? In brief, because we undermine the protective wall of national separation between Mexico and the United States; we deconstruct the fictions of exclusivity necessary for Mexicans to go on seeing themseles in terms of a solidified absolute. (58)

La cultura chicana se halla en constante oposición entre las tradiciones heredadas por la familia mexicana y las influencia de la cultura norteamericana. No obstante, estas oposiciones según evalúa Marcienne Rocard son favorables para el desarrollo de una contracultura que se maneja entre dos perspectivas opuestas:

The guardian of traditional values, and the dominant Anglo society modulates into a series of oppositions: the opposition between yesterday (the Mexican past) and today (the Anglo reality) between today (a grim present) and tomorrow (a hopefully better future). (34)

Tal como lo proyecta este largometraje, María y José no perciben las diferencias culturales entre sí mismos y sus hijos, aún a pesar de los conflictos generacionales, ambos padres respetan y tienen un gran amor por cada uno de ellos. La única instancia en el cual el afecto paternal se ve desafiado es cuando Toni convence a Jimmy que se case con Isabel, una refugiada salvadoreña, quien necesita una visa para radicar en los Estados Unidos. Los Sánchez reaccionan alarmados a la falta de escrúpulos de sus dos hijos, pero sobretodo por la falta de respeto hacia la institución matrimonial que ellos estiman sagrada. Este conflicto se resuelve cuando Jimmy, al enamorarse de Isabel, adquiere el incentivo necesario para reintegrarse a la sociedad y empezar a trabajar para mantener a una familia propia. Por desgracia, al dar a luz, la joven muere en el parto del primer hijo y esta crisis vuelve a arrojar a Jimmy fuera del núcleo familiar y social. Una vez más roba y se deja atrapar, buscando refugio en la cárcel. Cumplida su sentencia, Jimmy viene a despedirse de sus padres para marcharse a Texas. En esta oportunidad conoce por primera vez a Carlitos, su hijo. Al sentir el peso de la paternidad, Jimmy toma conciencia de su error y decide hacerse cargo del niño, pero éste lo rechaza como padre hasta que finalmente, Jimmy comprende que sólo con el amor, la perseverancia y el diálogo podrá ganarse el afecto y la confianza de su hijo. Una vez que hijo y nieto se han marchado, José ve la figura de otro ángel entre las nubes que viene a traerle paz. En la última escena, los Sánchez, ya ancianos, reevalúan satisfechos sus experiencias de vida y los logros de su familia.

My Family se encuentra entre las producciones cinematográficas que mejor reflejan la dinámica afectiva de la familia chicana y su énfasis en el sistema patriarcal que acentúa las relaciones entre padres e hijos, el orgullo familiar, la familia numerosa, y el culto a los antepasados. Según evalúa Alvarez Jr., "The family is considered the single most important institution in the social organization of Hispanics. It is throughout the family and its activities that all people relate to significant others in their lives, and it is through the family that people articulate with society" (147). Además, este largometraje destaca con precisa claridad la situación subcultural de la comunidad chicana dentro del marco social imperante. En el transcurso de la película, la presencia del Otro/Other se manifiesta mediante metáforas que proyectan la noción del cruce de puentes y fronteras tanto físicas como socio-culturales. Esta dialéctica invariable entre "nosotros y ellos" es reflejada a veces con cierto dramatismo, aunque sin llegar a caer en lo melodramático, y otras, con una alta dosis de ironía y un gran sentido del humor. Por ejemplo, cuando José cuenta a la familia de la prometida de Memo que su tío Californio se encuentra enterrado en el jardín, su hijo no sólo reniega de la veracidad de la historia, sino que avergonzado obliga a su padre a admitir que se trata únicamente de un rumor. Las nuevas generaciones de inmigrantes chicanos se niegan a aceptar e incorporar determinados aspectos culturales y sociales de sus ancestros por considerarlos fuera de foco con su propia realidad. Sobre este punto, Manuel Martín-Rodríguez opina que la mayoría de los grupos minoritarios residentes en los Estados Unidos reniegan de los mitos, tradiciones y creencias de su colectividad porque sufren el estigma de su raza ante la postura crítica de la cultura hegemónica. Suárez-Orozco considera que la brecha cultural causa una ruptura en la familia, dado que los hijos se acde también más rápidamente que los padres, y ésto provoca conflictos a todo nivel. En este debate, los padres acusan a los hijos de haberse americanizado demasiado, mientras que los hijos acusan a sus padres de ser demasiado mexicanos. "All too often, a pattern emerges whereby Hispanic immigrants parents become 'frozen in time' rigidifying some world-view and value orientations" (143). No obstante, psicólogos como Buriel aseguran que:

> Individuals who are closely aligned with their traditional culture
> are aware of the many rewarding and constructive elements of
> their culture and use these as a frame of reference to guide their

thinking and behavior. As a result, these individuals do not readily succumb to damaging stereotypes, which they know from their own personal experiencies to be unsubstantiated, and false. (126)

Durante años, el campo de la sociología ha examinado las deficiencias culturales de la herencia mexicana concluyendo que, al contrario de lo asumido generalmente, las familias chicanas que mantienen sus tradiciones culturales reflejan con frecuencia gran capacidad de adaptación a los constantes cambios socio-económicos. "What were once labeled culturally deficient family patterns may now be viewed as family strategies that serve as solutions to constraints imposed by economic and social structures in the wider society" (Baca Zinn 166). La sociología y psicología contemporánea han demostrado también que, contrario a la creencia popular, el sistema de familia chicana no es netamente patricarcal, sino que se basa en la distribución equitativa de las responsabilidades de cada uno de los géneros. A partir de la década de los 90, se ha concluido que el machismo hispano no es más que un estereotipo racista y no un indicador del todo válido para calificar a una cultura y su gente. "Marital role relationships in Mexican-origin families are neither male dominated nor egalitarian, but like families in general, they reveal a range of patterns between these opposing models" (Baca Zinn 169). Dentro del núcleo familiar y, tal como lo proyectan estas tres películas, las mujeres trabajan a la par de los hombres y simultáneamente son las encargadas de transmitir y mantener las tradiciones culturales que fundamentan y perpetúan la cosmovisión del grupo. En la opinión de Mirandé y Enríquez:

> As the center of the family and mainstay of the culture and tradition, the Chicana has helped counter the insidious and pervasive encroachment of colonial institutions. The Chicano family has proved remarkably resilient and impervious to external forces, and the preservation of cultural values and language are a tribute to her at its center. (116)

Tal como percibe Paz y se manifiesta en estas obras, las mujeres mexicanas son un símbolo que representa la estabilidad y continuidad de la raza. A su significación cósmica, según evalúa Paz, se amalgama la significación social como agente ejecutor de la ley y el orden en la vida diaria, aunque jamás se olvida de conservar su piedad y dulzura (34). Como sabia mediadora entre los espíritus ancestrales y el acelerado paso la sociedad contemporánea, la imagen de la mujer-madre constituye el núcleo del ámbito familiar. Tanto en *Tierra* como en *My Family*, la figura materna no parece ser una persona de carne y hueso, sino una figura mítica que nunca se cansa y nunca se queja. En realidad, debemos tener en cuenta que estas películas se basan en la narración de los hijos varones, quienes perciben a sus madres como sufridas víctimas del medio social o familiar. En la apreciación de Alvarez Jr., a pesar de que existen diferentes niveles de autoritarianismo masculino:

> for the most part, women are strong contributors to decision making and often the internal authority figures in the family [...] In fact, one of the greatest of changes in the Hispanic family in the United States is in the woman's role. However, family ideology continues to be verbally expressed as a value and cultural norm, often in contradiction to actual family behavior. (149)

Las nuevas generaciones de Chicanas, tal como se ven representadas en los personajes de Irene y Toni, distan de ser figuras vulnerables y estoicas dado que al interactuar con el resto de la sociedad norteamericana, las mujeres han comenzado a modificar sus roles de género dentro y fuera del seno familiar. Irene Blea expone que: "As Chicanas interact with more dominant Americans, they learn and even internalize Anglo values, language norms, and roles. Social institutions promote this internalization of Anglo values at the same time that Chicano values are deemed unworthy, unscientific, old-fashioned, or impractical" (91). Las familias chicanas contemporáneas y, en particular, aquellas familias que llevan dos o más generaciones en los Estados Unidos, se adaptan gradualmente a formar parte de un sistema bicultural, pero lo que sí se perpetúa inalterablemente es el concepto fundamental de la ideología familiar:

> Family ideology among Hispanics sets the ideal and standards to which individuals aim; it is the guiding light to which all look and attempt to shape their behavior for themselves as well as for the perceptioin others have of them. For Hispanics, the ideal of family is that is the central and most important institution in life. It holds all individuals together and all individuals should put family before their own concerns. It is the means of social and cultural existence. Ideology also defines the ideal roles and behaviors of family members. (Alvarez Jr. 149)

En contraposición a las figuras femeninas, los largometrajes presentan dos tipos de personajes masculinos, aquellos quienes se ajustan a la dinámica afectiva del núcleo familiar o aquellos, como Chucho y Jimmy, quienes reniegan de éste, ya sea por resentimiento, estoicismo o simplemente por temor a aceptar su vulnerabilidad dentro de una cultura machista. Es interesante destacar que estas tres producciones se ocupan de desmitificar el concepto de que en la casa, 'el hombre es el que manda', corroborando con ello que las decisiones a nivel familiar son efectuadas en conjunto y que "although the Chicano family is ostensibly patriarchal, it is in fact mother-centered. The Chicano family has proved remarkable resilient and impervious to external forces, and the preservation of cultural values and language are a tribute to her at its center" (Mirandé y Enríquez 117). El proceso de aculturación ha modificado el comportamiento del hombre al igual que la mujer chicana y, como explica Blea, "As Chicano men have internalized more Anglo male values, their sexism manifests itself in numerous ways. Society has denied Chicano males its symbols of human worth: power, money and control of resources. The need for power forces the Chicano to exert power where he can" (94). Como se ha visto en estas obras, parte del proceso de crecimiento y madurez radica en el cuestionamiento de los valores heredados por parte de los hijos durante el momento de transcición de la pubertad a la adultez. Cuando esa transición llega satisfactoriamente a su fin, el joven narrador en *Tierra* y Jimmy en *My Family* no sólo reconocen e incorporan la sapiencia de la voz colectiva dentro de su cosmovisión personal, sino que además perciben la necesidad de mantener vivas las tradiciones culturales para traspasarlas tanto a sus hijos como al resto de la colectividad y la sociedad. Los jóvenes protagonistas en cada uno de estas producciones, al llegar a la madurez, han aprendido a valorarse a sí mismos en el reflejo de sus pares y han aprendido que ellos son parte de un eslabón cultural y social que no debe romperse aun dentro de los márgenes territoriales de otras fronteras. Pero, Chucho en *My Family* y los hermanos en *El Norte* optan por sacrificar su identidad personal y colectiva en pos del 'sueño americano', sufriendo un shock cultural que los aliena psicológicamente y que los distancia aún más de sus raíces originales. Desarraigados de sus tradiciones, víctimas de un profundo sentimiento de orfandad, estos jóvenes sufren lo que Armando Epple llama 'el exilio interno' (338), una crisis existencial sobre su identidad cultural y social que finalmente los lleva a la alienación total de sí mismos y del medio que los rodea.

Tomando como punto de referencia las relaciones entre un individuo con su núcleo familiar y social, las producciones aquí analizadas nos trasmiten un claro mensaje: la identidad personal del chicano se encuentra en estrecha relación con los miembros de su familia y su comunidad. Ambos sistemas proveen la estabilidad emocional que demanda el individuo para alcanzar la madurez psicológica y social necesaria para adaptarse a la constante simbiosis cultural. Al respecto, Gómez evalúa, "Despite my sense of failure or perhaps because of it, I became more aware of my strengths; more aware of the identity I had been born with and which I had rejected from the moment I had been brainwashed and conditioned by Anglo-society into thinking that white is good and brown and black are bad" (5). Durante las dos últimas décadas, las familias de ascendencia mexicana están enfrentando los mismos conflictos y las mismas etapas transicionales que las familias norteamericanas. Sin embargo, y a pesar de los constantes cambios sociales, la cultura Chicana aún se mantiene como un sólido grupo étnico, aun cuando ha perdido el contacto con las raíces mexicanas y dominio del lenguaje español. En este punto, cabe acotar que la religión católica, los mitos y las tradiciones culturales continúan perpetúandose como lazo unificador que extiende la solidaridad entre familias y facilita el proceso de autoidentificación comunal. Dentro del tapiz social de la cultura mejicano-americana, el concepto de Raza o Chicanismo sirve también de pivote unificador para la comunidad, por cuanto abraza e incluye a varios grupos sociales y étnicos que de otra manera quedarían completamente marginados. Juan Bruce-Novoa confirma que a los chicanos, a partir de los 60, ya no les interesa pertenecer a un segmento cultural determinado, dado que se reconocen como una cultura híbrida producto de las cultura hispánica, indígena, mestiza y norteamericana. Autodefinéndose como un organismo en expansión con la capacidad de absorber, discriminar, rechazar y retener las porciones favorables o aceptables de todas estas culturas sin tener que limitarse, los chicanos ofrecen una síntesis entre el centro y la periferia con tremendo potencial de desarrollar nuevas y trascendentes formaciones sociales (59-60).

En estas representaciones cinematográficas, ni la familia y ni la comunidad son idealizadas; por el contrario, los conflictos y la realidad socio-política de los individuos que conforman estas colectividades se reflejan con claridad y sin embellezamientos romanticistas. Lo que percibimos como críticos y/o espectadores es la consistente percepción interna y reflección externa por parte de artistas y escritores de la gran influencia que ejerce la colectividad y el núcleo familiar en la vida del individuo. La dinámica que se traduce en cada una de estas producciones tal vez no cambia pero, sin duda, amplía la cosmovisión de los espectadores con respecto al viaje existencial, los ritos de iniciación, los logros y los dramas de los inmigrantes y los chicanos en particular. Tal como evalúa Baca Zinn, el estudio de las familias minoritarias puede contribuir enormemente en el campo de la sociología en lo que se refiere al proceso de adaptación cultural:

> These are truly extraordinary times for family study. Accelerated social changes that are affecting families in all racial categories are creating widespread variation in "the American family." [...] Contemporary family studies have taken insufficient account of the Mexican experience. Mainstream scholarship has not questined how the study of minority families can generate insights for family dynamics in general. Mexican-origin families can teach us much about the interplay between families and society, about how people with severely constrained options and choices, nevertheless forge family lives that are suited to their own needs and lifestyles. (171)

En definitiva y tal como se ha mencionado al principio de este ensayo, el metadiscurso de la literatura y el arte chicano es el de enfatizar la relevancia de la raza y de las tradiciones culturales heredadas. En este sentido, cada una de estas producciones refleja la intención de los escritores, productores y artistas de sentar un vivo testimonio sobre las experiencias de vida de las sucesivas generaciones de inmigrantes y sus dificultades de adaptación a la cultura norteamericana. Simultáneamente, el cine chicano no sólo busca lograr un mayor reconocimiento dentro del contexto de la cultura anglo-parlante, sino que también se interesa por despertar un sentimiento de conciencia nacional entre las diversas colectividades de ascendencia mexicana con el fin de lograr su mutuo reconocimiento y aceptación. Dada la oralidad de la cultura indígena, el alto nivel de analfabetismo y los escasos medios económicos de estas colectividades, la cinematografía y el arte documental son quizás los medios más efectivos para captar la historia, el lenguaje y las tradiciones culturales de estos grupos minoritarios en constante transformación. Estos tres largometrajes de gran sensibilidad y fuerte mensaje político son un fiel legado que nos alcanza las voces y las experiencias de una riquísima comunidad en constante crecimiento. Sin duda, y a pesar de los impedimentos socio-económicos, el movimiento cinematográfico chicano hoy en día se ubica a la vanguardia del medio explorando nuevas y más efectivas formas de expresión de esta multifacética cultura.

Obras Citadas

Alicea, Marisa. "The Latino Inmigration Experience: The Case of Mexicanos, Puertorriqueños and Cubanos." *Handbook of Hispanic Cultures in the United States.* Ed. Félix Padilla et al. Vol. 3. Houston: Arte Público P, 1994. 35-55.

Alvarez, Jr. Robert R. "Changing Patterns of Family and Ideology among Latino Cultures in the United States." *Handbook of Hispanic Cultures in the United States.* Ed. Thomas Weaver et al. Vol. 4. Houston: Arte Público P, 1994. 147-67.

Anaya, Rudolfo A. "Aztlan: A Homeland Without Boundaries." *Aztlan:Essays on the Chicano Homeland.* Eds. Rudolfo Anaya and Francisco Lomelí. Albuquerque: U. of New Mexico P, 1991. 230-71.

Baca Zinn, Maxine. "Mexican-Heritage Families in the United States." *Handbook of Hispanic Cultures in the United States.* Ed. Félix Padilla et al. Vol. 3. Houston: Arte Público P, 1994. 161-172.

Blea, Irene I. *La Chicana and the Intersection of Race, class, and Gender.* New York: Praeger, 1992.

Bruce-Novoa, Juan. *Chicano Authors: Inquiry by Interview.* Austin: U of Texas P, 1980.

---, ed. "Chicanos in Mexican Literature." *Missions in Conflict: Essays on U.S.-Mexican Relations and Chicano Culture.* Tubingen: Gunter Narr Verlag Tubingen, 1986. 54-64.

Buriel, Raymond. "Traditional Culture Integration and Adjustment." *Chicano Psychology.* Orlando: Academic P, 1984.

Ebert, Roger. "El Norte" *Cinemania 95.* CD-ROM. Microsoft Corporation. 1994.

Epple, Juan A. "Hispanic Exile in the United States." *Handbook of Hispanic Cultures in the United States.* Ed. Francisco Lomelí et al. Vol. 1. Houston: Arte Público P, 1994. 333-359.

Fredericksen, Brooke. "Cuando lleguemos/When we arrive: The Paradox of Migration in Tomás Rivera's "... Y no se lo tragó la tierra." *The Bilingual Review. La Revista bilingue* 19 (1994): 142-150.

Gómez, David F. *Somos Chicanos: Strangers in Our Own Land.* Boston, M.A.: Beacon P, 1973.

González, César. "Archetypes of Integration in Chicano Literature: Tomás Rivera's *Tierra*". *Confluencia* 5 (1989): 85-90.

Heller, Mary. "Mexican American Youth." *The Forgotten at the Crossroads.* New York: Random House, 1966.

Karrer, Betty. "Families of Mexican Descent: A Contextual Approach." *Family and Medicine.* Ed. R.B. Birrer. New York: Springer-Verlaag, 1987. 228-32.

Lomelí, Francisco A. y Urioste, Donaldo W. *Chicano Perspectives in Literature.* Albuquerque, N.M.: Pajarito Publications, 1976.

Maciel, David. "Latino Cinema." *Handbook of Hispanic Cultures in the United States.* Ed. Félix Padilla et al. Vol. 1. Houston: Arte Público P, 1993. 312-322.

Martín-Rodriguez, Manuel. "El tema de la culpa en cuatro novelistas chicanos." *Hispanic Journal* 10 (1988):133-142.

----. "Aesthetic Concepts of Hispanics in the United States." *Handbook of Hispanic Cultures in the United States.* Ed. Francisco Lomelí et al. Vol. 1. Houston: Arte Público P, 1994. 109-32.

Martínez, Joe L. Jr. y Mendoza, Richard H. eds. *Chicano Psychology.* Orlando: Academic P, 1984.

Mindel, Charles H. "Extended Families among Urban Mexican-Americans, Anglos and Blacks." *Hispanic Journal of Behavioral Sciences* 2 (1980). 21-34.

Mirandé, Alfredo y Enríquez, Evangelina. *La Chicana : The Mexian-American Woman.* Chicago: The University of Chicago P, 1979.

Montoya, José. "Chicano Art: Resistance in Isolation 'Aquí estamos y no nos vamos.'" *Missions in Conflict: Essays on U.S.-Mexican Relations and Chicano Culture.* Tubingen: Gunter Narr Verlag Tubingen, 1986. 25-30.

Olivares, Julián. "The Search for Being, Identity and Form in the Work of Tomás Rivera." *Revista Chicano – Riqueña* 13 (1985): 66-80.

--- Ed. *Tomás Rivera: The Complete Works.* Houston: Arte Público P, 1992.

Paz, Octavio. *El laberinto de la soledad.* México: Fondo de Cultura Económica, 1986.

Rivera, Tomás. *...y no se lo tragó la tierra/... And the Earth Did Not Devour Him.* Houston: Arte Público P, 1992.

Rocard, Marcienne. "The Chicano: A Minority in Search of a Proper Literary Medium for Self- Affirmation." *Missions in Conflict: Essays on U.S.-Mexican Relations and Chicano Culture.* Tubingen: Gunter Narr Verlag Tubingen, 1986. 31-40.

Rodríguez, Joe D. "God's Silence and The Shrill of Ethnicity in the Chicano Novel." *Explorations in Ethnic Studies* 4 (1981): 14-25.

Rulfo, Juan. *El llano en llamas.* México: Fondo de Cultura Económica, 1955.

Saldívar, José D. "The Ideological and the Utopian in Tomás Rivera's ... *y no se lo tragó la tierra* and Ron Arias' *The Road to Tamazunchale.*" *Tomás Rivera: The Complete Works.* Ed. Julián Olivares. Houston: Arte Público P, 1992. 203-214.

Stevens, Donald F. Ed. *Based on a True Story : Latin American History at the Movies.* Wilmington-DE: Scholarly Resources, 1997.

Suárez-Orozco, Carola y Suárez-Orozco, Marcelo. "The Cultural Psychology of Hispanic Immigrants." *Handbook of Hispanic Cultures in the United States.* Ed. Thomas Weaver et al. Vol. 4. Houston: Arte Público P, 1994. 129-46.

Treviño, Jesús S. "Chicano Cinema." *New Scholar* 8 1982. 140-48.

Weaver, Thomas. "The Culture of Latinos in the United States." *Handbook of Hispanic Cultures in the United States*. Ed. Thomas Weaver et al. Vol. 4. Houston: Arte Público P, 1994. 15-58.

7

Celestino antes del alba:
The Family as Agent of the Community

Dinora Cardoso

Foucault states, "[Sexuality is] an especially dense transfer point for relations of power: between men and women, young people and old people, parents and offspring, teachers and students, priests and laity, administration and a population" (103). The struggle around power and sexuality is particularly evident in the domain of the traditional family system. The Cuban family of the thirties and forties still followed principles set by the Spanish Civil Code. The Code's two primary principles were the absolute authority of the head of the house and the husband's property rights. The wife could only dispose of or manage her own property with the consent of the husband. In addition, a double standard of morality allowed men to carry on discreet, adulterous relationships as long as they did not cause a scandal, while the wife was barred from such behavior. The behavior of women was controlled through the family structure and dynamics as well as through legal means. Even children did not escape the arbitrary nature of society. The legitimacy of children empowered them while the "illegitimate" or "natural" children were discarded and/or stripped of their birthrights. Reinaldo Arenas' *Celestino antes del alba* exposes the type of hierarchy based on gender and sexual preference that has been established by Cuban society and is taught within the home. In the novel the unconventional behavior of women and homosexuals is castigated not by society at large, but rather by a dictatorial and patriarchal male figure who, in a sense, simply perpetuates the prevalent family patterns.

Sexual activity has, traditionally, been one area that is used to repress people's individual power by restricting their choices and channeling sexual energy into specific, society-endorsed actions--like marriage and, through it, monogamy. When women began to explore the other sexual possibilities that existed, a long-standing and pejorative terminology surfaced to describe the woman's sexual freedom. The use of words such as *whore* or *prostitute* became a method of restricting behavior by placing derogatory connotations on any departure from the norms set by patriarchal society.[1] In this way the dominant discourse stabilized the status quo in society and family. On the other hand, it is by codifying, writing, and leaving a historical account of the alternate experiences, in the language of the oppressor, that some modification of the system has been made. Foucault discusses this dilemma: "discourse can be both an instrument and an effect of power, but also a hindrance, stumbling-block, a point of resistance and a starting point for an opposing strategy" (101).

The purpose of feminist theory has been, above all, to expose and resist the sexual inequities that have been built into the social order. Arenas did not experience, first-hand, the life of Cuban women, but he was a witness to his mother's and his aunts' perception of the world. As an illegitimate child, he must have been aware of the problems that his mother's flagrant sexuality brought for both of them. Octavio Paz writes of the stigma associated with female sexuality in Latin America in his essay regarding the birth of the Mexican nation in *El laberinto de la soledad*. Malintzin's (a. k. a. Doña Marina, La Malinche) betrayal of the tribes that had mistreated her symbolized the illegitimate birth of the Mexican nation. The sexual domination of Malintzin by Hernán Cortez, symbolic of the Spanish conquest of the Indians, has other implications: Malinche, later referred to as *la chingada* (the violated) by Paz, did not have control over her own sexuality. Instead, she is perceived as having been raped. It seems to be more palatable to view the woman as a victim than as a real source of power, and more specifically, sexual power. Patriarchal society, in the past, chose to disregard a woman's control over her own body; therefore, the only acceptable alternative was for the illegitimate birth to come from a rape rather than from a woman's choice to exercise her sexuality.

While women have long been denied control over their sexuality, the issue of control over one's own body is one which male homosexuals also face. The stigma that has been associated with a sexually liberated woman in the past sometimes is applied to gay males. As Tomás Almaguer points out, "it may be noted that the Spanish feminine word *puta* refers to a female prostitute while its male form *puto* refers to a passive homosexual, not a male prostitute. It is significant that the cultural equation made between the feminine, anal-receptive homosexual man and the most culturally stigmatized female in Mexican society (the whore) share a common semantic base" (260). Freedom to govern one's own body is the common goal of the two groups. Each group searches for its autonomy from a society that imposes a sexual behavior without giving the individual a choice.

Despite the strength and activism of many Latina women, the radical feminist agenda engenders fear and distrust in Latin American society. For example, Mexican women shy away from self-applying the feminist label in fear of being perceived as lesbian. Debra Castillo has pointed out that "This misreading of feminist activism as a specific preference for same-sex relations is, I submit, only the first and least crucial of the critical misprisions. More importantly, the lesbian, or perceived lesbian, falls into the category of women exempt from the respect mandated for decent women" (22). Because there is a tendency to equate homosexuality with an immoral act, sexual discrimination has been endured not just by women but also by homosexuals (male and female) in society. And as Castillo points out, homosexuality is farther down the hierarchy of socially acceptable behavior.

Although Cuban women are not as likely to shy away from the feminist label as their Mexican counterparts, and they have achieved a great deal in terms of women's rights in the past forty years, they are still expected to put the needs of family and the nation ahead of their own personal desires. Moreover, the Revolution has not been as concerned with individual rights as with social and material rights. The treatment of homosexuals is "conditioned by the machismo that has pervaded Cuban culture for generations and that the present government has not done enough to challenge" (Lumsden 27). In this novel, which takes place before the Revolution, Arenas offers a look into alternate sexualities and voices the inequalities suffered by those deviating from what the patriarchy considers the norm. In *Celestino antes del alba*, the family becomes one source of education as to the standards set by the community.

Within a very dysfunctional family setting, *Celestino* demonstrates the subservient role of the woman and, because of their emerging homosexuality, of the children. The free expression of women's sexuality leads to their communal degradation, and keeping them powerless, both economically and socially, reinforces the repression of their sexuality. The children, usually powerless entities in most societies, further endanger their position by exhibiting an unconventional femininity; therefore, both children, Celestino and his cousin, are punished in hopes of rectifying what the community believes to be aberrant behavior.

The nameless narrator and his cousin, Celestino, have been identified in a study by Perla Rozencvaig to be doubles[2]. Both boys suffer the same fate in their sexual journey, which would lead us to confirm Rozencvaig's theory. The first two sexual references are inexorably linked with the creative act of writing,

> Esta casa siempre ha sido un infierno. . . Pero cuando las cosas se pusieron malas de verdad fue cuando a Celestino le dio por hacer poesías. . .
> "Eso es mariconería", dijo mi madre cuando se enteró de la escribidera de Celestino. Y esa fue la primera vez que se tiró al pozo.
> "Antes de tener un hijo así, prefiero la muerte." Y el agua del pozo subió de nivel.
> [This house has always been hell... But things got really bad when Celestino devoted himself to writing poetry...
> "That's faggottry," my mother said when she found out about Celestino's writing. And that was the first time that she threw herself in the well.
> "Rather than having a son like that, I prefer to die." And the water level in the well rose.] (*Celestino* 15-16)

Homosexuality[3] and creativity are considered in the same pejorative light by the mother who, although also a victim, represents the machista, patriarchal structure present in this rural community. The family's tendency to behave as a unit has been called "family homeostasis," and according to Virginia Satir, whenever one family member tries to break the patterns established, the others "exert much effort to maintain it" (2). The mother's severe disapproval of the writing and homosexuality is revealed, not only through her words, but also by her action--throwing herself into the well. The mother becomes the first to reinforce the community's morals within the family structure, through a type of psychological blackmail. Her passive-aggressive behavior, which physically wounds her, is meant to wound and control her son psychologically while preserving her role as the self-sacrificing mother. Interestingly, the narrator goes to the well and drinks from it, comparing himself to a bird, *pájaro*. Of course, one connotation of *pájaro* in Spanish is homosexual, so her tactic does not have the effect desired, and the boy (or boys, if they are doubles) continues to write poetry on the tree trunks. The fact that the writing takes place on the trees creates a space between the public areas normally associated with the community and the private space of the family home. This space is symbolic of the links between our private lives and our public persona. The first encounter that the child narrator has with sexuality in the community is at school. When he and Celestino are sent to school, the poetic writing that Celestino has done on the surface of the tree trunks in his grandfather's farm has already earned him the title of *mariquita*. The other boys scorn them and smear them with excrement. It is unclear whether the other boys are also forcing them to have sexual intercourse or whether they are urinating on them:

> --¡Maten al sijú platanero!. . .
> --¡Llora como una mujer!
> --¡El hijo de la lagartija está llorando como una mujer!
> --Es de la misma calaña que Celestino: ¡pantalones por fuera, pero sayas por dentro!
>
> --¡Es el primo de Celestino!. . .
> --¡El primo de Celestino el loco! ¡El primo de Celestino, el que escribe poesías en los troncos de las matas!. . .
> --¡Los dos son mariquitas!
> --¡Mariquitas! ¡Mariquitas!
> . . .
> --¡Ciérrense las portañuelas!. . .
> [--Kill the gnome owl!...
> --He cries like a woman!
> --That son of a rascal[4] is crying like a woman!
> --He is the same type as Celestino: pants on the outside and skirts on the inside!
>
> --He's Celestino's cousin!...
> --He's crazy Celestino's cousin! Celestino's cousin, the one who writes poetry on the tree trunks!...
> --The two of them are fags!
> --Fags! Fags!
> . . .
> --Close your flies!] (*Celestino* 32-33)

Whether they are forced to have intercourse or are merely being punished for being artistic and, therefore, different from the traditional masculine image, the two boys suffer verbal and physical abuse. In this case, the dominant discourse of scorn and shame is offered as a concrete punishment. From the start, Celestino is involved in a feminized and therefore marginalized writing, an activity equated with homosexuality, an effeminate, and therefore negative, activity. Here, the production of poetry is physically punished; neither Celestino nor the narrator is allowed to control his own body or his choice of vocation. The schoolboys act as agents of the community, reinforcing the mother's sanctions. The schoolboys' violence is directed explicitly and the mother's violence implicitly at Celestino and his cousin.

This pattern of violence is repeated within the family as a reflection of its role as an agent of the community. The grandfather beats and berates Celestino for the same reason that the boys suffered the derision of the schoolboys: the poetry that Celestino must express. However, the lexicon that the grandfather uses to refer to him becomes an obsession for the narrator. His grandfather describes an unacceptable expression of sexuality that the boy doesn't know how to interpret.

> . . . sé que él me la tiene desde el día en que abuelo me
> levantó por el cuello y me dijo: "Hijo de puta y de matojo: aquí
> tú comes porque yo quiero. Así que ve a buscar los terneros si
> no quieres que te saque a ti y a tu madre a patadas de esta casa."
> ... Lo de puta no me importa porque lo sé. Pero eso de "matojo".
> ¿Qué querrá decir eso de "matojo"?
> [...I know that he has had it in for me ever since the day
> that grandfather lifted me by the neck and said: "Son of a bitch
> and of a bush: here, you eat because I will it. So go look for
> those calves unless you want me to literally kick you and your
> mother out of this house. ... The stuff about bitch, that I don't
> care about because I know. But that "bush." I wonder what he
> means with that "bush" thing.] (*Celestino* 35)[5]

By censuring the mother and including the boy, the grandfather begins to teach both Celestino and the nameless grandchild about the power of words and the hierarchy that exists within this family. As Satir explains, both the sender and the receiver of the messages must fulfill certain roles, if clear and understandable communication is to occur. Both the adult and the child fail to execute their parts: the first by not being clear, and the second by failing to ask for clarification. Of course, Celestino's inability to transmit or receive information simply reflects that he has learned well the family's prohibition of transparent communication. Curiously enough, it is the power of the words that Celestino uses in his poetry that the grandfather himself fears. The character that becomes the dictator of the family is afraid of Celestino's written discourse because, just as he has used language as a weapon with the children, language can be turned against him. This fear of language is reflected not just in the lives of the children. The community, with its silences and discourse, can control the whole family--which is an extension of the grandfather--; consequently, the lesson learned in the family is only practice for what will take place within the larger community.

The mother's sexual indiscretion has been censured by the community, "Aunque a mamá no la saludaban desde mucho antes; desde que mi padre (que yo no sé ni quién es) la trajo un día. . . Desde entonces nadie en todo el barrio le da ni los buenos días a mi madre, pues ellos dicen que cuando un hombre bota a una mujer es porque ésta hizo algo malo" [Although they didn't greet mom since way before that; since my father (I don't know who he is) brought her back one day... Since that day no one in the whole neighborhood even says good day to my mother, well they say that when a man dumps a woman is because she did something wrong] (*Celestino* 75). The "popular wisdom" of the community automatically blames the woman for the failure of the union. Consequently, through words or silences, the community can pressure its members to act according to the established code. As this type of censorship is applied, the discipline acts as a lesson to others about the consequences of straying from the expected behavior. As the community shuns her, the woman's dependence on the grandfather becomes greater, thereby reinforcing the family's hierarchy and creating a circle of power that is not easily broken by the errant individual, again maintaining the family homeostasis and the community norms.

The *machismo* that this segment of Cuban society exhibits is reflected in the role of the grandfather. His power over all the women and children in the family can be observed throughout the novel. For example, the aunts were restricted by the grandfather if they were single or abandoned by their husbands. Moreover, all of the women in this novel have been subjected to the will of the men around them in some form or another. In this case, the grandfather reinforces the societal norms that had already been applied.

The sexual histories of both Eulogia and Carmelina, the narrator's cousin and Celestino's mother respectively, are woven into the plot as a testimony to the fate of women. Interestingly, although they were mistreated and subjugated, each found an escape from the family and community that denied them a basic right to control their own fates and bodies. Eulogia's story can be read as one of incest:

Pobre Eulogia. . . Cuando salió para el monte yo vi que
iba llorando. . . Si ella no fuera tan boba como es no hubiera
dejado que abuelo se le encaramase encima, como lo hizo. Pero
es la esclava de esta casa y todo el mundo se le encarama
encima. Y hacen de ella lo que les da la gana. Hasta yo una
tarde tumbé a Eulogia detrás del guaninal y me le encaramé
arriba. Ella no dijo ni pizca de palabra. . .

[Poor Eulogia... When she left to go to the mountain, I
saw that she was crying... If she were not as foolish as she is,
she wouldn't have allowed grandfather to climb on top of her, as
she did. But she is the slave of this house and everybody climbs
on top of her. And they do with her whatever they want. Even I
knocked down Eulogia, behind the palm tree thicket and got on
top of her. She didn't say a word...] (*Celestino* 23)

The woman must run away from home in order to escape the
injustices that she suffers at the hands of all of the members of the
household. Being single does not exempt her from a man's domination.
Instead it subjects her to her father's wishes for a longer period of time:
the result is incest. Eulogia is not allowed to reject or denounce the
sexual advances by the grandfather; this injustice highlights and
parallels what a woman's relationships with her husband would be. The
community teaches women to bear their burdens in silence, unless they
want to be ridiculed.

On the other hand, Carmelina's story is one of rape and possibly
domestic violence. The parallel between her story and Eulogia's is
drawn when she leaves her father's home and is subject to the will of
her husband. Carmelina is, in effect, modeling her mother's role in her
parents' marriage and may be perpetuating transgenerational family
patterns. One character informs us of her fate:

--A Carmelina la volvió a dejar el marido y se pegó
candela. ¡Ay, pobre de mi hermana! Que en paz descanse.
Todos los hombres abusaron de ella. Cuando íbamos a la feria
la arrinconaba para lo oscuro, y ya. . .

. . . Al menos eso fue lo que me dijo el que trajo la
noticia del ahorcamiento de Carmelina, porque no solamente se
dio candela, sino que cuando estaba ya con la soga al cuello,
cogió una botella de alcohol y se lo roció. ¡La pobre! No me
explico cómo es posible que una persona se ahorque y se dé
candela al mismo tiempo. . . Eso sí que está raro. ¿No sería
que alguien después que ella se ahorcó le pegó candela por hacer
la maldad?. . .

[Once again Carmelina's husband left her and she set
herself on fire. Oh, my poor sister! May she rest in peace. All
the men took advantage of her. When we would to go to the
festivals, they would corner her in the dark, and that was it...
... At least that was what the guy who brought the news
of Carmelina's hanging told me, because not only did she set
herself on fire but rather when she already had the rope around
her neck, she took a bottle of alcohol and doused herself with it.
Poor woman! I can't explain how it's possible for a person to
hang herself and set herself on fire at the same time... That's
very strange. I wonder if someone, after she hung herself, didn't
set her on fire out of spite.] (*Celestino* 42-43)

The narrator's confusion (or facetiousness) exemplifies the self-
censorship established within the family and community. Physical
impossibility is easier to explain away than any logical sequence of
events that would be incongruent with or threaten the family fiction.
Perhaps the answer sought by this character lies with Carmelina's
husband, who could have been responsible for her death. The readers
never know why she was mistreated, just that she was. Wife abuse is
recurrent throughout this novel. Not only are the women subjected to
the restrictions imposed by words but also by physical abuse, just as
Celestino and his cousin were.

Shortly after this passage, the narrator's mother also confesses
that she has thought about suicide but has not had the courage to do it.
In other words, she too has seen death as an escape from the abuse
suffered within the family. However, even the women themselves
reinforce the restrictions of society and family and attempt to impose
them on each other: "¡Yo no le veo ningún mérito [al suicidio de
Carmelina]! Lo que merece es que la desenterremos y le digamos
'cabrona, cómo te atreves a matarte si tienes un hijo' [I don't see any
merit (in Carmelina's suicide)! What she deserves is that we dig her up
and say 'Bugger, how dare you kill yourself if you have a son']"
(*Celestino* 47). According to the doctrine of the Catholic Church,
suicide is an unpardonable sin, but the mores implied by these women
take on a more practical character. The child is the woman's
responsibility, not the father's; therefore, it is her duty to suffer in order
to give the child adequate care. Sacrificing for the sake of others has
been one lesson taught verbally and through example to women by
patriarchal society but, more specifically, by other women in their
families. Again, the woman's life is not her own, but rather it belongs
to those around her, for whom she must sacrifice. The mores of
society, reflected in the family, rob the women's right to safety and to

control their own bodies. The two boys' role models are the grandfather, who abuses his power, and these women who suffer injustices, sometimes silently.

Another example of *machismo* in this Cuban community is the relationship between the grandfather and grandmother. Although this marriage is not analyzed from a sexual point of view, the connection and subjugation is based on the biological sex of the two people involved. The grandmother suffers abuses at the hand of her husband and responds in a passive-aggressive manner:

> . . . Y por llevarle la contraria a abuela (ya que a él no le importan las matas y le da lo mismo que en el corredor haya una de tulipán o una de guao), le dijo: "Cuidado con tocar una de esas matas". Y por ahí empezó la bronca. Y desde entonces abuela le ha cogido un odio a las matas del corredor que no las puede ver. Y un día yo vi cómo ella le echaba agua hirviendo al tronco de los tulipanes para que se secaran. Entonces yo fui corriendo y se lo dije al abuelo; y él la cogió por el moño y la llevó hasta el fogón, y agarrándole las dos manos, se las zambulló entre el agua que borbotoneaba en la olla. Abuela se quejó con un resoplido fuerte, como una vaca cuando le dan una pedrada en el pecho. Pero no volvió a echarles agua hirviendo a las matas del corredor.
>
> [... And just to be adversarial (because he didn't care about the plants and it's all the same to him if there are tulips or guao trees in the hallway), he said: "Careful not to touch any of those plants." And that's when the quarrel began. And since then grandmother has taken to hating the plants in the hallway, so much so that she can't even look at them. And one day I saw her putting boiling water on the tulip stalks so that they would dry up. Then, I went running and told grandfather; and he took her by her hair bun and dragged her to the stove, and grabbing both of her hands, he plunged them into the water bubbling in the pot. Grandmother complained with a strong snort, like a cow when it's hit in the chest with a stone. But she didn't water the hallway plants with boiling water again.] (*Celestino* 28)

The narrator's nonchalant description of this spiteful and violent episode illuminates the depravity and emotional cutoff fostered in the family sphere. In a classic example of triangulation, the family members conspire against one another, building brief, intergenerational alliances, but the ultimate authority is the grandfather. Just like everyone else, the grandmother must conform to the desires of the man of the house. The hierarchy represented in the family conforms to that of the community.

The grandmother has little influence over economic decisions, although she, along with the other women and children, is forced to work in the fields:

> Ya sé por qué abuela no quiere que la ayude: ella no está limpiando nada, sino que lo que hace es arrancar las matas de maíz. Sí, ya me he dado cuenta del truco; abuela coge y arranca la mata, trozándola por el tallo, y luego hace como si la sembrara de nuevo. La mata se queda muy parada y cualquiera diría que está bien sembrada, pero por debajo está trozada y en cuanto le den dos o tres soles se seca. . .
> [I know why grandmother doesn't want me to help her: she is not weeding anything, but what she is doing is pulling the corn stalks. Yeah, I figured out her trick; grandmother takes and pulls the plant, breaking it, and later makes as if she were replanting it. The plant stands very straight and anyone would assume that it's planted correctly, but underneath it's broken and as soon as it's been in the sun a few times it dries up...]
> (*Celestino* 51)

However, indirect vengeance and attempts at control are an ingrained part of the family pattern.

> . . . todavía le tiene un poco de respeto al viejo. Y es que cuando él se pone furioso no cree ni en la madre que lo parió. Ayer mismo cuando fuimos a tomar café con leche se ardió los labios, pues abuela (y yo creo que lo hizo adrede) se lo dio que echaba chispas; entonces él cogió el jarro de café con leche hirviendo y se lo hizo tragar a la abuela, así, encendido, y sin parar.
> [... she still has some respect left for the old man. And it's because when he gets furious he doesn't even believe in the mother who bore him. Just yesterday when we went to have some coffee with milk, he burned his lips because grandmother (and I think she did it on purpose) gave it to him too hot; then he took the pitcher of boiling coffee and made grandmother swallow it down without stopping, just like that, burning.]
> (*Celestino* 48)

The grandfather's overt action, which shows the inequity of the relationship between him and his wife, produces a covert reaction that subverts the efforts of the man. In other words, the passive reception of the abuse later becomes an aggressive response to the suffering.

In the midst of the violence and chaos, one character continues to mold and shape a powerful discourse that can both reflect and resist the reality. Celestino's writing points to how the family can be a prison, if the individual dares to dream outside of the narrow scope of acceptable societal behaviors. One of Celestino's creations is a play of about twenty pages, which is included in the last section of the novel. All of the characters, whether real or imagined by the child narrator, take part in this play, which documents all of the narrator's insecurities, hopes, and dreams. The stage directions give some insight:

> *(El abuelo se vuelve rápido y te mira. Tú aún estás con el cuchillo en alto. Tú vas a clavarle el cuchillo en la cara. El abuelo te sonríe. El cuchillo cae al suelo...)*
> Tú--*(Con un brazo levantado en el aire.)* Perdóname que no te haya podido salvar. Perdóname, pero cuando le iba a clavar el cuchillo en la cara, me miró, y me sonrió...
> Coro de primos muertos-- *(Siempre con el brazo en el aire.)* Me miró y me sonrió. A mí, que nunca nadie me ha sonreído.
> [(The grandfather quickly turns around and looks at you. You're still holding the knife overhead. You're going to stick the knife in his face. Grandfather smiles at you. The knife falls to the floor...)
> You: (With your arm in the air.) Forgive me because I have been unable to save you. Forgive me, but when I was about to stick the knife in his face, he looked at me, and he smiled...
> Chorus of dead cousins: (All with their arms in the air.) He looked at me, and he smiled. At me, who never has been smiled at before.] *(Celestino* 153)

The overwhelming power of the grandfather comes, not only from the violence that he can inflict, but also from the few acts of kindness that are experienced by the characters. The community also functions in this way, through a system of punishment and rewards. As with kidnapping victims or abandoned children, any demonstration of love or approval by the abuser paradoxically can provoke a strong positive identification with that individual.

The grandfather, symbolically, tries to keep Celestino and his cousin in the closet; he tries to hide the proverbial "writing on the wall" regarding the children's homosexuality by chopping down the trees on which Celestino has recorded his poems. The grandfather's hatchet, which is used to cut down the trees on which Celestino has recorded his poems, is symbolic not just of the grandfather's authority, but as Arenas explains: "en el medio campesino cubano, el hacha es el instrumento que representa la violencia por excelencia... [in the environment of the Cuban farmer, the hatchet is the premier instrument that represents violence]" (Rozencvaig 42). The hatchet is, then, spatially represented in the text, creating the image of a hatchet with the word "hacha." In an interview the author suggests that, "Su proliferación representa un poco su posibilidad de escape. Es la liberación por la violencia ya que en un medio así no existe otro medio de alcanzarla. [Its proliferation represents, a bit, the possibility of escape. It is liberation through violence since in such a medium as that there is not other method of achieving it...]" (Rozencvaig 42). The only way to escape this family is through violence, by death. The hatchet is a method used to curtail the boys' aspirations of becoming writers. These dreams are not acceptable to the grandfather as the representative of the community because of the connotation that the community itself has given to writing poetry. This sentiment is echoed in the voices of the schoolboys who assault Celestino and the narrator. Moreover, the grandfather must cleanse this symbolic place between private and public spaces in order to keep the public image of the family intact. The cleansing is ultimately effective, in that the erasure of the boys' alternative discourse removes their last site of resistance. In the third and final ending, the narrator's suicide by jumping into the well becomes the only escape for Celestino and his cousin, because the two (or one, if one subscribes to Rozencvaig's theory) cannot live within the confines of the societal and family codes.

None of the relationships that could serve as models for the two young boys were "normal" or what we would call healthy. Each interaction in the novel points out an injustice, whether it is forcing boys into sexual relationships or beating the children for their creative powers, or displaying women who are trapped in subservient roles or in incestuous relationships. The dysfunctional acts of this family take place, mostly, around the central figure, the head of the house. Violence is one method of control, but one has to question how effective it continues to be. It takes the help of the other members to maintain family homeostasis. Both the children and the women help the grandfather, the only adult male, to propagate the societal norms. Often the family is viewed as shelter from the outside world; on the other hand, in this case it becomes an agent of the community. Arena's subversive act, which is not able to be erased or chopped down, is to voice all inequalities in the family based on sex, age, or sexual preference.

NOTES

[1] In discussing sexuality, the terms *homosexual* and *gay* will be used interchangeably; both are accepted by the gay community according to Mark Lilly. There are several words that are used in a derogatory sense to refer to homosexuals, such as *maricón* (faggot), and *mariquita* (fag), that will be used in the study as part of quotations or in referring to those segments of the novels.

[2] These "doubles" are the psychological complements of one another, according to Rosencvaig. This is similar to split personalities in that the boys help each other cope in this dysfunctional setting; however, unlike split personalities the two boys are very aware of each other's existence and do not inhabit the same body.

[3] Almaguer says, "Although the stigma accompanies homosexual practices in Latin culture, it does not equally adhere to both partners. It is primarily the anal-passive individual. . . who is stigmatized for playing the subservient, feminine role" (257). The emphasis here is how both the receptive homosexual and the women are thought to be inferior to the heterosexual male.

[4] "Lagartija" has two meanings according to *Simon and Schuster's International Dictionary*: 1. wall lizard. 2. (Amer.) rogue, rascal.

[5] In Spanish, *matojo* can be taken two ways. First, a traditional Cuban meaning is the sprout of a plant that has been cut down. Second, it can be interpreted to mean scrub or weeds. Here the grandfather clearly is referring to Celestino's parentage. The mother has been discarded by her husband, brought back to the family, and is regarded as less than whole; therefore, the grandfather projects her faults onto the child.

Works Cited

Abelove, Henry, Michèle Aina Barale, and David M. Halperin, eds. *The Lesbian and Gay Studies Reader*. New York: Routledge, 1993.

Almaguer, Tomás. "Chicano Men: A Cartography of Homosexual Identity and Behavior." Abelove, Barale, and Halperin, 255-73.

Arenas, Reinaldo. *Celestino antes del alba*. Buenos Aires: Editorial Brújula, 1968.

Castillo, Debra. *Talking Back: Toward a Latin American Feminist Literary Criticism*. Ithaca: Cornell UP, 1992.

Foucault, Michel. *The History of Sexuality*. Trans. Robert Hurley. 3 vols. New York: Random House, 1980.

de Gámez, Tana. *Simon and Schuster's International Dictionary*. New York: Simon and Schuster, 1973.

Hernández Miyares, Julio E., and Perla Rozencvaig, comp. *Reinaldo Arenas: Alucinaciones, fantasía y realidad.* Glenview, IL: Scott Foresman, 1990.

Leiner, Marvin. *Sexual Politics in Cuba: Machismo, Homosexuality, and AIDS.* Boulder: Westview P, 1994.

Lilly, Mark. *Gay Men's Literature in the Twentieth Century.* New York: New York UP, 1993.

Lumsden, Ian. *Machos, Maricones and Gays: Cuba and Homosexuality.* Philadelphia: Temple UP, 1996.

Murray, Stephen O. *Latin American Male Homosexualities.* Albuquerque: U of New Mexico P, 1995.

Rodríguez, Alicia. "La mujer en la obra de Reinaldo Arenas." Sánchez 151-159.

Rosencvaig, Perla. *Reinaldo Arenas: Narrativa de transgresión.* Oaxaca: Editorial Oasis, 1986.

Sánchez, Reinaldo, ed. *Reinaldo Arenas: Recuerdo y presencia.* Miami: Ediciones Universal, 1994.

Satir, Virginia. *Conjoint Family Therapy.* (1964) Palo Alto, CA: Science and Behavior Books, Inc. 1983.

Schwartz, Kessel. "Maternidad e incesto: fantasías en la narrativa de Reinaldo Arenas." Hernández Miyares and Rozencvaig 19-28.

Soto, Francisco. "*Celestino antes del alba:* escritura subersiva/sexualidad transgresiva." *Revista Iberoamericana* 57 (1991): 345-54.

---. "*Celestino antes del alba, El palacio de las blanquísimas mofetas,* and *Otra vez el mar:* The Struggle for Self-Expression." *Hispania* 75 (1992): 60-68.

---. *Reinaldo Arenas: The Pentagonía.* Gainesville: UP of Florida, 1994.

8

Family in Levi Calderón's *Dos mujeres*: Post-Traumatic Stress or Lesbian Utopia?

Sara E. Cooper

Sara Levi Calderón's best-selling first novel, *Dos mujeres* (1990), translated and revised by the author as *The Two Mujeres* (1991), shocked Mexican society by portraying the love of upper middle-class Valeria for her bohemian painter friend Genovesa. Although *Dos mujeres* without a doubt breaks ground in its portrayal of sexual agency by women (and by lesbians), there is some disagreement about just how revolutionary the novel is. Claudia Schaefer-Rodríguez, author of the few existing critical articles on Levi Calderón's first novel, is especially concerned with its placement within the ever-evolving nationalist discourse of Mexico. In "Monobodies, Antibodies, and the Body Politic: Sara Levi Calderón's *Dos mujeres*," she argues that on the surface Levi Calderón's work could be seen as a substantial challenge to the sociopolitical platform of "a horizon of progress for the individual and the family" held by the political party in power, a position described in the speeches by the former president of Mexico, Carlos Salinas de Gortari (223). The novel represents a non-homogenous Mexican people in terms of ethnicity and religion, class, and sexual preference, and as such diverges from the nationalist agenda that represents a unified people moving together toward socioeconomic stability and entrance to the technological age and the global arena. By the same token, the novel directly confronts the existence of violence and discrimination present in Mexican society, if only on a microsystemic level. However, Schaefer points out that contrary to what one might expect, the novel was widely accepted in the very society that it exposed. However, she concludes that the framing of the novel as a love story and the relative isolation of the two protagonists permits viewing the novel as basically inoffensive ("Monobodies" 225-27). For Schaefer, *Dos mujeres* loses political agency because of the isolation and specificity of the newly created family. Schaefer posits that the lesbian relationship is framed completely outside of the realm of universal or human experience, so it does not intrude on the dominant social order. In response to her conclusion, I would submit that Levi Calderón's novel, although it does allow this non-threatening integration by the reader, works on a deeper level to criticize and systematically break down the traditional notions of family espoused by the conservative Mexican discourse. The alternative family system created and maintained by the protagonist is shown to be a major rupture with the social norm, not only because it is composed of two lesbians, but because it provides an example of functionality and loving support of individualism that is lacking in the protagonist's other family systems. The intricacy of the narrative structure and style allows this direct social affront to be perceived as indirect or nonexistent, resulting in the widespread acceptance of the novel.

Dos Mujeres is semi-autobiographical in its portrayal of a young woman who struggles with the lack of acceptance and tolerance shown by her family and society as she comes out as a lesbian (Schaefer "Levi Calderón"). As an underlying premise of the novel, Valeria must choose between her traditional family--her parents, her children, and a planned conventional marriage--and a new form of kinship based on something other than custom or procreation. Schaefer comments in *Danger Zones*: "How the biological body (in the form of family), the productive body (the realm of work), and the libidinal body (desire and fantasy) are experienced by the characters Genovesa and Valeria forms the core of this narrative" (92). As *Dos Mujeres* slowly presents what is growing between the two women, juxtaposed against violent and stifling images of the traditional family, the novel facilitates an undermining of the definition of family, with a subsequent exploration of how family systems respond when, in full crisis, their very function and configuration begin to be questioned.

Valeria --the first-person narrator-- is obsessed with the idea of family. Her own history with her biological and procreative families, the familiar connections of her acquaintances, and even the structure and workings of the family are of the utmost importance to her. On the novel's second page she says of her friend Morena, her future lover's cousin, that "Our difference in age made me old enough to be her mother. But we never talked about that" (3). The statement is fairly banal if not seen in the larger context of the entire novel, but in the 237 pages of this work this is only the first of more than fifty passages referring directly to family, a sign of the thematic importance of the topic. Moreover, in that short citation Valeria alludes to her own characteristic role for over forty years--a silent and compliant onlooker in the face of any situation even related to family.

The narrated action begins when Valeria is thirty-nine years old, divorced, and supposedly liberated, but in reality is still living beneath a reign of terror instilled by her own two sons. She says that she barely dares to bring Morena home with her for a meal, because:

> My sons thought she was weird. "Why is she always wearing huaraches?" they would ask. "Doesn't she have any money to buy shoes?" They despised her looks and they couldn't understand why she was my friend. Morena stared at me. "Aren't you scared of going back?" "I'm not scared, I'm panicked." (6)

And of course, when the two arrive, Valeria's sons (already grown, more than twenty years old) behave rudely, speaking only in monosyllables, reading the newspaper at the dinner table, and interrupting the maid so that she attends to them before helping their mother. First Valeria maintains her accustomed silence, and when she finally opens her mouth it is only to make excuses for them. Then, when Genovesa visits for the first time, the scene plays out similarly:

> Alberto, my son, walked quickly in and looked at my guests from head to toe. I introduced them; he hardly answered back. His arrogance got on my nerves, but I decided to simply invite him in. "Have a drink with us," I said. He wouldn't accept. He just turned and walked out, slamming the door. . . . Genovesa was pale with rage; she questioned my son's right to judge his mother's friends. I argued that it had been I who had invested him with that right after my divorce. (17)

Although Alberto is now a young man, within his position as child he has been given a jurisdiction that is theoretically reserved for the parental figures. This is not surprising, given the cultural tradition that until recently left women under the legal control of their nearest male relative. However, from a more contemporary perspective, the right to presume a moral authority --in this case for Valeria's son to judge his mother's friends-- carries with it a power of domination that should be tempered by the responsibility to act in concordance with the wisdom gained through age and experience. That he doesn't act so is illustrative of the imbalance created by this element of the family dynamic.

Whereas Valeria has managed to break free from her marriage, in some ways she still conforms to the role she has always played, the role handed down from her mother, and from previous generations. In a classic example of the transgenerational repetition compulsion, this is the pattern that will repeat itself throughout almost the entire novel: the familiar, comfortable and traditional design in which the self-effacing woman submits to masculine excess, a behavior taught to her since childhood.[1] This describes Valeria's biological family, even more so her first marriage to Luis (who wanted to teach her by the rod to be a "real woman" 130), and it would also be the family she would form if she were to marry her petulant, arrogant current suitor, Alejandro. This seeming inability to skirt disaster, the pull to return to a familiar abusive system is not at all incomprehensible, in that even *discomfort* may contain the *comfort* of familiarity, and even the violent patterns that one knows how to respond to may hold less fear than a calmer or less volatile situation. The fact that Genovesa questions this pattern from the very beginning hints that a different sort of dynamic is entirely possible.

Valeria's cyclic return to old family patterns is further emphasized in the novel's structure, a weaving of concentric circles that expands to bring in a wider expanse of time and perspective. The second section of the novel brings us back to the narrator's youth, where we witness the early manifestation of her cycle of abusive family systems. The flashback is an effective technique that not only provides a backdrop for the present-time narration, but in rare moments allows the realistic appearance of a child's narrative voice that can communicate her fear and confusion in a palpable manner. What emerges from the child's perspective is that Valeria's mother exerted control using her delicate health, her father with out-of-control rage, and her brother by adopting an arch-conservatism. Valeria says of herself, "There my destiny was defined: to be silent, always silent" (96).[2] This is the configuration of family homeostasis, silent or manipulating women and men who allow no challenge to their authority; any threat to the system provokes a violent and immediate reaction.[3] When Valeria's brother insists upon becoming a priest instead of a businessman, he is sent to a military academy; when Valeria falls in love with a young man whose mother's reputation is tainted, she is prohibited from seeing him again, and her family finds her a more acceptable fiancé. Her family tries to enforce the boundaries of a closed system, one that lacks the ability to incorporate or adapt to new or foreign circumstances, and one in which the needs of individuals are ignored if they in any way interfere with the rigid rules of family interactions.[4]

The same tendency toward systemic rigidity is encountered from the very first in Valeria's marriage to Luis, when he attempts to remold her into a carbon copy of his own mother, and "the first thing he demanded was that I stay away from my parents" (130). A typical response of perpetrators of abuse, her husband prohibits contact with anyone who might question or challenge his perspective, a good way to achieve his ends. Valeria is immediately isolated from any possible support or emotional aid, leaving her completely vulnerable to her husband's tirades, unreasonable expectations, and physical mistreatment. Ironically, she is even shut off from the very system that prepared her to accept such treatment, her own family. In a closed system there is no room for even the least contradictory information--it is necessary to close off all means of outside interference.

As often happens in life, this desire for control degenerates into domestic violence in *Dos Mujeres*. It is interesting to note that the novel is described as "an out of the ordinary story, a love that faces an antagonism with society and that expresses itself uniquely in a thousand different ways" (back jacket). Antagonism seems a vague and almost bland word to express the extent of physical and emotional violence perpetrated against the two protagonists, and it is surprising that this level of abuse receives no comment outright. By the same token, to say that the women's love faces *society's* antagonism is misleading, in that the novel depicts almost no occurrences of anti-homosexual episodes in the public sphere. Startlingly, in Levi Calderon's novel, practically all of the violence suffered by the two protagonists is at the hands of other family members. As a little girl Valeria is beaten by both brother and father for having been coerced by schoolmates into sexual behavior, her husband hits her to make her a "better wife," and the cycle continues with the brutality of her sons and other male family members. The level of violence escalates after her family realizes the depth and scope of her relationship with Genovesa.

Particularly striking is the narration of one act of physical cruelty perpetrated by Valeria's elder son, which occurs as she comes out from showering with her lover:

> Ricky walks out through the dining room. He stops in front of the glass cabinet to stare at the menorah that my mother had given me as a wedding present. He tries to pull it out but the small door won't open; he searches for a key but can't find it. He shatters the glass with an elbow and takes hold of it. I hear his footsteps on the staircase as he comes up to my bedroom. I go out to receive him, dripping wet. He raises the menorah above his head as high as he can and smashes it over my head. (76)

The present tense narration and simply structured phrases lend immediacy to the passage. At the same time, the absence of any emotional reaction on the part of the narrator reflects a carefully controlled and distanced stance. The cold, impassive recounting chills and shocks the reader, urging a closer exploration of the situation. While the attack on Valeria does not explicitly include rape, her state of undress suggests a sexual vulnerability that is violated by her son's brutality. Moreover, I propose that Valeria's recent proximity to her lover in the shower implicitly links both women as intended victims. The son's violent intrusion into his mother's personal and sexual life can be seen as a patriarchal attempt to infiltrate the sacred and almost utopic women's space established by the lovers. What is most threatening to the status quo must be attacked, and the fact that two women might not need men in their life for economic, emotional, or physical fulfillment is discordant with the Mexican code of morality and gender roles. This symbolic and physical transgression against Valeria's privacy, which in obedience to the established pattern will never again be mentioned, can also be seen as another desperate attempt to reestablish the family homeostasis. While on some level Ricky is trying to put his household back into a recognizable order, he is also acting on behalf of his family, and even on behalf of the sociocultural belief system that condemns Valeria's deviation from the established norm.

Of course, other attempts to reclaim the accustomed family system will follow. Genovesa's automobile is vandalized, Valeria's bank account is illegally plundered, and Valeria receives multiple threats to her physical safety as well as her economic security. Valeria's family begins to ostracize her, threatening to cut her off completely from her inheritance, not to mention any comfort to be garnered from familial solidarity. While these attacks serve a purpose in the family system, that of bolstering the homeostasis that has been endangered by Valeria's rebellion, they are destructive on every possible level and do not strengthen or protect the family members. The family experience that Valeria must endure is, more than merely patriarchal, so permeated by violence that it must be qualified as dysfunctional.[5]

Fortunately, from the first there are indications that Valeria will eventually break with tradition in order to create her own competing version of a family system, albeit without cognizance of the symbolic weight of her actions. Before even meeting Genovesa, and in a prefiguring moment of self-awareness she thinks:

> I often had the need to go back and search into my blood ties. Not long ago, I had discovered a treasure, a series of photographs that had belonged to my grandmother. I found a picture of two old-fashioned beauties, my grandmother and my mother, at a time in their lives when they still believed that age couldn't leave its mark on their faces. (8)

Valeria suddenly realizes that she, as a woman, also is losing her social power as she ages.   Being that historically much of women's power has centered in their ability to demonstrate femininity, especially physical beauty and social deference to men, women begin to lose their attraction as they become older, or even worse, wiser.[6] Since Valeria has returned to her studies and question the reality of her dependency on the men in her life, she is in danger of becoming something both dangerous and repulsive in upper-class society--the crone.   Her response is immediate and severe, if appropriate: "Rage burst from my left temple. Furious, I hurled the photographs to the floor, then tried to stop the album from falling but it was too late. I had also knocked over a vase filled with roses and water on top of my visual legacy. And I did nothing to rescue it" (8).   The feminist epiphany of the injustice inherent in contemporary society thus allows Valeria to not "correct" what she does by accident--figuratively cut the always existent and strangling ties with her photographic family tradition.   Perhaps a recovery of the momentum garnered for her divorce, this willingness to face, and even break patterns is unfamiliar territory for Valeria. Nonetheless, the trend intensifies as she severs her connection with her family system by starting a romantic relationship with Genovesa. Although she has rebelled in some instances before, this is the first time that her opposition is sustained.   In the face of her family's insistence that she break off with her new lover, Valeria steadfastly refuses, again deciding against rescuing the doubtful "treasure" of tradition and dysfunctionality.   While Valeria has no idea of the repercussions that will ensue, as the rest of the family fights to reestablish the equilibrium that sacrifices her identity and safety to maintain coherence, she embarks on a course of revolution.

In the new system --a dyad owing to the fact that all the other family members begin to ostracize the two women-- Valeria finally dares to say and do what she wants, a radical deviation from her former behavior.   The strength and rebellion emerging in this lesbian family shows that it is more than the sum of its parts.   And even though some might be skeptical about defining two lovers as a family, social psychologists consider a pair as a valid familial structure.[7] Valeria and Genovesa's newly formed relationship is one of many alternative family systems depicted in contemporary Latin American literature.[8] Here, the alternative family fulfills many of the functions that had been fulfilled only sketchily, if at all, in Valeria's previous family systems. She experiences emotional support and acceptance as well as the encouragement to become the most self-actualized and fulfilled person she can be.   She even continues to change in her role as daughter, neither permitting her father to hit her, nor allowing herself to be controlled by family expectations or even the temptation of financial security. Valeria's newfound strength is reflected in the narrative style of the novel's second and third parts; she speaks more vigorously, describing herself in heroic terms and refusing to hide even behind a verbal passivity. Her communication style becomes more clear and direct; whereas before her sentences might trail off, to be finished by Genovesa, more and more she takes full responsibility for her thoughts and feelings. At the same time, she allows the poetry of her spirit to begin to invade her speech, making the narrative voice more lyrical.

The shift in the narrative voice is the first indication that Valeria's new family is more healthy and functioning than her traditional family. As a writer and a woman, she explores and revels in her own identity, textually represented by the more creative and beautiful prose. However, not only the writing style undergoes a radical change. This developing relationship with herself gives her the fortitude to deal with the increasingly intolerable conditions of her life. The dynamic between her and her sons also undergoes a shift:

> With the strength of a goddess, I refused to be walked on by my sons. Serious problems arose: the boys claimed they weren't meant for domestic labor. This claim symbolically closed the circle my father had spun around me when I was born. The price of freedom would be a heartrending break. (175)

Terrified but determined, she continues on. Her now ex-boyfriend says that she seems like another woman (198) and almost at the end of the novel her father questions confusedly "What kind of strength is this you've acquired with Genovesa? I don't understand" (202). In the new relationship/family, there is communication, negotiation, and flexibility; the two women do not have fixed or predetermined roles, but rather either one may instigate a controversy, make a decision, and ask for or accept help. According to Minuchin, it is important for a family to have not only the adaptability to face new challenges together, but also to be able to weather crisis and conflict without always staying in the conflictual mode. "Flexibility in [a family's] transactions. . .[such as] bickering and competition alternat[ing] with periods of sharing, confidence and cooperation. . .is a good indicator of a healthy family organization" (*Kaleidoscope* 34). As does any relationship, this one suffers unpleasant moments, separations, and periods of alienation; however, it is a more permeable system and thus much more adaptable. There is not the necessity to resort to violence in order to perpetuate a fixed code of behavior or beliefs, and not every question or comment is seen as an infringement upon or threat to the system.

Sometimes, says Minuchin, the rejection of the family of origin together with a focus on the opportunities offered by the change can create a model of individual development through what he terms *dismemberment* (*Kaleidoscope* 42). In spite of the violent connotations of this word, Minuchin stresses the positive aspects of detaching cleanly and completely from other family members when the situation is extreme enough to warrant such an action. And truthfully, it is with the radical change represented by her love for another woman that Valeria finally succeeds in questioning the authority that until then had always defined family, and subsequently her own role as woman. Only when offered the hope of a viable alternative can she separate herself from the escalating violence and oppression that so obviously threatens her life, not to mention her self-expression.

In the final third of the novel, Genovesa also has to free herself from a dysfunctional family entanglement, the caretaking of her heroin-addicted cousin Morena. The intensity and futility of Genovesa's attempt to save Morena results in her temporary emotional withdrawal. This is a clear strain on her romantic relationship with Valeria, who struggles to remain patient and supportive. Finally she returns to her lover, choosing a support system that values her as an artist and a person rather than a caretaker. Valeria narrates:

> "Life has its do-re-mi flats," Genovesa said, feeling threads and ropes loosen. She had finally freed herself from what had tied her to her cousin. My house was filled with *Siglos*, luscious food and joy. We loved each other again, and once more, fear vanished. We began a new cycle. (173)

Toward the end of the novel, Levi Calderón allows a subtler, lighter, and more dreamlike quality to enter the narration, indicative of the psychological and physical shifts experienced by the main character. Under the now fluid paradigm of family and prose, Valeria goes to the point of imposing herself as authority and recuperates her voice completely when she finishes writing the novel that is her and Genovesa's love story. Valeria's new approach to life is a radical re-writing of herself and her family history, as she exclaims, "Masks off!" (194) She refuses to hide herself or act as an accomplice in the distorted narration that would portray her family of origin as ideal. Here the reader notices an intensification of the subtle interplay between narrator and author, as the narrator (Valeria) assumes authorship, and Levi Calderón's intimate and semi-autobiographical connection to the novel is more poignant than ever. This intersection of narration and recovery of self is essential to Levi Calderón's novel, as Valeria redefines herself as a writing subject. Thus she affirms her experience as a woman, a lesbian, a mother, a daughter, a lover, a survivor of abuse, and a wealth of strength and hope for others. Zimmerman stresses the importance and cultural relevance of this type of writing:

> Fiction is a particularly useful medium through which to shape a new lesbian consciousness, for fiction, of all literary forms, makes the most complex and detailed use of historical events and social discourse. By incorporating many interacting voices and points of view, novelists give the appearance of reality to a variety of imaginary worlds. Novels can show us as we were, as we are, and as we would like to be. This is a potent combination for a group whose very existence has been either suppressed or distorted. (2)

Valeria is no longer hiding in the closet, allowing the traditional cultural and literary distortions to define her and her idea of family. She speaks what she has always kept silent, what her family has tried to keep unspoken, what Mexican society has labeled as deviant or nonexistent, and so mines the therapeutic power of narration, as introduced by psychologist Michael White. Clearly, Valeria's writing is as revolutionary as her pursuit of a lesbian family to fulfill her emotional, psychological, physical, and economical needs.

In reference to the revolutionary quality of the novel, Schaefer asks whether "alterity and resistance are [. . .] defused through their incorporation into a false space within the liberal community" -- "the book is there, the women are not" ("Monobodies" 100) or "whether Levi Calderón's narrator is permitted to speak of her desire for another woman because, after all, this is the story of *only* two women" ("Monobodies" 102). Schaefer sees the novel's ending as both utopian and distanced from reality, and therefore less effective as social criticism. The novel never does incorporate the idea of a lesbian community, nor does it suggest what sort of continued support will sustain the new family as it struggles to survive. Without a doubt, the reader must ask herself what the implications are of the lack of community in *Dos Mujeres*. While the novel doesn't represent explicit negative effects of Valeria's and Genovesa's isolation, it is clear that there is no "Lesbian Nation" to support them.

I propose that the disconnection of this lesbian family is the one element that specifically argues against reading the novel as utopian. The lesbian utopian novel usually constructs a community of like-minded individuals who together will effect social change. However, it is still possible that Levi Calderón is participating in what Zimmerman calls lesbian mythmaking, "a political project aimed at overturning the patriarchal domination of culture and language," (21). As the novel progresses, the protagonist looses any external controls over her body or her voice, unleashing a powerful feminine-centered identity and narration. The ambiguous and dreamlike ending that Schaefer reads as a self-imposed exile or utopian escape ("Monobodies" 89) could also be viewed as a novelistic denouement that Valeria wishfully inserts in lieu of her own unknown future. At the very least, it must be seen as a transition period, which will be followed with more struggles and different panoramas, as suggested by the final words: "The sounds harmonize, break, fade. The sea, again, comes into focus. The linear turns concentric" (211). If this is not technically utopian, it still offers a striking difference from the rigid boundaries and restrictions imposed by the family, particularly by the men who wish to retain dominance.

Although the contrast is strong, almost unsettling, I believe that in *Dos Mujeres* there is no attempt to introduce a lesbian utopia in direct contraposition to a dysfunctional heterosexuality. As mentioned before, the two women have arguments and separations; they do not, however, resort to acts to violence. In the new *pas de deux* family, the most important factor is that between the two women there exist love and mutual respect, just as one supposes would have happened if Valeria had married the young man with whom she had fallen in love, only to have him rejected by her family. By no means do I see a categorical negation of heterosexuality, but rather a criticism of violence and oppression in any relationship. In the end, the critical reader must concede that the establishment of a lesbian family breaks radically with the rigidity of the prevailing social system. *Dos Mujeres* demonstrates the necessity to create a system of kinship that values all of the family members in their diversity. In the context of Latin American cultural production, where the traditional family has long been sacred, Levi Calderón's novel offers a revolutionary definition of family based not on legality or the necessity to reproduce, but like the definition in Kath Weston's *Families We Choose*, based on love, responsibility, emotional support, and the continuous creativity of a relationship in constant change. Whether or not the alternative families are presented as utopic, they serve as a constant undermining of the patriarchal structure and oppressive dynamic that for some people still define the traditional, mythical Latin American family.

NOTES

[1] Minuchin's conception of the transgenerational repetition compulsion, which Bowen calls the multigenerational transmission process, refers to the unplanned and perhaps complete unconscious repetition of patterns over the generations of a family. Children will often communicate, interact in society, and raise children in a fashion reminiscent of their parents'. This is not merely imitation, and may occur in subtle ways despite a firm resolve to avoid the repetition.

[2] Valeria's position in the family is determined by her age and her gender. In this case, as in others, the family acts as an agent of society to perpetuate restrictions that are mostly unwritten. Her silence at the public level is emblematic of that of all Latin American women, or of women in general. Her voice, or her "ability to participate in activities of discourse" (Lindstrom 15) is limited to the private sphere, and even there is severely limited. Only as she gains more personal freedom does she develop a personal and public voice. For more discussion of women's voice in literature, see Pratt and/or Lindstrom.

[3] See Jackson on homeostasis, a process in which a family naturally attempts to sustain a balance in relationships; the first reaction to change will be an instinct to try vigorously to preserve the status quo.

[4] Margaret Hall explains that Bowen, one of the most influential theorists in Family Systems Theories, views all processes within the family dynamic, as well as the family system itself, as on a continuum of open and permeable to closed and rigid. Says Hall, "One of Bowen's related hypotheses is that both individuals and families are more effective or more viable when the systemness of their functioning is relatively open rather than relatively closed" (22). In this way families can adapt to changing circumstances, additions or losses within the family, etc., with a minimum of chaos and crisis.

[5] Kerr and Bowen posit that family functioning was more a continuum than an easily divisible dichotomy of "sick" and "healthy" or "functional" and "dysfunctional." They elucidate that in general, relationships are governed by the (im)balance of two equally crucial life forces, individuality --the wish and ability to follow one's own directives --and togetherness-- the wish and ability to follow the directives of others (Kerr & Bowen 64-65). High functionality would be indicated in part by the ability to maintain a balance between individuality and togetherness.

[6] See Brownmiller on elements of femininity and their historical relationship to power.

[7] As discussed in Allen and Demo, Scanzoni and Marsiglio (1993) proposed a theoretical framework for incorporating and valuing a variety of family structures, including same-sex couples, a framework intended to replace "'the prevailing dichotomy of benchmark family versus deviant alternative family" (119).

[8] See Cooper on alternative family systems in Marilene Felinto and Cristina Peri Rossi. "Forging a Family Discourse in Marilene Felinto's *The Women of Tijucopapo*." *Reading the Family Dance: Family Systems Therapy and the Literary Study*. Eds. John V. Knapp and Kenneth Womack. 36 ms. pages. Forthcoming from U of Delaware Press Spring 2003; "The Lesbian family in Christina Peri Rossi's 'El testigo': A Study in Utopia and Infiltration." *Tortilleras: Hispanic and Latina Lesbian Expression*. Eds. Lourdes Torres and Inmaculada Pertusa. 35 ms. pages. Forthcoming from Temple Press Spring 2003.

Works Cited

Bowen, Murray. *Family Therapy in Clinical Practice.* New York: Jason Aronson, 1978.

Brownmiller, Susan. *Femininity.* New York: Fawcett Comlumbine, 1984.

Hall, C. Margaret. "Family Systems: A Developing Trend in Family Theory." *The Sociology of the Family (Sociological Review* Monograph 28) Ed. Chris Harris. Staffordshire: U of Keele, 1979.

Jackson, Don D. "The Question of Family Homeostasis." *Psychiatric Quarterly Supplement* 31 (1957): 79-90.

Kerr, Michael E., and Murray Bowen. *Family Evaluation: An Approach Based on Bowen Theory.* New York: W.W. Norton, 1988.

Levi Calderón, Sara. *Dos mujeres.* México: Diana, 1990.

---. *The Two Mujeres.* Trans. Gina Kaufer. San Francisco: Aunt Lute Books, 1991.

Lindstrom, Naomi. *Women's Voice in Latin American Literature.* Washington, D.C.: Three Continents P, 1989.

Minuchin, Salvador. *Family Kaleidoscope.* Cambridge: Harvard UP, 1984.

Pratt, Mary Louise. *Toward a Speech Act Theory of Literary Discourse.* Bloomington: Indiana U P. 1978

Schaefer, Claudia. "The Body Politic: Calderón's *Dos mujeres.*" *Bodies and Biases: Sexualities in Hispanic Cultures and Literatures.* Eds. David William Foster, and Roberto Reis. Minneapolis: U of Minnesota P, 1996. 217-37.

---. "Monobodies, Antibodies, and the Body Politic: Sara Levi Calderón's *Dos mujeres.*" *Danger Zones: Homosexuality, National Identity, and Mexican Culture.* Tuscon: U of Arizona P, 1996. 81-106.

---. "Sara Levi Calderón." Foster *Latin American Writers* 199-202.

Weston, Kath. *Families We Choose: Lesbians, Gays, Kinship.* New York: Columbia UP, 1991.

Zimmerman, Bonnie. *The Safe Sea of Women: Lesbian Fiction 1969-1989.* Boston: Beacon P, 1990.

Appendix

Viability of Family Systems Theory for Latin America

Sara E. Cooper

One central concern that arises in the application of social or psychological criticism to literature is that of the validity of any particular approach in the cultural context of the body of works. In the case of Family Systems Theory being applied to Latin American narrative fiction, several relevant questions must be addressed. These questions are more sociological than psychological in nature. First of all, FST was initially developed in the United States, primarily by English-speakers, for use with families of their own culture. Subsequently, in the literary arena, FST has most frequently been utilized in conjunction with Anglophone texts from the United States and England. Thus it is necessary to explore the extent to which one may compare the family in the United States and the *familia* in Latin America: are they similar enough to warrant the transference, borrowing, or adaptation of the analytical tool of one in order to better view the other? And how can we be convinced that a psychological approach created for one culture may be applied as effectively to another--what evidence is there that FST is accepted as valid and used by experts on the family in Latin America? Finally, even if the composition, power structure, and mode of communication epitomized in the United States family myth were very unlike the family patterns found in Mexico, Argentina, or Brazil, how would FST still be useful in understanding the latter? Addressing these issues is a vital component of this chapter, because only when it is established that there is indeed compatibility between FST psychology and the target cultural context will it be viable to continue with the development and application of a FST methodology to Latin American literature.

In the first place, then, let us delve into a brief comparison of the family of the United States, the family system of which write Bateson, Satir, and their colleagues, with the Latin American family, which provides a skeletal social model for those families found in works by García Márquez, Lispector, and many other writers. Let us first turn to a sociological perspective of family. Such a discussion will be necessarily incomplete, as it is far beyond the scope of this work to provide an in-depth comparative study of the sociology of family. In addition, to attempt one definition of family doesn't fully take into account such factors as class, ethnicity, education, and geographical placement, which in truth make the continuum of family very difficult to pin down. Nonetheless, one may speak of certain relevant data reflected in the considerable research on the family, keeping in mind that these are generalizations that do not necessarily fit all families. As demonstrated in the introductory chapter, the definition of family not only has changed over the centuries, but also has differed widely depending upon any number of factors. Nonetheless, in order for sociologists to study the family, in order for psychologists to develop any critical device that may aid in its interpretation, and in order for great writers to chronicle the family experience, working with these generalities has been inevitable. That being said, what I hope to accomplish here is to outline a few similarities, in my view unarguable, that emerge in a glance at contemporary family sociology.

First, I should reiterate that the form and function of family is changing and becoming more complicated throughout the world. The mythical ideal of the "American Family" in the United States, as discussed earlier, is no longer that of Mother, Father and two or three children in the clearly defined roles and hierarchy promulgated and popularized in the media. The 1950s television programs *Father Knows Best, Donna Reed* and *Leave it to Beaver* were the first wave of shows to mirror and instruct the public "as to how it should understand the relations of the private" (Heller xii), as 90% of households were tuning in an average of five hours a day by the 1960s (Heller 40). Of course most people today realize that the family landscape is much more complex than that of the "perfect" post-war nuclear family. The domestic space is not the natural environment for all women, many families will never have two-story houses with picket fences, and at least one child out of ten will be abused by a member of his or her immediate domestic circle.[1] But as Dana Heller proposes in *Family Plots: The De-Oedipalization of Popular Culture* (1995), the 1990s have spawned a culture that still views the old sitcoms with "a cool, ironic detachment that culturally decontextualizes specific programming while reinforcing viewers' unity of experience and commitment to the dominant fantasies of the television dreamscape" (41). Heller argues that while the practical and academic definition of family has evolved to reflect a diversity of forms, structures, and dynamics, nostalgia for the old myths still has a firm hold on the general public. Many of the current family configurations are considered incomplete or aberrant by the most conservative sociologists and laypersons; for instance, some degree of stigma is placed on the single-parent family, divorced and remarried "step-family," or gay family. By the same token, while changing economics has necessitated the geographical separation of extended family and the development of the two-earner family, such manifestations are often faulted for the corruption of our youth and the destruction of the family's moral fiber. In this manner, the inherent contradictions in the messages we receive through family socialization, education, and the communications media operate as a kind of double bind. In an increasingly urban society, we are urged to retain (up to a certain point) social and emotional constraints born of a rural and agrarian culture. We must adapt to the changing economy and its repercussions in the family structure and dynamic, but we are warned against losing the family values that reflect a previous reality. In general, the family is being shown multiple and mutually contradictory models of an ideal within which it must formulate its identity and/or judge its functionality, a daunting position that necessarily takes its toll on each member as well as the entire system. This postmodern familial dilemma is played out in countless works, such as Toni Morrison's novel *Beloved* (1987), and *Bastard Out of Carolina* (1992), a novel by Dorothy Allison.

A similar proliferation of contrasting takes on kinship can be seen in a glance at contemporary sociological studies of the Latin American family. In Lila Ruiz de Mateo Alonso's 1986 study *Dinámica de los grupos familiares dentro de la estructura social venezolana* (Dynamic of family groups inside the Venezuelan social structure), which significantly is informed by a systems approach, a listing of possible categorizations of family structures includes the following: traditional nuclear family, married couple, dual-income family, single-parent, three-generational, cooperative (including non-married members), and institutional (orphanages, correctional) (25). Ruiz adds to this list some other new, experimental structures that she defines in the following manner:

--*Communal family.* A home with more than one monogamous couple with children, where all share the edifices, resources, and experiences: the socialization of the child is a group activity.
--*Single mother with children.* Family generally composed of mother and child, marriage is unwanted or impossible.
--*Unmarried couple with a child.* Family composed of a couple living out of wedlock with a biological or informally adopted child.
--*Family of homosexual couple with a child.* Family composed of a gay couple and an informally or legally adopted child. (25-26)

Interestingly enough, although Ruiz is scrupulous in admitting the existence of these family structures, she does not go so far as to discuss most of them within the Venezuelan context. Nonetheless, she does particularly point to one new form which is quite common in both Venezuela and the rest of Latin America, that of a mother and her children (perhaps of diverse fathers), in which the mother carries out all material and spiritual responsibilities and the father(s) play a secondary and negligible role within the family dynamic (38).[2] Definitely a recurring theme in Latin American literature (e.g. Magali García Ramis's *Felices días, Tío Sergio* 1986), the matriarchal family that makes little note of the errant father's place is also common in some segments of United States culture.[3]

Ruiz's detailed and conspicuously non-judgmental chronicling of the family panorama in Venezuela is in divergence with texts such as Guillermo Paez Morales' *Sociología de la familia* (1984; Family sociology), in which a more emotional rhetoric problematizes such occurrences as the single-parent family. Indeed, one of the most striking elements of this text is an extreme conservatism that upholds the most traditional of views in terms of family. It should be noted, however, that his conservatism does not inhibit his being influenced by systems philosophy, such as in his definition of family and his review of current psychological approaches to family (25, 81-83). For instance, Paez Morales proposes rigid gender definitions in which the father is the most powerful person, both *de facto* and *de jure*, and the woman rightfully takes her inferior position, thereby modeling for the child what the social situation will be outside the family (27-28). Throughout the text, Paez Morales describes fairly common changes that have been occurring all through the Americas in the industrialization, urbanization, and now the technological transformation of the modern (or post-modern) society.[4] Nonetheless, being of a conservative bent, Paez Morales mentions many of the modern characteristics as elements contributing to the crisis in the family today. For example, among other things, he cites as problematic the move toward a more urban, nuclear family in which the woman has more rights in terms of birth control and dissolution of marital ties (412). To reiterate, such a view of the family crisis is not at all foreign to the sociocultural context in the United States, where the New Right and other self-defined defenders of the family have vociferously opposed the Equal Rights Amendment, abortion, and gay rights (Thorne 1).

It is clear that at least in some elemental aspects the US and Latin American families do have some basis for comparison--they are all in the process of evolving, forming alternative family systems and changing functional focus in accordance to the changing social needs. By the same token, families in both areas are facing some of the same stressors, such as the need to adapt to an increasingly industrial and technological world and the contradictory pressure to conform to traditional stereotypes of the perfect family. If this suggests that a similar family psychology could be valid in both cultures, even more persuasive arguments exist to substantiate such a belief. Even a cursory review of the current psychological trends in Latin America gives credence to the idea that FST is a viable tool for gaining perspective on the Latin American family. In their "Bibliografía de terapia y psicología familiar en español" (1989; Bibliography of family therapy and psychology in Spanish) Guillermo Bernal and Ana Isabel Alvarez have compiled citations of books, professional journals, monographic studies, dissertations and conference proceedings in Spanish which deal with the topics of family therapy and/or family psychology. Among the 428 bibliographical entries included, 33 contain a specific reference to family systems in the title, and at least 131 more from the bibliography are authored by known proponents of FST or are included in the specialized journal *Sistemas Familiares* (Buenos Aires; Family systems). [5]

While the Bernal/Alvarez study only looks at production between the years of 1954 and 1988, for the last couple of decades FST has by no means waned in popularity in Latin America. Appearing frequently are journal articles that chronicle the current foci and usage of systems models, and indeed it appears that in some psychological communities FST has influenced most of the major trends. For example, a study based on Edwin Fernández Bauzó's interviews of seven prominent Puerto Rican professionals in psychology, psychiatry and social work shows that the six therapeutic models presently being used on the island include: the Familiar/Personal influenced by Ackerman and Satir, an eclectic model based on Whitaker's vital cycle and another on psycho education, Minuchin's Structural/Strategic, Bateson's Systemic/ Communication, and the Systemic/Interactional which stems directly from General Systems Theory. Upon reviewing the influences and bases of the models being utilized it is obvious that all but the psychoeducational has a strong affinity or a complete founding in the systems perspectives (and according to the article, even the psychoeducational application includes a touch of Minuchin) (24). The brief descriptions of each approach point strongly to such a connection to FST, reflecting the current preoccupation with communicational patterns, power structures, coalitions, larger social contexts, and the here and now (24-27).

Evident from the list of FST-focused articles and books is that interest in the subject surfaced in the early 1980s, gaining momentum through the decade. The titles show the early tendency toward the discussion and debate of systemic theories, with fewer texts disseminating case histories in which FST informed the therapist's interventions and treatment. Increasingly the object of interest in psychological communities in the 1980s, many Family Systems theoretical and practical models originating in the US have been judged sufficiently apt or modifiable to be applied to families in Latin American countries. Notably, it has been experts in the family who first made this judgment, which seems to have held up under critical view, as more current psychological journals continue to chronicle the usage and discussion of the systems perspectives. Nonetheless, some Latin Americans do subject contemporary psychological models like FST to intense critical scrutiny, questioning certain elements as being incongruent with their cultural context. Bauzó delineates three limitations that he perceives in the imported theories: the homeostatic vision, the individualism, and the tendency to view human nature as universal and ahistoric (28-29). With respect to homeostatic vision, Bauzó voices the following complaint:

> This vision guides us to value as undesirable and bad all which signifies disequilibrium, crisis, and conflict. Even worse, the homeostatic vision places us within a conceptual frame that makes extremely difficult the possibility of rejecting the established social order and supporting the social struggles of

the people, because these inevitably occasion disequilibrium. (28)

While these concerns must be addressed, I believe that Bauzó's comments reflect an incomplete understanding of family systems. As outlined in the introductory chapter, homeostasis is the default system of relationships and roles within a family; it is what is familiar and customary for the members. When a system's homeostasis is threatened by some new or altered element, the first instinct of the system is to preserve or restore what is familiar. However, this does not necessarily signify a value judgment of the "disequilibrium" or "interruption" of the familiar, either by the family itself, by an attending psychologist, or by society at large. In fact, it is generally accepted that systemic change is absolutely necessary, inevitable, and many times advantageous to the family, as when children marry or leave home or when an alcoholic seeks treatment for her excessive, problematic drinking. Often times for this to happen there must have been some crisis or "disequilibrium" in the system to spur the change. Dr. Dora Fried Schnitman explains, "evolution happens through fluctuations. [. . .] Only when a system operates in a sufficiently unpredictable manner can there develop a differentiation between past and future. ... [Thus] crises acquire a fundamental importance in evolution" (740). Based on this premise, informs Schnitman, therapists may themselves intervene and attempt to precipitate crises that challenge the family paradigm when these are not forthcoming within the family in treatment (77-78). In light of these reflections, I argue that far from stigmatizing family or social revolution, Family Systems Theories support a fluid and evolving system that can effectively transcend and even utilize the conflicts that arise.

By the same token, I disagree with Bauzó's other claims against current psychological trends in Puerto Rico. His preoccupation with a supposed inherent individualism and universalism seems equally indefensible in that his argument rests on a conception of therapeutic models that ignore the family system's social context. On the contrary, one of the basic tenets of FST is that while each family is a system, it also is comprised of subsystems (e.g. the parental or the sibling subsystem) and itself is only a subsystem of larger systems such as the extended family, the immediate community, and the society at large. Indeed, Bauzó's description of the Systemic-Interaction orientation explicitly recognizes that fact: "At the same time the therapist observes the family system and how the relations between family members are affected by hierarchically superior systems such as the juridical, cultural, political and economic systems" (26). Although I would not propose that every theoretical inconsistency is so easily refuted, I must reiterate that a thorough knowledge of Family Systems, in all its various manifestations, confers a realization of its extreme adaptability and combinatory potential. Indeed, rather than a single theory or practical model, it should be clear that Family Systems is a general perspective, a paradigm that recognizes the systemic properties of family. While the entire work of any one systems theorist may not be applicable to the Latin American context, the proliferation of subtly distinct approaches by US and Latin American psychologists alike is an indication of the flexible nature of FST.

According to data from the Bernal/Alvarez bibliography, some of the theorists and practitioners of Family Systems who are well known in Latin America include: Gregory Bateson, L. Bertanlafy, R. D. Laing, Salvador Minuchin, Virginia Satir, B. Keeney, A. Martínez Taboas, J. E. Maldonado, C. Ravazzolay, and C. Sluzki (123-142). (As is evident, among these names figure many of the same prominent psychologists whose work has informed the construction of this collection's critical methodology.) Indeed, some early systems theorists such as Satir have inspired entire hospital or clinic programs in Latin America to use their work as models for operation. Aside from the prominence of several US systems theorists, what stands out is that an equal number of Latin American specialists (particularly Argentines) have turned their critical and professional attention to the study and use of Family Systems. Such an embracing of the conceptual framework originally laid out by practitioners from another culture is quite telling; if the systems theories had not proven useful in the new cultural context, undoubtedly they would have been abandoned rather than incorporated into the vast panorama of psychological approaches now being utilized in the Americas.

The essays in this collection principally will refer to systems scholars who did their training and research in the United States, simply because they were the founding thinkers in the field and thus so far have been more prolific and influential. Even so, there is at least one of this group who has more than a casual comprehension of the Latin American cultural mosaic--the Argentine Salvador Minuchin. While Minuchin was born in and spent his youth in his native land, he then moved to the United States to continue his studies and practice psychology. Indeed, his is one of the most notable names in Family Systems. He went on to practice family therapy with an emphasis on cross-cultural adaptation and flexibility, and his contributions toward a culturally broad-based Family Systems therapy are considerable. Says

Minuchin, "The family is a social unit that faces a series of developmental tasks. These differ along the parameters of cultural differences, but they have universal roots" (*Families 16*). Along with other systems psychologists, Minuchin stresses that one of the family's most pressing functions is to prepare its members to live and adapt within their existing socio-economic culture "in transition" (46-47). Subsequently, the composition of and tasks that define each family system will reflect not only its own particular idiosyncrasies, but also the cultural community to which it belongs. Certainly other systems theorists address this issue specifically, for instance the Turkish psychologist Guler Fisek.[6] Notwithstanding, Minuchin like perhaps no other understands the necessity of developing a flexible, adaptable approach to each family that validates its own cultural values and even admits the possibility of *learning from* the family in therapy.

> Every family has elements in their own culture which, if understood and utilized, can become levers to actualize and expand the family members' behavioral repertory. Unfortunately, we therapists have not assimilated this axiom. Though we pay lip service to the strengths of the family, and talk about it as the matrix of development and healing, we are trained as psychological sleuths. Our instincts are to "search and destroy": Pinpoint the psychological disorder, label it, and eradicate it. We are the "experts." We are the specialized personnel who have earned our credentials to defend the normal by developing and maintaining a typology that frames deviancy as mental illness. Ironically, this job of policing deviance is organized in relation to a model of normal that is vague and undifferentiated at best. (Minuchin and Fishman 262-63)

As Minuchin goes on to suggest a reframing of the psychological lens with which to view families, he emphasizes both differences and similarities across cultures:

> The small transactions that occur. . .the preparing of food, the sitting silently together, the giving up of ordinary routines to care for a relative in need--all these are familiar elements of family life that exist anywhere. Nick Gage's family in Worcester is, in this respect, very similar to the Minuchin family in Argentina, in Israel, and in the United States, to Bell's families in Camaroon, [etc.]. (Minuchin and Fishman 267)

Rather than impose any one model of form or functionality, FST thus explicitly and systematically requires that family evaluation include an awareness of and sensitivity to cultural difference, greatly facilitating its application to families outside of the United States.

In summary, there are many valid points to the argument that FST can be applied in the Latin American cultural context, and by extension, to Latin American literature. Since the mid-1980s, Family Systems Theories have become a strong influence in the psychological communities of Latin America, and there are psychologists throughout the Americas who are applying systems perspectives to families as diverse as those from Argentina, Puerto Rico, and Spanish-speaking families in US. communities. One of the reasons that this has been possible is that FST does not assume that families in the Spanish-speaking world are just like those in the United States or any other first-world nation, but rather that they have their own values and traditions that must be taken into consideration before an accurate psychological analysis can be made. It is this flexibility and respect that has also made FST a valuable psychological tool with marginalized population inside of the United States. Nancy Boyd-Franklin and Nydia García-Preto state that the structural therapy theorized by Minuchin, Haley, and Aponte is "most useful in working with African American and Hispanic women. . .[because] women are helped to redefine their roles and shift responsibilities in relationship patterns" (241). These authors also suggest that Bowenian paradigms can be helpful with the same populations (242).

FST concentrates on viewing the here and now, the communication (or lack thereof) between family members, the power structure made apparent by the family interactions, and the participation of all family members in the cycles of dysfunction or oppression that exist in the system. All of these are phenomena that do certainly occur in families across national borders. In a text such as Van Steen's short story "Cio," in which the fragmented narrative structure and style mirror the dysfunctional communication, transitioning form, and limited functionality of the protagonist's family --within the changing social milieu in Brazil--, family systems goes beyond a reading that is merely linguistic, descriptive, or intrapsychic, and ultimately facilitates the exploration of all of these complex intersections. If it is at all appropriate to use a psychological paradigm in the study of families in Latin American literature, then it seems befitting to employ one that encourages the very cautions that exist in a good literary analysis to begin with, one that gives narrative voice to the rich diversity of family within its culture.

NOTES

[1]The figure of occurrences of child abuse in the United States was reported in a feature story aired on National Public Radio news on October 10, 1997.

[2]Alonso also adds that this family structure is denotated as "atypic" and disastrous to the culture by sociologist José Luis Vethencourt. (38 footnote)

[3]For example, the black ghetto households described by Carol Stack can best be described as an extended kinship network made up mostly of the female family members.

[4]Paez Morales does not address the differences in psychological impact that these shifts must occasion in such distinct cultures as those of Latin America (encompassing so many cultures itself, after all) and of the United States (which also must be recognized as heterogeneous). Nonetheless, Family Systems tries for a flexibility that can facilitate the perception and interpretation of these elements on an individual basis.

[5]Among these are authors such as Gregory Bateson and Salvador Minuchin.

[6]In keeping with the general precept that "Meaningful cross-cultural application of family therapy theories requires that basic assumptions about normal family functioning be made explicit, and contextual factors be incorporated into the theories" (121), Fisek goes on to demonstrate that within a sampling of Turkish factors it was culturally inappropriate to assess hierarchical immobility as family dysfunction because of a strong Turkish social code that "surpresses variation" in this element of family dynamic (121).

Works Cited

Bateson, G., et al. "Toward a Theory of Schizophrenia." *Behavioral Science* 1 (1956): 251-64.

Bauzó, Edwin B. Fernández. "La terapia familiar en el contexto puertorriqueño." *Revista Interamericana de Psicología* 23.1-2 (1989): 21-32.

Bernal, Guillermo, and Ana Isabel Alvarez. "Bibliografía de terapia y psicología familiar en español." *Revista Interamericana de Psicología* 23.1-2 (1989): 119-49.

Boyd-Franklin, Nancy, and Nydia García-Preto. "Family Therapy: A Closer Look at African American and Hispanic Women." *Women of Color: Integrating Ethnic and Gender Identities in Psychotherapy*. Lilian Comas-Díaz and Beverly Greene, eds. New York: Guilford, 1994. 239-264.

Fisek, Guler Okman. "A Cross-Cultural Examination of Proximity and Hierarchy as Dimensions of Family Structure." *Family Process* 30 (March 1991): 121-33.

Heller, Dana. *Family Plots: The De-Oedipalization of Popular Culture*. Philadelphia : University of Pennsylvania Press 1995.

Minuchin, Salvador. *Families and Family Therapy.* Cambridge: Harvard UP, 1974.

Minuchin, Salvador and H. Charles Fishman. *Family Therapy Techniques.* Cambridge: Harvard UP, 1981.

Paez Morales, Guillermo. *Sociología de la familia*: *Elementos de análisis en Colombia y América Latina.* Bogotá: U Santo Tomás Centro de Enseñanza Desescolarizada, 1984.

Ruiz de Mateo Alonso, Lila. *Dinámica de los grupos familiares dentro de la estructura social venezolana.* Caracas: U Central de Venezuela, 1986.

Satir, Virginia. *Conjoint Family Therapy.* Palo Alto: Science and Behavior Books: 1964.

Schnitman, Dora Fried. "Paradigma y crisis familiar." *Revista Argentina de Psicología* 19 (1987): 73-88.

Thorne, Barrie. "Feminist Rethinking of the Family: An Overview." Barrie Thorne and Marilyn Yalom. *Rethinking the Family: Some Feminist Questions.* New York: Longman, 1982. 1-24.

Index

EDITOR

SARA COOPER is currently an Assistant Professor of Spanish and Women's Studies at California State University, Chico. She has presented papers on alternative family systems and queer theory at conferences in Cuba, Mexico, and the United States. Her publications appear in *Confluencia, Ciberletras, Dactylus, Tortilleras: Hispanic and Latina Lesbian Expression* (Eds. Lourdes Torres and Inmaculada Pertusa) and *The Family, and Dance: Family Systems Therapy and the Literary Study,* (Eds. John V. Knapp and Kenneth Womack) as well as a forthcoming article in *Women's Issues in North America and the Caribbean* (Editor-in-Chief Cheryl Kalny). Her current projects include a critical analysis of queer family in Latin American literature and the editing of a collection of translated short stories, *Havana is a Really Big City*, by the Cuban writer Mirta Yañez.

CONTRIBUTORS

ELLEN MAYOCK: Associate Professor of Spanish at Washington and Lee University, Mayock has published numerous articles on women writers of Spain, Latin America, and the United States (U.S./Latina), as well as others on naturalism in Spain and Spanish America. She has just finished a manuscript that examines the female protagonist in Spanish novels written by women between 1939 and 2001. Mayock's research interests also include Spanish film and twentieth-century Catalan narrative.

DONALD MILLER: Assistant Professor of Spanish at California State University, Chico, Miller has been a Fulbright Fellow in Madrid and also has taught at the University of Alabama (Birmingham) and Brigham Young University. His research interests include theatrical, narrative, and cinematographic representations of historical female figures of the Spanish Golden Age, as well as the historical, socio-political, and artistic ramifications of gender and family law in early modern through nineteenth-century Spain. He co-edited the volume *A Society on Stage: Essays on Golden Age Drama* with Edward H. Friedman and H.J. Manzari, and has published on the subject of dramatic representations of false piety in Mira de Amescua's *Vida y muerte de la monja de Portugal* and social and gender ideologies in colonial Mexican theater of evangelism.

MIRYAM CRIADO-REYES is an Assistant Professor of Spanish at Hanover College, Indiana. She received her M.A. degree from Pennsylvania State University and her PhD. from Rutgers, The State University of New Jersey. Her research focuses on the relation between gender and discourse and mother-daughter relationships as portrayed by contemporary Spanish American, Iberian, and Latina women writers. She has published "Lenguaje y otredad sexual/cultural en *How the Garcia Girls Lost their Accents* por Julia Alvarez" (*The Bilingual Review Press*) as well as several articles in *The Feminist Encyclopedia of Latin American Literature*. She is currently working on a textbook entitled *Mujeres de hoy: textos, voces e imágenes*.

LEA RAMSDELL is an Assistant Professor of Spanish at Towson University in Baltimore, MD. Dr. Ramsdell received her Ph.D. in Romance Languages from the University of New Mexico in 1997. Her dissertation, entitled *The Family Narrative as an Oral and Written Genre of Female Resistance in Latin American Cultures*, examines women's family narratives within a theoretical framework encompassing aspects of feminist ethnography, post-colonial literary criticism, reader-response theory, and performative studies. Her current work investigates the role of the family narrative in the formation of Latina identities in the United States.

MARÍA CLAUDIA ANDRÉ is an Associate Professor of Hispanic American Lietrature and Latin American Studies at Hope College, Holland, Michigan. She holds a Ph.D. in Latin American and Spanish Literature from the State University of New York, Albany (1995) and is a professional translator and interpreter certified by Universidad del Salvador, Argentina as well as the Unified Court System in New York. She has presented papers at national and international conferences and published articles in *Confluencia, Letras Femeninas, Alba de América, Revista Hispánica* y *Atenea* de Chile. She is the editor of *Chicanas and Latin American Women Writers: Exploring the Realm of the Kitchen as a Self-Empowering Site* (Edwin Mellon Press, 2001) and currently she is finishing *Antología de Escritoras Argentinas Contemporáneas* and co-editing *De musas, amigas y amantes: Relaciones e influencias en el discurso femenino/feminista latinoamericano*, both texts forthcoming in 2003.

DINORA C. CARDOSO was born in Havana, Cuba. Her family immigrated to the United States in 1968. Dr. Cardoso received a B.A.

from Calvin College, a M. A. from the University of South Florida, and a Ph. D. from the University of Texas at Austin. Dr. Cardoso has published translations, short stories, and scholarly papers in a variety of mediums. She is currently Professor of Spanish at Pepperdine University.